THE
Summertime
of Our Lives

THE Summertime of Our Lives

STORIES FROM A MARRIAGE

NYLE KARDATZKE

ALL RIGHTS RESERVED. No part of this work covered by the copyright hereon may be reproduced, transcribed, or used in any form or by any means—graphic, electronic, or mechanical, including photocopying, recording, taping, Web distribution, or information and retrieval systems—without permission.

Unless otherwise stated, biblical quotations are from THE HOLY BIBLE, NEW INTERNATIONAL VERSION®, NIV® Copyright © 1978 by New York International Society. Used by permission of Zondervan. All rights reserved worldwide.

Editorial Services: Karen Roberts, RQuest, LLC

Cover Photo: Deposit Photos
Back Cover Photo: by Author

Other Photos by Author

Printed in the United States of America

For permission to use material, contact:
Nyle Kardatzke
Email: nylebk@gmail.com

Copyright © 2019 by Nyle Kardatzke
All rights reserved.

ISBNs: 978-1-7328222-0-7 (print)
         978-1-7328222-1-4 (eBook)

Dedication

This book is dedicated to the memory of Darlene Sayers Kardatzke, MD, 1945–2010. It is a gift to her children and grandchildren, her sisters and others who knew her, and to some who never knew her but may find this book meaningful. I hope that Darlene can see the book and smile from where she is now so happy.

Contents

Foreword	xi
A Tribute to a Friend	xiii
Preface	xv
Acknowledgments	xvii
Prologue	xix

Part One—Springtime in Indiana: 1965 to 1967   **1**

1	How We Met	3
2	Spring Tornados	6
3	Romance, Rabbit, Death, and Life	8
4	The Fox in the Henhouse	10
5	Kinfolk from Kentucky	12
6	"Papa Huffman" and an Uncle Named "Uncle"	20
7	Homes in Indiana	23
8	The Broken Swing	27
9	The Burning Car	30
10	Grada's Gold Mine	32
11	Career Decisions	36
12	Our Roads Diverge	39

Part Two—California Callings: 1967 to 1974   **43**

13	Our Roads Converge	45
14	First Tent Camping Trip	50
15	Engaged on Interstate 10	53

16	Wedding Day	57
17	"Missing the Boat"	61
18	Migration to California	63
19	Children of "Troubles"	66
20	How the Kittens Got Their Names	68
21	A Cat Named "Eight"	70
22	Yosemite and the Road to the Sea	72
23	Internship and Residency	76
24	Saved by an Apple Pie	79
25	"Visiting" Presbyterians	81
26	Our Mostly Quiet Second Apartment	83
27	The Big Tent	86
28	Burnt Sugar Cake	89
29	Taking Off Our Wedding Rings	92
30	Hitting the Job Market	94
31	A Glimpse into the Future	97
32	Leaving California	99

Part Three—Summertime Years in Wisconsin: 1974 to 1992 — **103**

33	Milwaukee Migration	105
34	First Autumn in Wisconsin	108
35	Wisconsin Snows	113
36	Accidental Methodists	116
37	Discovering Elmbrook Church	118
38	Our New Church Home	121
39	From Sierra to Summit	124
40	New House, New Baby	127
41	Jenny Elizabeth: March 30, 1977	129
42	Anna Katherine: February 15, 1980	134
43	Matthew August: July 22, 1983	138
44	Birthday Cakes and Parties	144
45	The Great Midwest Triangle	146
46	The Climbing Tree	148
47	The Tree Row	150

48	Tree Row Relatives	152
49	From Professor to Headmaster	156
50	Mothering and Doctoring	160

Part Four—Autumn: 1992 to 2009 — 165

51	Wichita Calls	167
52	The Kansas Detour	170
53	Home Again in Indiana	176
54	Autumn's Harvest	179
55	First Decade as Hoosiers	184
56	Halcyon Days of Camping	189
57	Bad News Breaks In	192
58	Telling the Children	196
59	Preparing for Treatment	199
60	Chemo Begins	201
61	Laughter in the Midst of Cancer	203
62	Hair Loss and More	205
63	Mastectomy and More Bad News	208
64	More Passages	215
65	Radiation and "Normal Life"	217
66	The Seven-Hour Hike	219
67	A Wedding and a Gift	225
68	The Road Clears	227
69	The First Grandchild	230
70	The Big 2005 Trip	232
71	Peaceful Years 2005 to 2008	236
72	Late Autumn: March 2009	244

Part Five—Wintertime: 2009 and 2010 — 247

73	Cancer Returns	249
74	Gruesome Procedures	253
75	Darlene's Retirement	258
76	Chemotherapy Again	261
77	CaringBridge	264
78	Alumna of the Year	265

79 New Grandchildren	268
80 Returning to Colorado	271
81 My Retirement	274
82 A Celebration of Life	278
83 Deep Conversations	280
84 Milestones of 2010	283
85 Final Camping Trip	286
86 The Last Summertime	290
87 The Trip Not Taken	295
88 Nearing the End	299
89 The Baby Gate Crisis	302
90 Looking Toward the End	304
91 Last Day at Home	307
92 Second to Last Conscious Day	312
93 Resurrection Day	315
94 The Kiss Test	324
95 The Benediction	326
96 The Aftermath	330
97 Memorial Service	331
98 Closing Words	335
Epilogue	338
Chronology	342
Appendix	344
In Her Own Words	349
About the Author	355

Foreword

Darlene Sayers Kardatzke and I shared many life experiences beginning with our high school years in Indianapolis. Just a year apart, we went through high school, college, and medical school. We also both attended the Garfield Park Church of God and participated in many of the same youth activities, including youth camps and youth conventions.

I graduated from Southport High School on the south side of Indianapolis in 1962, and Darlene graduated in 1963. I attended Anderson College (now Anderson University in Anderson, Indiana) and graduated in 1966, and Darlene attended there and graduated in 1967. We both earned our medical degrees at the Indiana University School of Medicine. I graduated in 1970, and Darlene graduated in 1971.

Darlene met Nyle while she was a student at Anderson, and they were married the day after her medical school graduation. She went on to complete her pediatrics residency at the UCLA Medical Center in 1974. The young couple then moved from Los Angeles to a Milwaukee suburb and formed a family there while experiencing other major life changes that are recounted in this book.

In 1993, Darlene and Nyle moved with their three children to Indianapolis, where Darlene had been offered a fellowship in Developmental and Behavioral Pediatrics. She began a distinguished career at the Riley Hospital for Children, part of the Indiana University School of Medicine. Her devotion and dedication to her patients and her calm temperament were so valued by her colleagues that they initiated a lecture series in her honor in the last year of her life.

Shortly before Darlene died in 2010 at the age of 64, she told Nyle she regretted that her grandchildren would not know her. The stories in this book offer them and other readers the chance to know her in a very personal way, and probably more intimately than most readers know their own parents and grandparents. Here readers will learn of her relatives in Kentucky and her parents' lean years in Indianapolis before they began to thrive. They will read about Nyle's first pursuit of Darlene and how he spent his first summer with her. Their very short engagement after a very long courtship led to a long, loving marriage nourished by their shared beliefs and their mutual enjoyment of travel and tent camping.

Nyle's description of the last days of Darlene's life is poignant and riveting. Darlene's cancer returned in 2009 after the original diagnosis and heavy treatment in 2003. The intimate interchange of husband and wife in her final months will be an inspiration to other couples and to those who have experienced cancer themselves or in family members. The way she faced her own death can have special meaning to every reader.

It was my pleasure to know Darlene as a young woman in school and church as well as a medical doctor and friend. The time you spend in this book will be rewarding for the way it shares a life well lived by the person who knew her best.

Guy Perry, MD
Indianapolis, Indiana

A Tribute to a Friend

I don't know when or how our friendship started.

As a pastor at a megachurch, it was always intriguing to me when someone with professional credentials would volunteer for a position that brought no applause. I mean when an attorney chose to serve coffee or an administrator sharpened pencils in the Sunday school supply office. Or when Darlene, a pediatrician, changed diapers in the church nursery. As a pastor of children's ministry, I recognized her as a resource for challenges that come as part of working with children.

It was convenient that she lived just up the hill from the church. I would call and ask if she had time to talk. Her response was always an eager "Yes!" We would then meet, usually within minutes, at a corner restaurant where we ordered coffee and a muffin. We always ordered the same thing.

I don't think our meeting times together grew into a friendship. I think, rather, that we were given the gift of an instant friendship that grew deeper and stronger through the years. We trusted each other with things that were too small or too big to share with anyone else. We cherished our time together. We laughed easily and spent little time trying to fix that which only God can fix.

An indelible memory for me is the day, at this same restaurant, that Darlene updated me on the progression of her breast cancer. As I listened through the ears of my nursing background, I knew she was telling me that she was dying.

I gripped the table, looked deeply into her eyes, and said, "It sounds like you're telling me about somebody else."

It was not that she showed no emotion, but rather that her trust in the sovereignty of God gave her lenses to see eternity.

My last conversation with her on this earth is also etched in my memory. It happened only hours before she would be in the arms of Jesus. Hearing that the time for her to be freed from her "tent" was short, I called and asked if I should drive the miles that separated us to say good-bye.

"No, Roselyn, we are going to do this by phone."

The strength of her voice and her calmness was decisive. It wasn't a rejection of a visit but rather a mutual knowing that we had already said everything that could be said.

Maybe a way to describe a friendship such as ours is "a mutual knowing."

Roselyn Aronson Staples, Pastor, Brookfield, Wisconsin
May 2018

Preface

Most of us have heard people say something like this: "I never knew my grandparents. They died before I was born. I wish I could have known them." Sometimes the speakers say they knew one or more grandparents, but only in a fleeting, superficial way. In either case, something is missing from their lives without personal contact with grandparents.

Where did I come from? Who were those people who gave me my parents? Are there traces of my grandparents' lives in my family traditions? Am I affected by genes that have been pulsing through human bodies for thousands of years, long before I was conceived? Do some of my thoughts, feelings, likes, and dislikes reflect traits from my grandparents or more ancient ancestors?

Questions like these reflect our need to see our lives as part of a larger picture, part of an ongoing story. Very often, only the smallest traces of those family stories have survived.

In her last few months of life, Darlene said, "My only regret is that my grandchildren won't know me."

That comment came from her love for family and children. She intended that her life would be one worth her grandchildren knowing. When she made that statement, she was looking into the empty space that would be created for them by her early departure. She could see that her passing would affect her grandchildren, including those not yet born. On December 5, 2010, a little more than a month after her death, I wrote on a desk blotter, "Darlene's Life Story," a reminder to write this book. The note is still there.

When Darlene died, she was just short of her sixty-fifth birthday. We had been married thirty-nine years, and we had only four of our present ten grandchildren. Only our eldest grandson, who was five years old at the time, remembers "Grandma Darlene." Even so, our adult children mention "Grandma Darlene" in dinnertime conversations and family stories, especially on holidays and birthdays. On trips like those she used to enjoy, they often mention events and facts from "Grandma Darlene's" life and travels that they remember, passing along those memories to Darlene's grandchildren. But I have noticed that, in the haste of life, they and even I include fewer and fewer memories of Darlene in our conversations and storytelling.

Although Darlene regretted that she wouldn't know each of her grandchildren here in this life, she was confident that she would "see" them through something like a Polaroid lens she believed separates heaven from earth—a lens that filters out the evil on earth and allows only joyful scenes to enter heaven. She expected to see her grandchildren through that lens and also later, in person with her in heaven.

It is my hope that, by reading this book or having it read to them, each of our grandchildren will learn stories about Grandma Darlene's life and hear her voice through the direct quotations from her. One day they may even remember some stories to tell *their* children and even their grandchildren. Most of all, I hope these stories help them discover ways to live their own lives.

Our oldest grandchild turned twelve years old on April 8, 2017. The youngest was born the next day, April 9, 2017, as I was writing this book. It will be many years before the youngest one can read and remember stories from the life of Grandma Darlene. In their busy years ahead, the older ones may have little time to reflect on these stories of their ancestors. My wish is that each will somehow know her better for having read this book about her and our life together.

This book is also for members of our extended families and Darlene's friends from childhood through adulthood, including friends from churches we attended, colleges and universities where we earned our degrees, and my work and Darlene's medical practice years. Others such as cancer survivors, patients, and those close to them may find value in Darlene's life journey.

The stories of our marriage in this book may resonate with some readers and contrast sharply with the experience of others. I hope it will be entertaining, moving, and meaningful in some way to every reader.

Acknowledgments

Above all, I must acknowledge the role of my wife, Darlene, in my writing this book. She shared her life with me from our first date until her last breath, even during the four years we were studying half a continent apart. She loved me with an all-encompassing love that looked beyond our occasional irritations with each other and habits of mine that she quietly endured. She was tolerant of my diary keeping that has been so valuable in clarifying events, thoughts, and feelings that I have shared here. She didn't know I was going to write about her. That's probably fortunate; she might have put a stop to this project if she had the chance.

Several family members and friends have contributed memories and corrections for this book. My children, who are named in the book, have read portions of it and have answered many questions by phone and email. Their value in Darlene's life and mine cannot be overstated.

We are grateful to the doctors and nurses at the Simon Cancer Center, Indianapolis, and especially Darlene's oncologist, Dr. Anna Maria Storniolo, for expert, compassionate care during her two episodes of cancer treatment.

I am indebted to Darlene's sister Evelyn Sayers Eldridge, who shared her extensive writing about her family's history and made several valuable corrections in my manuscript. Her sister Beverly Sayers Guffy also commented on a segment of the book.

A childhood friend of Darlene, Sunny Sutton-Martinez, read an early draft of a portion of the book and provided valuable comments on its tone. She said she didn't want the book to sound like a long obituary. Another childhood friend, Connie Pavey Anderson, shared memories from the childhood she shared with Darlene. Zola Troutman Noble, one of Darlene's college roommates, established facts about her college years that had been hazy to me.

Karen Roberts, my editor, worked patiently through several drafts, helping me shape the sequence of events for clarity and saving me from many blunders of poor expression.

I'm still trying to think of people to blame for errors that remain in this book. For the time being, I'll admit that I had many chances to make things right.

Prologue

*I*n December 2009, Darlene and I went from Indiana to Wisconsin for a weekend funeral. We had lived in that state for eighteen years, so the trip was a sentimental journey as well as a time of respect and remembrance for Stewart Davis, Board Chairman at Brookfield Academy, who had died of cancer at age sixty. As we stood in a very long reception line at the viewing, we talked of our own life journey. In 2003, Darlene was first diagnosed with cancer, and in 2009, the cancer returned. Within a year of our trip to Wisconsin, the scene we were part of that day would be repeated for Darlene.

One of my journal entries on that trip contained words to each other that would echo throughout the months ahead and beyond.

December 19, 2009. Brookfield, Wisconsin: *Yesterday at Stew Davis' viewing, Darlene said, "The years we spent here were the summertime of our lives." I loved the phrase, and I repeated it several times. I told her that our years after we left Wisconsin were an "autumn of life" when we worked very hard to bring in the harvest, and we were now in "the winter of our lives." She agreed.*

The years Darlene referred to as "the summertime of our lives" were from 1974 to 1992, when we bought our first house, planted our first garden, brought all our children into the world, experienced an awakening and deepening of our faith, and spent many hours gazing from our hilltop house in Waukesha, Wisconsin, on scenery that we believed foretold a beautiful future.

Darlene's phrase describing those years was so felicitous that I have repeated it often since the day she coined it. Now, as the title of this book, it applies to all our life together: spring, summer, autumn, and winter. The later seasons gain their fullest meaning only in light of the earlier spring and summertime.

PART ONE

*Springtime in Indiana:
1965 to 1967*

1

How We Met

Darlene Sayers and I met on March 20, 1965, and we had our first date that same day. Ever after, March 20 was a significant calendar date in our lives.

On that spring day in Indiana, Darlene was nineteen years old, and I was twenty-five. She was a sophomore at Anderson College, now Anderson University. I was working there for Dean of Students Norman Beard. I had graduated in 1962 and had spent two years teaching in Ethiopia in the Peace Corps before returning to campus, taking a job that would offer me an opportunity to sort out the next steps of my career. I hoped to find a wife.

In the late afternoon, I was sitting as usual in my tiny office in Old Main, the original building that once housed all of Anderson College, working on some now forgotten task. My office door opened directly onto a busy hallway, allowing me to see students passing by between classes. Just in time, I looked up to see a lovely, dark-haired young woman glide past. She definitely merited a second look.

I quickly but calmly rose from my desk and followed her, trying to be suave. When she paused to read academic announcements on a bulletin board, I sauntered up and pretended to study the bulletins with her.

"There's a lot to learn here," I said with all the charm and confidence I could muster.

"It pays to read the bulletin board once in a while," she said with a side glance.

We're off to an exciting start, I thought. I assumed she knew my name because I had been in the campus news several times.

"What's your name?" I asked.

"Darlene Sayers," she said, still studying the bulletin board.

Having made such progress, I blurted, "Would you like to go to a movie tonight?"

She turned to face me directly and smiled. "Yes, I think I could. What's showing?"

I wasn't prepared for her question. "I'll have to check the paper. Do you want to take a chance on it?"

She agreed, and I said I could pick her up at 5:00 p.m. in time for dinner at the Alibi Restaurant in downtown Anderson. The Alibi at that time had an extensive menu and was known for excellent pies. After dinner, we would go to one of the two movie theatres in downtown Anderson.

A light freezing drizzle was settling on the streets, trees, and lampposts on the evening of our date, but we were not to be deterred. I picked her up at her dormitory right on time. Once again I noticed her serene beauty as I led her to my distinctly unromantic 1960 green Pontiac station wagon.

During dinner, I talked about my two years in the Peace Corps, something I hoped she would find interesting. I also told her about some trouble I was having with a student organization at the college. She listened calmly and attentively, and she encouraged me to keep talking. The more I talked, the more confident and calm I became. Other girls had jangled my nerves and sometimes even upset my stomach; Darlene calmed me. I hadn't been that calm on a date in a long time, maybe not ever. I'm sure she talked, too, but I mainly remember her calm, patient listening.

The movie we saw was *How to Murder Your Wife*. Yes, that's how our dating life began, the first step toward a friendship that would last forty-five years and a marriage of thirty-nine years. Many years later, I bought a VHS tape recording of that movie so we could watch it again. We were appalled at the shallow story line and the stilted acting. How could we have begun our life together watching such a low-grade movie?

When we emerged from the theater that night, the streets were covered in ice. At a crosswalk on the way back to my car, I stepped behind her and grasped her elbows. "Stand straight, and I'll slide you across the street!" I said.

She held her feet together and made her body rigid. "Whee!" she yelled as I glided her across. If she had fallen, she might have wondered years later if I *had* been planning to murder my wife on our first date!

I can't say whether we fell in love that first night, but I can say we "fell deeply in like."

After that first date, Darlene informed her parents that she had "met someone" and was dating. Her father was naturally suspicious of such an "old man" six years her senior dating his daughter. I learned many years later that he contacted my boss at Anderson College to learn whether I was to be trusted. Mr. Beard had gone out on a limb and vouched for me. Grada Sayers must have remained skeptical for a time, but he accepted me as his daughter's boyfriend and then later as her husband.

2

Spring Tornados

A few weeks after my first date with Darlene, Indiana experienced its greatest tornado outbreak up to that time. On Palm Sunday, April 11, 1965, forty-seven tornados roared through the Midwest, killing 271 people and injuring about 1,500 more. During the storms, Darlene was on her way home from Chicago after a student recruitment trip with her traveling trio, the Envoys. I had offered to take her to her parents' home after she returned to campus, so I was at her dorm at the scheduled time.

The tornados tore across the trio's route home, and the rain, hail, and fallen trees delayed their return. Meanwhile, radio news reported on devastating tornados between Anderson and Chicago. Eventually, someone traveling with the trio found a pay phone and called the college to report that the group was okay but would be late. I returned to my apartment to await further news.

Darlene phoned when she reached her dorm, and I drove back to the college. Lightning flickered in distant clouds as I walked her out to my car. She talked excitedly of the traffic they had crept through and the storm damage they had seen. It was after 11:00 p.m. when we reached her parents' apartment building, which was forty-five miles southwest from the college. That night we heard that fifty miles northwest of Anderson, the small town of Russiaville had been struck by one of the state's eight powerful F-4 tornados. Three people had been killed there, and 90 percent of the buildings were damaged or destroyed.

The next weekend, on Easter Saturday, Darlene and I joined about a dozen other students and staff members from Anderson College to help with cleanup in Russiaville. Our group focused on a farm where the house, barn, and outbuildings had been destroyed. Wallpaper and furniture dangled from the standing half of the two-story house. Little could be done except concentrate on moving some of the broken timber and pieces of furniture so the heavy equipment coming later could remove the rubble. The owner, an older man in bib overalls, wandered in a daze as we tried to be useful. Someone took a photo of Darlene pitching hay from a mound of wreckage we were clearing.

On the way back to Anderson, Darlene and I talked about the work we had done and the troubles still ahead for the people at that farm. Darlene was thinking deeply about our day when she said, "I just wanted to do something to show my concern for the people there."

Her comment surprised and impressed me. I had thought of our work there in practical terms, to *fix* things the tornado had damaged, but she had understood the need better than I.

3

Romance, Rabbit, Death, and Life

*O*ne romantic night in autumn 1965, Darlene and I went out for a drive in the countryside in my new 1966 Volkswagen Beetle, the only new car I ever bought. We wandered around some winding country roads, talking about life and the future. We stopped somewhere and talked in the quiet, humid night.

At about 9:30, we started back toward Anderson. As we cruised along the edge of a field of tall corn, a rabbit bounded into the road. THUMP! We had hit the rabbit.

"Stop! Stop!" Darlene yelled.

I pulled over, and we saw the rabbit twitching behind the car in the glow of the taillights.

"Let's take him to Dr. Stevenson!" Darlene exclaimed. "This is great! We can dissect him. We needed an animal like this, and this is better than one in formaldehyde."

Had it not been so dark, I might have glanced at her in disbelief. But she was the scientist, so I picked up the rabbit and placed it in the VW.

When we were back in the city, Darlene somehow contacted Dr. Stevenson even though it was late evening. The three of us met in the biology lab at the college, and the two scientists eagerly sliced into the rabbit. I had skinned rabbits while hunting as a boy in Ohio, so I wasn't squeamish. Neither were the two of them. As I watched, they peeled back the rabbit's skin, going deeper to see its inner organs. It was as though they were unwrapping a birthday present.

"Look at this," Dr. Stevenson said as he opened the rabbit's body cavity. "Do you see that motion? Look at the intestines."

Darlene and I looked, and to our surprise we could see the rabbit's intestines clenching and unclenching. Other muscles twitched nearby.

"The rabbit is technically dead," Dr. Stevenson said, "because its heart isn't beating, and I'm sure its brain isn't working either. In a human situation, we would pronounce the person dead. But look at those intestines and muscles still moving. They aren't dead yet."

It was a revelation. I had thought that life ended instantly, like an electric light turning off. But we were seeing in this rabbit's body that death is a longer process. Some semblance of life can go on for hours, maybe even for days.

Dr. Stevenson then amazed us even more. "One measure of death is a heartbeat. In a hospital, doctors can simulate life in a person almost indefinitely by keeping the heart beating and by providing breathing support with a ventilator. The brain may have ceased to operate and could never recover, but some signs of life can be maintained mechanically. It's difficult to know when to stop."

We stood silently for minutes, watching parts of the rabbit's body still functioning while other parts were motionless, cooling, and becoming rigid.

What I learned that night may not have been new information to Darlene the scientist, but it was a revelation for me. We both learned something that night about the difficult decisions of life and death that would become more common for doctors and families in the years that followed.

4

The Fox in the Henhouse

Most people these days are far from their ancestors' farm roots and don't know that it was common for foxes to raid chicken houses. The foxes would kill the chickens and eat them on the spot or drag the bodies away to some secret place. Foxes were not to be trusted around chickens. I admit once being like a fox in a henhouse. I knew what I wanted, and I would find a way to get it.

Two months after I met Darlene and we began dating, I was asked to be the chaperone for a girls' trio that would travel to about forty churches in the northeastern United States over summer break to recruit students for Anderson College. Darlene was a member of that trio. There I was, a single young man, assigned to guard a trio of young women and their pianist, and I had already begun dating one of the women, a fact unknown to the College staff member who had assigned me the job. Since she was a student and I was a staff member, Darlene and I had agreed to keep our relationship a secret from others on campus. We had managed to do so successfully. Now we would need to be secretive on the tour.

Even though I was looking forward to having so much time with Darlene, I was dreading the summer ahead of being cooped up in a car, spending nearly every evening in a church service, and hearing the girls sing the same songs over and over every night. It would be difficult to keep our romance a secret from the other girls and from the people in the churches we visited. If they knew, the church people might be shocked by this "fox in the henhouse" situation. The other girls in the troupe probably suspected we were dating.

In late spring, before the big summer tour began, the trio was sent to sing on a weekend at a church near my home outside Elmore, Ohio. Darlene had already gone there with me to meet my parents, so she knew about the pond next to my childhood home and other delights there. When the troupe stopped at the house that Sunday afternoon, all the girls roamed the yard and asked questions. Darlene acted curious about the place, as though she had never been there before. I was impressed by her intelligence and sly acting. At least for a while longer, our secret was intact.

That summer of 1965 was a blur of driving, church services, talking to people about Anderson College, and a few sightseeing afternoons. For the most part, things went well, but we were late for church services a couple of times. Once the girls nearly missed their singing engagement at a church in the Bronx in New York City; somehow we all showed up, out of breath, at the last moment. On the Fourth of July, Darlene and I sat on a hillside alone somewhere in Upstate New York to watch the fireworks. None of the adventures or dull days on the road mattered as much as the fact that Darlene and I were able to spend our first summer together on a college-sponsored trip with three other girls who guarded her from "the fox" while he guarded the hens.

5

Kinfolk from Kentucky

Darlene was born in Lebanon, Indiana, on November 3, 1945, but her parents were from a rural area in Kentucky. Darlene's long view of life and her self-discipline owed much to her kinfolk and family roots in Kentucky. She was determined to lead her life with the perseverance she had seen in her parents.

Grada and Virginia, Darlene's parents, moved north to Indianapolis to look for work, bringing with them some of the Southern flavor of Kentucky. They were almost like immigrants to the new, urban setting, and they fit a historic pattern. Indiana had been settled mainly from south to north, rather than from east to west like its neighboring states. Emigration such as theirs was a pattern repeated thousands of times.

Virginia Huffman, Darlene's mother, was born February 21, 1909, on the family farm near Three Forks, Kentucky, which is not far from Bowling Green, Kentucky. Grada Sayers, Darlene's father, was born about three months later, May 14, 1909, in a rural farmhouse at Merry Oaks, Kentucky, which is near Glasgow, Kentucky. After they married, Grada jokingly moaned and complained every year on Virginia's birthday about being married to "an older woman." Each year Virginia scowled and shook her head, the helpless victim of his teasing. To his credit, Grada dropped his complaints after his birthday in May each year.

Grada and Virginia had very different temperaments. Steady and imperturbable, Grada was a man who refused to worry about anything, preferring to deal with things *after* they happened, always looking for solutions. During stressful times, he simply did his best to solve the problem and left the rest to God. In contrast, Virginia was inclined to be apprehensive and worry about possible outcomes. As she grew older, she seemed to dread the world around her—a contrast to her earlier, outgoing years.

Darlene admired her father's serenity, perhaps more than I knew. She grew to be a woman who maintained her non-anxious temperament in nearly all situations, just as she knew he would have. More than once, including very late in her life, she told me she "took after Daddy" when facing major decisions and alarming times. She must have inherited her desire to be an accomplished and independent woman from her mother's early career as a college student and schoolteacher.

For Grada Sayers, Kentucky was a place of wretched poverty. His parents and siblings (thirteen children in all, with Grada as number twelve) worked hard on their tiny farm but often ate only corn, beans, collard greens, and cheap cuts of pork. They were sometimes isolated for weeks at a time when heavy rains made it impossible even to walk to the nearest farm through sticky mud, let alone go to town for supplies.

As his older brothers and sisters left the farm to marry and start their lives, Grada and his youngest two brothers had to take on more work on the family farm. Their small farm could barely support the remaining family members. To Grada, there seemed to be no end to the heavy manual farm work and no way to get ahead.

The cycle of farm work could hold a man all his life, but it could not hold Grada. One hot summer day as he trudged behind a team of mules and a single-bottom plow, he paused to rest on the plow handles. He wiped his face and gazed a few minutes at the partially plowed field. He thought of the hot, tiring days ahead and endless meals of cornbread, greens, and pork belly.

"There must be a better way of making a livin' than this," he said aloud to the mules. That moment was decisive, and he soon left the farm and moved to Indianapolis to find work. He intended never again to live on a farm, and he never again ate corn, not even in the city.

Darlene didn't know many details of her father's early life in Indianapolis, but she did know that he married a woman named Nola in 1927. After only two years of marriage, Grada and Nola divorced. Nola kept their infant son, Orval (born 1929), and Grada provided financial help for Orval into his adult life. Orval died in 1972.

Virginia Huffman was an educated and poised lady. In a day and time when a girl married young and started her own family and household, Virginia took a very different path. When she graduated from the eighth grade in 1923, she did not want to end her schooling as so many young people (even the boys) did in that time. Going to high school meant going to Smith Grove, Kentucky, the closest high school but some distance from her home. Since travel was still mostly by horse and buggy, arrangements were made for her to live with a lady in Smith Grove during the school week and come home on weekends. Virginia did housework and chores, and her parents paid the lady 25 cents a week for Virginia to stay there. She graduated from Smith Grove High School on May 23, 1927.

That fall she enrolled at Western Kentucky State Normal School and Teachers College, now Western Kentucky University. She received her first two-year teaching license in 1931 and graduated from Western with a bachelor's degree on June 1, 1934. From 1927 to 1934, she would teach for a few months and then attend college for a semester. During her teaching career, Virginia taught in a one-room school and later a two-room schoolhouse, where she served as principal as well as the teacher. She taught grades one through eight in the one-room school and high school subjects in the two-room schoolhouse.

Virginia was an independent woman who made her own money, had a car, and assisted her parents by giving them money to supplement the farm income. If she had completed the 1933–34 school year as a teacher or completed another semester at Western College, she would have had a lifetime teaching license in Kentucky. But teaching was not her ultimate goal in life. Like most young women at that time, she wanted more than anything to marry, have children, and be a mother. On a visit to Indianapolis, Virginia heard of Grada through other Kentuckians, but when a friend tried to arrange a blind date for her with him, she refused.

"I can't date him!" she said. "He's a married man!"

The friend explained that Grada had divorced in 1929, and he was a reliable, Christian man. Sometime in 1933, friends arranged for Grada to meet Virginia. Four of them went to Riverside Amusement Park on the northwest side of downtown Indianapolis. That day Virginia saw Grada's good looks, and she must have sensed his intelligence, honesty, and energy. Grada must have been bold enough that day to convey to her his strength of character as well, overcoming her earlier resistance to dating a divorced man. As for Grada, he was smitten by Virginia's beauty, poise, and intelligence.

Grada and Virginia were married on December 21, 1934, in a double ceremony with their friends Aubrey and Winnie Duckett. The simple ceremony was performed at Franklin, Kentucky, before a Justice of the Peace. They were both twenty-five years old.

In their first years of marriage, Grada worked as a day laborer at a factory a bus ride away from their apartment. He would show up in the morning and wait to be called in for work. The foreman soon learned that Grada was hard-working and reliable, so he called on him as often as possible. It was a ten- to thirteen-hour-day with travel time, and the pay was $5 a day, but that was enough to pay the rent and buy groceries.

As World War II was beginning in Europe in the late 1930s, Grada took a job at Allison Transmissions, where transmissions for military tanks and trucks were made and prototype jet engines were being tested. The pay was better and the hours were more reliable. When the United States entered the war, Grada tried to enlist in the Army, but he was told his work at Allison was more valuable to the war effort than any soldiering he might have done. He continued at Allison throughout the war. Although he had gone only through the eighth grade in school, he quickly learned engineering concepts and skills at Allison. At Virginia's insistence, he took classes at the Purdue Extension in Indianapolis to enhance his knowledge. He later became a builder and contractor, making him prosperous beyond what he had hoped on that hot summer day in Kentucky when he spoke to the team of mules.

Compared to his earlier life in Kentucky, Grada was prosperous in Indianapolis. After the war, he worked at Polar Ice, an important business that supplied blocks of ice to kept people's ice boxes cold. He learned enough about refrigeration at Polar Ice to help keep the company's ice plant running as refrigeration was being introduced, and his knowledge of refrigeration helped later when air conditioning became standard in homes.

Leaving Kentucky did not mean abandoning it. Though they made their home in Indiana, Grada and Virginia's hearts were still in Kentucky. They made frequent trips to Kentucky for the rest of their lives. Both had strong ties to their siblings and older relatives living south of the Ohio River.

Darlene's family trips to Kentucky during her childhood included many visits to Aunt Lois (pronounced "Loyce") Smith, Virginia's older sister. She and William Smith lived in a farmhouse a few miles beyond the end of the paved road with their young daughters. Darlene and her two sisters were usually asleep in the back seat of the family car late on those Friday evenings when the rumble of gravel under the car announced that they had left the pavement and were near Aunt Lois' house. Fun and food were just ahead.

Aunt Lois did not have electricity, so she would light kerosene lamps and put food on the table that she had prepared on her wood-burning stove. She couldn't offer toast for breakfast in the morning, so she fried bread in a pan for her city-raised nieces. They thought it was a beautiful treat. Because of Aunt Lois, on camping trips many years later, Darlene made fried toast for our children on our gas camp stove just as Aunt Lois had done many years earlier for her.

Grada and Virginia's Kentucky relatives visited Indianapolis, too, and sometimes they came without writing or calling ahead. A carload of relatives might burst into the kitchen during breakfast, having left Bowling Green in the wee hours of the morning. "We in time for breakfast?" they'd ask, and Virginia always managed to feed them.

Throughout their lives, Grada and Virginia provided hospitality, advice, and financial help for their siblings. Virginia was an excellent cook, and she could put food on the table with the best of them when company came from Kentucky. Her standard breakfast included bacon, sausage patties, scrambled eggs, and Hungry Jack biscuits from a can.

Years later, when Darlene and I and our children came to visit, Virginia put a similar spread on the table. I was surprised that an excellent Southern cook did not make her own biscuits from scratch, nor did she ever make gravy when I was there. Perhaps she made those changes from the standard cooking fare of Kentucky when she moved to Indianapolis. I never asked about biscuits or the absence of gravy; I was too busy enjoying the food she did provide.

During spring break in March 1991, we drove to Florida for some of the standard sights and amusement. While we were there, we visited Rev. Larry Reynolds, the pastor who had performed our wedding twenty years earlier. He was dying of cancer, but he greeted us warmly.

"Is our marriage still under warranty?" Darlene asked, repeating our standard joke for Rev. Reynolds.

"It's good as the day I tied the knot for you," he laughed and leaned back on his pillows.

That was his last good day. In a week, he was beyond this life in the presence of God.

Our family visited Grada and Virginia in June 1991. I went with Grada on some of his errands, and on one very hot day, he and I climbed the stairs to the apartment where they had lived when I first dated Darlene. He worked on a window air conditioner there in sweltering heat. It was an effort, but his stamina was good.

The next morning, while Darlene and I were at the breakfast table, Grada came from the bathroom off the kitchen and nearly collapsed. Darlene helped him to a chair and started a medical interview. His symptoms were serious. She took him to the nearest hospital, and he was admitted for testing. Within a few days, the diagnosis was clear: He had an advanced case of pancreatic cancer. The date was June 20.

Grada was sent home to be cared for by his three daughters. Virginia was already weakened by age, and the shock of his illness left her dazed. Grada could join us at the table at meals and was able to settle several major business matters that summer. He lived as normally as possible, even while his strength was ebbing away.

Grada showed the matter-of-fact approach that Darlene would emulate near the end of her own life. One morning he and I were at the breakfast table alone. The phone at his side rang. He picked it up and listened as the caller told her story. It was one of the elderly women who rented a small house from him. The pilot light had gone out on her water heater.

"Can you come over this morning and light the pilot light?" she asked.

Grada squirmed a bit and simply explained softly, "Why no, I can't do that. I'm over here dying of cancer!"

We didn't hear the woman's response, but the conversation ended there. It must have been one of the last requests for his help.

On August 20, 1991, Grada died at the age of eighty-two at home on Walnut Street with his wife and children around him. After he stopped breathing, Darlene, the only medical doctor present, felt his pulse. It became weaker and weaker until it finally stopped.

"Daddy is now with God," she said calmly to her mother and sisters.

After Grada's death, Virginia moved to a senior living place in Greenwood, Indiana, where she felt safe and was well cared for. Darlene's sister Beverly became her main caregiver, but Darlene and her other sister Evelyn visited often. All three sisters spent Virginia's last night by her side at her nursing home. She died on October 12, 1994, at the age of eighty-five. At her funeral, Darlene and I both choked up in tears as we tried to sing her favorite hymn, "I'll Meet You in the Morning."

The Garfield Park Church of God on the south side of Indianapolis was the center of their social and spiritual life in Indianapolis. Grada's niece, Virgie Cline, had introduced Grada and Virginia to that church early in their married life. Virgie was Grada's niece, the daughter of one of his much older sisters. She was several years older than Grada, so she was always known to Darlene and her sisters as "Aunt Virgie." The girls loved her for her sweet disposition and warm smile that belied the tragedies of her life. Virgie's devotion to the church was an example that Grada and Virginia followed all their lives.

Throughout their years, Grada and Virginia were strong in their faith and tireless in their support of the church. Their hearts were "fixed on Jesus," as an old song goes, and their devotion to God was evident in their care for others and for the church. Darlene and her sisters all became Christians and were baptized there. She and her sisters sang in the choir from age eleven through their high school years.

Church dinners were a favorite memory of Darlene's. No pitch-in meal was complete without two or three of her mother's delicious dishes, including at least one dessert. She was well-known for her well-done green beans and her yellow cake with chocolate frosting. As for Grada, the church building itself might have flooded, burned, suffered loss of water or heat, or simply fallen down had it not been for his constant ministry of volunteer maintenance work.

Some who remember the history of Garfield Church of God, still standing in 2018 but now closed, may know what the church did in return for Grada and Virginia Sayers and their three daughters. Darlene always felt a tie to the Garfield Park Church, even when we attended other churches far away. She knew that her character and outlook on life were shaped by that congregation, as well as by her parents. She was thankful for that heritage.

6

"Papa Huffman" and an Uncle Named "Uncle"

My first visit with Darlene's Kentucky kinfolk was in the summer of 1972, a year after she and I were married. During a visit to Indianapolis from Los Angeles, Darlene's Uncle William died. Darlene and I decided to go to the funeral with her parents. It was my first chance to meet her Kentucky relatives.

As we traveled across the border, I noticed how the Kentucky countryside was dotted with ominous-looking black barns that were unlike the red and white barns I was familiar with. Tobacco was one of Kentucky's main cash crops, and these barns were used for drying and curing tobacco. The small frame houses that clung to hillsides near those barns were surrounded by corn cribs and hog lots. I was beginning to learn about the culture that Darlene's parents left behind but still loved.

On that trip I met many relatives, including Darlene's cousin Edwin. He was a genial man of about forty-five whose most valued possession was a red 1965 Ford in perfect, new condition. He kept the car in his barn up on blocks off the ground most of the time to preserve the tires as it aged. His quiet demeanor belied the fact that he had been an Army Ranger during

World War II. He didn't speak of his experiences, and I learned that he was reluctant to talk about those days with anyone.

I also met Uncle John and Aunt Hattie Sayers, an elderly childless couple who were notorious for their housekeeping. Darlene's mother was revolted by the sight of the dishpan of cold, gray water and stacks of unwashed dishes. She did not allow Darlene or her sisters to eat anything at John and Hattie's house because of obvious lapses in sanitation.

During our trip, Uncle Frank and Aunt Mae Sayers invited Uncle John and Aunt Hattie to join us for lunch at their rigorously clean farmhouse. Aunt Mae famously could put an elaborate meal on the table with no advance notice. She cooked up one of her celebrated feasts that day, and Uncle John and Aunt Hattie were delighted. They ate like teenagers and seemed not to have eaten in a long time. Aunt Hattie was nearly blind by then, and Uncle John was frail. They giggled and talked and showed wonderful appreciation by eating so much of the food set before them. Though the day was hot, Uncle John wore a food-splattered suit coat, and Aunt Hattie had a knit cap pulled down to her eyebrows.

On the same trip, I met Uncle Eldon Huffman and Aunt Rea (short for Marie). When Eldon was a young boy his two sisters called him "Brother." That became his name instead of Eldon. He was always called Brother until he became an uncle. Then he was simply known as "Uncle." For a number of years, Uncle worked as a cook at the Moose Lodge in Bowling Green, Kentucky. One evening Wilbur, Darlene's brother-in-law, needed to take him a message at the Lodge. When Wilbur arrived at the front desk and asked to see his uncle, the clerk asked for his uncle's name. Wilbur was at a loss.

"His name is Uncle," said Wilbur. "That's the only name I know."

The obliging desk clerk turned on the PA system and boomed out through the building, "Will *Uncle* please come to the front desk?"

Uncle soon appeared, laughing roundly, and the incident entered family folklore.

When I first met Uncle, he seemed to be the quintessential Kentucky "good old boy." He smoked cigars, raised 'maters in his garden, and loved fried catfish. He dressed carefully in well-pressed slacks and rather dressy casual shirts. One evening we went with Uncle and several family members to a popular catfish restaurant that sat right on the edge of the Barren River.

"Do you do much fishing, Uncle?" I asked.

"I ain't *nooo* fisherman!" he answered in an elegant drawl.

His reply became legendary.

On the same trip, I also met Darlene's grandfather, "Papa" Willie G. Huffman. To me he seemed like Colonel Sanders, the inventor of Kentucky Fried Chicken. Papa was kind and soft-spoken, and Darlene loved him dearly. Papa Huffman's wife, Mama Huffman (Donnie Bratton Huffman), had died in 1941. Papa was only about fifty-nine years old at that time, but he reasoned that he would die soon and sold his farm and all his household possessions. He would spend the rest of his life living with his three adult children on a rotating basis.

Papa Huffman came to Indianapolis once or twice a year and stayed about three months at a time with Virginia and Grada. On his visits, he would sit for hours in an antique rocking chair and chat with the family between naps. He rocked Darlene as a baby and played with her over the years as she grew from babyhood to childhood. He was her first real babysitter.

Papa Huffman was a well-groomed, fastidious, and gracious gentleman, but he had another side. He liked to attend professional wrestling matches, those over-acted dramas where huge, muscular men with ferocious names jump on each other and sometimes throw each other into the first three rows of the audience.

Whenever Papa Huffman was in Indianapolis, Grada or Darlene's brother-in-law, Wilbur, had the task of taking him to see professional wrestling in downtown Indianapolis. As soon as the wrestling matches began, Papa would begin raging and storming about the illegal hits, the bad job of the refs, and the ugliness of wrestlers he disliked. He would stand, shake his fists, and yell to direct the combat. Wilbur would sometimes become so embarrassed that he would go to the lobby until the end of the evening.

"It's all fake! It's all fake!" Papa Huffman would mutter later as he was guided out of the arena.

Papa Huffman died in early 1972, while Darlene was in her first year of internship at the UCLA Medical Center. She agonized about whether to travel from California to Kentucky for the funeral, but she decided she couldn't spare the time away from the hospital. She obeyed her call of duty, but sometimes in later years wished she had been there to honor her beloved Papa Huffman.

7

Homes in Indiana

*D*ating and marrying Darlene opened a whole new world of family for me. Darlene and I had much in common through our church and college experiences: Her parents and mine had strong marriages, but her upbringing was vastly different from mine. My family of four boys and two girls grew up in a rural area in northwestern Ohio. Darlene and her two sisters were raised in an urban setting in Indianapolis. My siblings and I roamed freely in the fields and lanes of the farms around us. Darlene and her sisters were under close and continuous supervision. My family was more rambunctious, and my siblings and I had far greater freedom to roam as "free-range children." With so many energetic children, my mother often preferred that we play outside, but we had to be home for meals and back in the house before dark.

Darlene's parents were happy to live in Indiana, and they were secure in their married life and family even though they lived through the Great Depression in their early years together. In their first years of marriage, they lived in a small rented house on Talbot Street. After the arrival of their first two daughters, Beverly and Evelyn, they moved to a larger rented house on Harlan Street near the Fountain Square area on the south side of Indianapolis. In 1943, to be closer to Grada's work at Allison's, the family moved west of Indianapolis to Brownsburg, Indiana.

Darlene's oldest sister, Beverly Louise, was born August 25, 1937. Seventeen months later, on January 26, 1939, Evelyn Marie was born, completing the family Grada and Virginia intended to have. Having just two girls was a blessing, they thought, and it would be challenge enough to raise them on Grada's income at the time from his work at Allison Transmissions.

Early in 1945, however, Virginia discovered she was pregnant. Baby Darlene was due in November and would be six years younger than Evelyn and eight years younger than Beverly. Childbirth for the first two had not been easy, and Virginia was thirty-six years old. Caring for a baby along with two elementary school-aged girls would be a physical and emotional challenge. But the prospect of another baby brought joy despite the challenges. Grada and Virginia thanked God and prayed for the baby's safe arrival.

Darlene Sayers was born on Saturday, November 3, 1945, at Witham Hospital in Lebanon, Indiana. The hospital was about thirty miles from the family home in Brownsburg, which meant a long drive for Grada and Virginia, but all other details of the day slipped into the mists of time. Darlene knew of no family connection to her name or other rationale for it, and she did not know why she was not given a middle name, unlike her sisters.

The Sayers girls spanned nearly nine years in age. The two older girls had a small society of their own. Being so much younger than the others, Darlene was in some ways raised like an only child. Beverly and Evelyn sometimes teased her when she interfered with their toys or their play by saying, "Mother and Daddy don't like you as much as they like us. You're *adopted!*"

Virginia's job raising the three girls was seldom easy. They pushed their mother to the edge. More than once, Grada told me about the challenges.

"Some days," he told me, "I'd come home, and Virginia would say to me, 'You take care of these girls. These kids is just about driving me crazy!'"

One thing Virginia delighted in was dressing her three daughters in identical outfits. She was an excellent seamstress, and she made most of their matching outfits. In the family's leanest years, whenever the girls got any new clothing, it was only because Virginia had found a bolt of cloth at a bargain price and made dresses for them.

Darlene was in significant trouble with her parents only once that I know of. In a test of wills with her mother, she refused to cooperate and probably said things she shouldn't have. To top it off, she threw something at her mother. Virginia reported the incident to Grada when he came home, and he demanded that Darlene apologize. She refused, and he took her over his lap and spanked her, telling her she had to apologize. She finally did. The incident became fixed in her memory as a crucial turning point in her behavior and her relationship with her parents.

When World War II ended and Grada's work at Allison's slowed, he went to work for Polar Ice and Fuel, where he helped oversee production of massive blocks of ice for home iceboxes. When he became upset about the lack of promotions at Polar Ice, he and Virginia decided to try to begin their own construction business. They chose the small town of Southport on the southern edge of Indianapolis. Later Grada would tell people that they chose that area because it was closer to Kentucky and had lots of cornfields.

Grada and a nephew of his began the business by building small "crackerbox" houses near Greenwood, Indiana. As soon as they built a group of homes, those houses sold. Most of them were snatched up by men returning home from the war. From 1950 to 1958, their construction business grew at a rapid pace, and Grada and Virginia became relatively prosperous compared to most of their relatives in Kentucky and many of their Indiana neighbors.

About 1952, Grada and Virginia bought a large building to house their growing business. Grada remodeled the second floor into a four-bedroom, two-bath living facility and moved the family there from Brownsburg. The second-floor apartment had a large kitchen and a large formal living room. "The building," as the family called it, was so important to Grada and Virginia's history that it was almost a member of the family. For Darlene, it was the only home she remembered well. She talked of her mother's cooking, her father's construction work, and visits from Kentucky relatives, especially Papa Huffman.

After Darlene's sisters married and moved away, Grada remodeled the building again, creating two apartments out of the area that had been the family home. Darlene had her parents to herself, and she became a darling of the lady who rented the other upstairs apartment.

In 1970, Grada built a small house on Walnut Street in Southport, where he and Virginia lived until his death. That little house often rocked with conversation when the whole family gathered for one of Virginia's culinary masterpieces. When Darlene and I brought our three children, there was just enough room for us in their spare bedroom and Virginia's sewing room. The kids had little room to play outside, but they delighted in the nearby miniature golf course, Dairy Queen, and walks to Long's Doughnuts. These were things we didn't have in my countryside home in Ohio farm country, nor did our kids have them in Wisconsin.

8

The Broken Swing

Darlene shared with me three dramatic episodes about her school-age years, stories that helped me understand the woman with whom I would spend the summertime of my life. The first story had to do with breaking a swing.

Darlene entered first grade in 1951 at the age of five and was one of the youngest in her class. She turned six in November. Southport Elementary was located on the south side of Southport Road, just across from "the building," which housed the family business and apartment. Living across the street from the school was a recreational advantage for Darlene because she could play on the school playground. She and friends often played on the swings on Saturdays and Sundays, testing their ability to pump them to dizzying heights and sometimes jumping off at the high end of the ride.

One Sunday afternoon while she was at the school with Connie Pavey, one of the girls had a rebellious thought: How about twisting a swing to get a spinning ride round and round? They wouldn't have done this on a school day because twisting the swings was against the school's rules. But the school rules were far from the girls' minds.

Darlene got on a swing, twisted it a few turns, and watched the world spin around her as the swing wound down. Connie did the same. To get a longer ride when it was her turn again, Connie twisted her swing two or three more turns than before. It writhed wildly to unwind, and she squealed with delight.

On her next turn, Darlene twisted the swing with all her might until the entire chain was twisted, right up to the crossbar above. The chain broke, Darlene and the swing dropped to the ground, and the entire chain flopped down with her.

"You broke the swing!" Connie yelled. "You broke the swing!"

Darlene fought back tears. She had never been in trouble at school, but she was certain she would be in trouble when the broken chain was discovered. Twisting that swing until the chain broke seemed to her to be the most serious thing anyone had ever done wrong at the school. Worst of all, she had done it. She had broken a rule that everyone knew.

That evening Virginia could see something was wrong with Darlene.

"What's wrong? You seem sad about something," she asked kindly.

"I broke the swing," she murmured.

"What swing?"

"One of the school swings. Connie and I were there, and we forgot and started twisting the swing to get a spinning ride. When it was my turn, the chain broke!"

"Oh, my! That's too bad!" her mother said. "You'll have to go right to Mr. Kirkman on Monday morning and tell him what happened."

"Mr. Kirkman! I don't want to tell him! He made the rule because other kids broke the swings. He will be really mad at Connie and me. He might kick us out of school!" Darlene wailed.

Virginia tried to keep a straight face. "Mr. Kirkman is a good man, and I think he's fair-minded. He won't kick you out of school, especially if you tell him what happened before he has to figure it out some other way. Just be sure you and Connie are there first thing Monday morning. I'll call Connie's mother. They are probably talking about this, too, right now."

On Monday morning, the two trembling girls were waiting at the principal's office when he arrived.

"Hi!" he called out to them with a laugh. "What a nice surprise! Two of my favorite girls are here to greet me on a Monday morning!"

The girls felt even worse when he said they were his favorites. Mr. Kirkman unlocked his office, and he noticed the girls still standing there.

"You still have some time to play outside," he said. "You might like a big ride on one of the swings."

Both girls gasped. *He must know! He's teasing us about it now,* they thought.

"We have something to tell you," Darlene managed to say, nearly choking.

"Good! I'll bet it's a nice surprise!" Mr. Kirkman said, still half laughing.

"We broke the swing!" Connie blurted out.

"We didn't mean to," Darlene added.

"What? Did you say you broke the swing? Just this morning?" He sat down at his desk with his mouth open.

"That was quick work," he stammered at last. "I haven't heard about a broken swing yet."

Both girls sobbed as they told how they had played on Sunday and forgot the rule, twisted the swing, and the chain broke. They looked up at Mr. Kirkman. He looked serious, but he was trying not to laugh.

"Well, girls," he began with the seriousness of a judge, "I guess you have learned a lesson, haven't you?"

Darlene and Connie nodded in unison.

"I think we can fix the swing. I'll ask Mr. Rigsby to take a look at it as soon as classes start. You girls did the right thing, coming to tell me what happened. That counts for a lot," he said. "Do your parents know about it?"

The girls nodded again in unison.

"That's another good thing. Now I can call your mothers and tell them you came to see me. I know your mothers. I know they will be proud of you. Your fathers too. Now you better get to your classroom before you're counted absent." Then he added, "One more thing, girls. Let's not twist the swings anymore."

Darlene and Connie had never been so happy to be sent to class. They were happy to be out of trouble, and they planned to stay out of trouble for a long time.

Darlene told the story of the swing when we were first dating, and I heard her tell it a few times to our kids. It was a big crime she remembered for a long time. She told it like a small catechism on the importance of honesty and repentance.

9

The Burning Car

The second story Darlene told me about her school-age years was something that happened during high school. She didn't burn up a car on purpose, but it did catch fire while she was driving it.

One Saturday morning after breakfast with her parents, Darlene asked to borrow their 1956 DeSoto sedan for a short errand. The DeSoto was a large, sleek car that looked somewhat like the Buicks of the time. On Madison Avenue near Southport Road, as she waited at the stoplight so she could turn left to go home, she noticed the paint on the car's hood bubbling up strangely. She had just enough time to jump out before the entire engine burst into flames. She was so close to home that she just left the flaming car in the street, ran there, clambered up the stairs, and burst into the apartment.

"The car is on fire!" Darlene yelled, crying hysterically. "I don't know what I did! The car is burning up! It's out in the street!"

"Where are you hurt?" Grada asked.

"I'm not hurt! I just jumped out of the car and ran home."

"Are you sure you're okay?" Virginia asked, looking her over carefully.

"I'm okay! I'm okay!" Darlene said.

"That's all that matters," Grada said. "They's a lot more cars in the world. Where's it at?"

"Out there," Darlene said, pointing toward Madison Avenue. She couldn't think of the street's name.

Grada joined the crowd of spectators and firemen at the car, followed by Darlene and her mother. Darlene had calmed down, but it was still a tragedy to her, burning up that beautiful, shiny maroon DeSoto. When the tow truck arrived, Grada identified himself as the car's owner.

"You can pull it right into that parking lot over there," he told the driver. "That's my building."

A policeman overheard Grada's directions to the driver.

"Sir, were you driving the car?"

"No, it was my daughter, the girl over there," Grada said, indicating Darlene. "She hasn't been driving but two months now."

The policeman went to Darlene, and she noticed he had a gun and handcuffs on his belt.

"Were you driving the car when it caught fire?" the policeman asked.

Darlene nodded. "Yes, I was," she admitted, "but I didn't do anything. It just started burning."

"Did you get burned?" the policeman continued.

"No. The paint on the engine started bubbling. Smoke came out. I just stopped and jumped out of the car and ran home, right over there," she said, pointing to the building.

"Well, that's about the best thing you could have done, young lady," the policeman said. "Good thinking!"

Darlene was so relieved that she wanted to hug the policeman. She had thought she might be arrested. She watched the DeSoto being towed away and the firemen hosing down the street. A beautiful car had been lost, but she had done the right thing and was alive and unharmed. It was still Saturday, and it was good to be alive.

10

Grada's Gold Mine

The third important story Darlene told me was the history of "the building" itself, the family home and the cornerstone of her father's business. The two-story frame structure was about 40 feet wide and 120 feet long. It was essential to the family's life and was also a landmark in the community.

The building originally stood within a few feet of the corner of Southport Road and Madison Avenue. Only a sidewalk separated it from those two busy streets. Behind it, the land sloped down to Buck Creek, a sleepy little stream in dry weather that became a raging torrent after heavy rains. When Grada bought the building to house his sizeable plumbing and construction business in 1951, he also bought the corner lot and the land behind it. The family lived in a large apartment upstairs, and his business filled the first floor. His panel trucks parked outside were painted with the words "Sayers Plumbing" to show off his success.

Grada's businesses grew rapidly in the early 1950s. He was a general contractor, a plumber, and a refrigeration specialist. Several men worked for him full-time, and he always had several construction projects under contract. In the early 1960s, however, the country experienced an economic downturn. Some of his customers were unable to make their payments. He was then unable to pay his suppliers, and his business empire began to shrink. To make matters worse, a business rival encouraged creditors to insist that Grada quickly repay his debts to them. It was the darkest time of his business life.

The family's income during that recovery time was perilously low. Darlene remembered going with her mother to the grocery store. Before leaving home, Virginia counted out every dollar bill and coin she had that day. The grocery bill would have to come in under that amount. As Darlene and her mother circled through the store, Virginia kept a running mental tally, trying to be sure they had not overspent. Still, when their groceries were totaled, it sometimes happened that they had more groceries than their money could cover. Humiliated, Virginia would send Darlene to put an item or two back on the shelf. When more prosperous times came, they remembered the sting of those hard times.

At one point, Grada had to seek bankruptcy protection to save the building, but he was a man of such integrity that he insisted on paying his creditors and suppliers. It was a long, nerve-racking process, but the loans and suppliers were paid. In four years, Grada was back on his feet financially, fully solvent but running a smaller empire. To some people, he again seemed wealthy. To all who knew him, he was most wealthy in integrity.

In about 1960, the city of Indianapolis made plans to widen the Madison Avenue and Southport Road intersection. The city initially offered Grada a small sum to buy just part of the building to make way for the widened street. For Grada, the whole building would have been ruined for his purposes if he had to sell just part of it, and he couldn't see how he could remodel the remaining portion for use. After further negotiation, however, he settled with the city for additional monies for the entire structure but retained the back portion of the corner lot.

The city intended to demolish the building. By law, the city's next step was to offer the building for sale at auction to the highest bidder, presumably to someone who would demolish it and salvage useable parts. Out of curiosity, Grada went to the auction that chilly morning and found there were only two or three other witnesses to the great event. When the auctioneer called for bidding to open, there was only silence. Men looked at each other.

Exasperated, the auctioneer yelled, "Won't *somebody* bid *something* on this building? Won't you bid *anything*?"

No one else spoke, so Grada raised his hand. "How about $450.00?" he said. Again no one else spoke.

Before Grada could change his mind, the auctioneer yelled, "Sold! Sold to that man for $450!" The auctioneer then said, "Aren't you the guy who sold this building to the city? What do you plan to do with it now?"

"Move it," Grada replied quietly.

No one believed it could be moved, and several at that sale spoke up to tell him it was impossible. But Grada had a new plan in mind that would turn it into what would one day become his personal gold mine. Since he still owned the land behind the building, he would move it to that open lot, keep his businesses in the building, and continue to live upstairs.

Grada hired a company that assured him the big, two-story building could be moved. The workers dug trenches around it, inserted steel beams underneath, jacked it up, and placed it on wheels. The whole thing then began a slow journey to its new location. Meanwhile, Grada, Virginia, and Darlene continued to live upstairs, spending nights there but leaving during the day.

It was early June 1961 when one morning as Darlene was finishing breakfast before school, she looked outside and noticed that a tall maple tree just outside the window was moving.

"Mother!" she yelled. "The tree is moving!"

"Oh, no!" Virginia gasped. "They're moving the building! Get your things! We have to get out!"

Darlene scampered off to school, and Virginia went to her job at L.S. Ayres in downtown Indianapolis. The movers continued the building's slow creep toward its new resting place. Eventually it was settled onto a new foundation, and members of Darlene's family continued to live in the building for nearly forty years.

Darlene and her parents were still living in the large second-floor apartment of the building when I met her. Grada was operating his plumbing and contracting business in the downstairs portion of the building, and he had rented the extra space to a beauty parlor, a lawyer, and another business. The family was truly "living above the store," as the saying goes.

I, too, have fond memories of the building. The main stair to the second floor had a small landing and a left-hand turn before reaching a lobby that served as the laundry room and the entrances to the apartment area. When we were first dating, Darlene and I sometimes sat on the landing late at night, whispering quietly to avoid attracting her parents' attention. She was always very careful to avoid displays of affection in her parents' presence, even after we were married.

The retirement house that Grada built in 1970 had three bedrooms and one-and-a-half baths. It was for Virginia and him in their old age, and they were then sixty-one. It had no stairs to climb and less space to maintain. Darlene and I visited her parents often at that sturdy, brick-clad house, and it was the only home where our children ever visited their Sayers grandparents.

Even after Grada and Virginia moved to Walnut Street, the building remained Grada's business center and his place of escape from the confines of home life. It must have been a sentimental place for him, though he seldom seemed sentimental. Late in life, he sometimes went to his office in the building for an hour or two alone with his tools and his memories.

Grada began negotiations for the final sale of the building again in the spring of 1991. He was diagnosed with pancreatic cancer in June that year, and he continued arrangements for the sale that summer. Upon his death in August of that year, the family completed the sale and held an auction to sell Grada's tools and plumbing supplies one cold, rainy November day. The building was soon demolished to make way for the Walgreens drugstore that still stands at that corner. Darlene and her sisters stood and cried as they watched the wrecking crew hack into their precious building with mechanical claws.

The story of "the building" was important to Darlene for several reasons, but perhaps most importantly because of what it taught her about facing life's challenges. She grew up seeing her father's example of unblinking steadiness, simple faith, and pure integrity. Those were traits for which she herself would be known.

11

Career Decisions

*O*ne sunny Sunday afternoon on the trio tour, Darlene and I had a picnic and a walk along a small creek in New York State. The afternoon sun shone through small trees and sparkled in the creek. It was a scene that could have made a beautiful painting. Since the other girls had graciously allowed us the time to be alone, we could talk freely, especially about the future. She was wrestling with thoughts about her career, thoughts that were better formed and more mature than my thoughts about my own future.

Darlene had decided in high school that she wanted to become a nurse. She volunteered as a "Candy Striper" in an Indianapolis hospital to gain practical experience and wore the red-and-white striped pinafore that gave her role its name. When she graduated from high school in 1963, she entered pre-nursing studies at Anderson College. In the fall of 1964, after one year of study at Anderson, she took the next step of her plan by enrolling in nurses' training at the Indiana University Medical School in Indianapolis. Only a few weeks of nursing school convinced Darlene she did not want to be a nurse after all.

Sometime that fall, Darlene had gone to Anderson College to see Dean of Students Norman Beard about returning there to study. I'd actually caught a glimpse of her on that day, not knowing who she was or what she would later mean to me, so the moment passed uneventfully. Only several months later did I remember that moment and realize it was the first time I had seen her.

That meeting with Dean Beard was a pivotal moment that led Darlene to return to Anderson College in January 1965. She was then halfway through her sophomore year, just nineteen years old at the time. She was undecided about medical school and thought perhaps a PhD in biology might fit her scientific interests better. Dean Beard had recommended choosing the path that would leave the most options open. She later heard the same advice from Dr. Jerry Stephenson, a medical doctor who had come to teach biology and related courses at the college. He pointed out that the MD degree was virtually assured once she was accepted into medical school, and she could go into either research or clinical work with that degree. In contrast, entry into a PhD program did not assure ultimately receiving that degree, and she could not have done clinical work with that degree.

That Sunday afternoon on the summer tour, the advice of these men must have been on her mind as we sat beside that quiet creek. Darlene was agonizing over her career direction. She had decided against a career in nursing. She knew what she *didn't want* to do, but what did she *want* to do? As we talked, medical school emerged as her more likely destination. The thought frightened both of us: It meant four more years of intense studies after college graduation, and that was still two years away. How could we be together while she finished college and later became absorbed in her medical training? Although we were excited about her prospect of becoming a medical doctor, we knew how hard it might be for us as a couple.

In the months ahead, we had other conversations about her medical future. None was as beautiful or as poignant as the one beside the creek that sunny Sunday afternoon. Our talks about the future became more and more painful as her decision hardened and she focused on her science studies and the medical career to which she felt God was calling her. We both believed we were meant for each other, but it would not be feasible to marry for several years.

When Darlene immersed herself in pre-med studies at Anderson College in September 1965, I began seeking my own direction, made more urgent by Darlene pursuing hers. I knew I wanted to do graduate work, but I didn't know what to study. I considered journalism, history, economics, and medicine.

Medicine attracted me, partly because of Darlene's decision to enter it, partly because three of my cousins were doctors, and partly because I liked the image of myself wearing a white coat and being called "Doctor." To test the waters, I signed up for a biology class with Dr. Marie Mayo, one of Darlene's favorite professors. My second-strongest interest was economics, so I enrolled in an economics class with Dr. Harold Linamen. Both courses were in the new science building at Anderson College, so my "commute" to class was only a walk across a parking lot from my office.

I lasted only two days in the biology class. The sessions I attended were introductions to DNA and RNA, the inner workings of living cells. The subject matter felt confining to me. In contrast, the principles of economics class with Dr. Linamen seemed to open the wide world I had begun to see in Ethiopia during my two years in the Peace Corps. Economics offered the mental tools I needed to think more clearly about the desperate poverty in Ethiopia and the relative abundance in the United States. I, too, had found my intellectual direction. Medical school was ahead for Darlene, and graduate study in economics was ahead for me.

12

Our Roads Diverge

Two roads diverged in a yellow wood,
And sorry I could not travel both
And be one traveler....

I shall be telling this with a sigh
Somewhere ages and ages hence:
Two roads diverged in a wood, and I—
I took the one less traveled by,
And that has made all the difference.

—From "The Road Not Taken" by Robert Frost

When Darlene made her firm decision to go to medical school, no clear path lay ahead for us. She was resolute in her decision, and I knew that tension and unhappiness would result if I tried to dissuade her. Besides, I was excited by the prospect of her taking on such an ambitious goal. It clearly seemed right to both of us, but what would become of "us"?

We continued to date each other in early 1966, but without a marriage commitment. We weren't sure we would ever marry. We both dated other people a couple of times, but we found no joy and no future in those experiences. In the summer of 1966, I was a co-leader of a student mission trip to Peru, while Darlene took summer classes to expedite her progress toward medical school. By the end of 1966, she had arranged to spend the first semester of 1967 as a research assistant at Argonne National Laboratories near Chicago.

While she was in Chicago, I remained on my job in Anderson and continued my studies for a career in economics. I took the Graduate Record Exam and applied for scholarships and admission to graduate schools. She applied to the Indiana University medical school in Indianapolis.

A massive blizzard struck Chicago in January 1967. It was a series of blizzards that dumped over thirty-six inches of snow on the city between January 26 and February 5. Both airports were shut down during the worst of it, and all other transportation was hampered or halted. When Chicago streets became just barely passable, Darlene's parents decided to visit her on the weekend of February 11 and 12, driving from their home in Indianapolis.

Coincidentally, I was scheduled for a scholarship interview with a University of Chicago professor that weekend. Scholarships were being offered by a national foundation, and the University of Chicago was the nearest interview site. UCLA, my first choice, was one of five universities where the scholarships could be used. Hearing of my plans, Grada and Virginia invited me to ride with them. They dropped me at my brother Merl's home in Chicago the day before my appointment at the university.

The next day, I hiked several blocks from the commuter train station to the professor's apartment for my scholarship interview. The streets around the University of Chicago were lined with cars buried deep in snow. I walked down the middle of deserted streets and arrived on time for my interview. The professor seemed surprised and a little amused that I had made it through the deep snow, but we had a fine conversation while he smoked his pipe and played classical music on a small record player next to his chair.

The blizzard and my intrepid hike may have had something to do with the scholarship I was awarded later that spring. I had found an unexpected "road in a yellow wood." Soon enough I would be leaving Anderson and entering graduate school at UCLA in Los Angeles.

I was not surprised when Darlene was accepted into medical school that spring, and I was sure she could accomplish whatever she wanted. Her "road in a yellow wood" would take her to the Indiana University School of Medicine. She was about to become the first woman from Anderson College to attend medical school.

PART TWO

*California Callings:
1967 to 1974*

13

Our Roads Converge

From the autumn of 1967 until 1971, four long but productive years, Darlene and I were separated by our respective graduate studies half a continent apart. We saw each other only briefly during summer breaks and each year at Christmas. We wrote letters and we sometimes spoke on the phone, but long-distance calls were so expensive then that we didn't talk often. We were both busy with our separate lives—hers in Indiana and mine in California.

I wrote many letters to her during those years, far more than I remembered. In 2013, I found a box in our basement in Indianapolis in which she had stored all of my letters. The most personal letters were on top, and they were in chronological order. Her saving the letters had been an act of love I learned about only when she was gone. Darlene wrote fewer letters to me, but from my letters, I can tell that she wrote more than I remembered. (I have yet to find my collection of her letters to me.)

My letters show that we were both agonizing over our separateness. In 1968, she considered transferring to UCLA to complete her MD, and she even thought of dropping out of medical school entirely. The letters, even now, help me understand how our lives finally converged in marriage.

In summer 1968, I led a group of college students to Uganda for the Experiment in International Living, and in 1969, I led a group to Tanzania for the Experiment. I talked to Darlene on the phone before those trips, and I saw her for a couple of evenings each time when I returned. Then I was off to Los Angeles again.

In January 1970, while Darlene was staying in a dormitory at the downtown Indianapolis campus of the Indiana University Medical Center, she awoke one morning to hear the Indianapolis weather report: "Today in the Circle City, the temperature is 17 degrees below zero, going to a high of 9 degrees above. The wind chill is 36 degrees below zero."

Darlene shuddered and continued to get dressed. She dreaded trudging across the campus on the ice that had formed two days earlier during a freezing rain. Then the announcer cheerfully continued.

"But in Los Angeles, it's a different story! Santa Ana winds are blowing into the LA basin from the deserts to the east. The high temperature in Los Angeles will be 95 degrees for the third time this week!"

When she told me later about her weather and what she had heard about mine, I shuddered too and felt a little guilty.

During that same cold winter of 1970, our relationship was heating up. My letters were even more frequent, revealing my excitement and passion. There was a possibility she would come to Los Angeles that spring, so I wrote openly of marriage and the hope that we would soon be together permanently. At that point, we had no formal agreement to marry.

Darlene had already started applying for internships in preparation for completing medical school in 1971. She was focusing on California medical schools, perhaps because of that frigid week in January or other reasons she didn't immediately divulge. She called in March 1970 to tell me she was planning a trip to San Francisco and Los Angeles in May for interviews. We made plans to see each other.

Her Los Angeles visit was during a time of national tension. On May 4, 1970, a few days after she arrived, we were having lunch with two economist friends when a student activist burst into the UCLA dining hall.

"Four dead at Kent State, strike now before it's too late!" the man chanted as he marched through the dining hall while patrons watched in varying states of mind.

Most of us hadn't yet heard that some young National Guardsmen had panicked in the face of demonstrators at Kent State University and had fired on the crowd. Soon the Kent State incident was the talk of the nation and was a catalyst for the activists at UCLA. Suddenly it didn't feel safe to walk across that beautiful campus. Police were present, and crowds of demonstrators congregated in front of the administration building. That afternoon I looked across the campus from my parking structure and saw smoke rising from the Student Center. Below where I stood were twenty armed policemen standing beside their motorcycles, waiting for orders.

Darlene's trip was the beginning of a new relationship between us. I took her to some of the standard sights around Los Angeles, and we toured the UCLA campus. She met some of my friends, and she visited the private home where I was renting rooms from Bess Cohn, an elderly Jewish lady. Mrs. Cohn approved of Darlene, and that was a good signal for me to give our relationship more attention. I sensed that we might find our way back together permanently if we could spend more time together.

After Darlene returned to Indiana, I decided to travel to the Midwest when I finished a set of PhD qualifying exams in June. I wanted to spend the summer seeing her in Indiana and my parents and other family in Ohio. I would look for summer work in Ohio, just as I had during college. A married couple from the Economics Department at UCLA was planning to deliver a car to New York City for a Los Angeles company, and when I shared my summer plans, they invited me to ride with them to Indianapolis. Their route took us from Los Angeles to Phoenix, Albuquerque, Amarillo, Oklahoma City, and Joplin, Missouri. After three days on the road, they delivered me at the door of Darlene's tiny apartment a few miles from the Medical Center. She took me to the apartment of a college friend who had agreed to share his apartment with me for a few weeks that summer.

After a week in Indianapolis, I left Darlene to her studies and took a Greyhound bus to Toledo, Ohio. I stayed with my parents in my boyhood country home near Elmore and relived some of the joys of childhood for a few days. I had left California with very little money, and it was running out. I landed a job at a ketchup and pickle factory in Oak Harbor.

At the factory, cucumbers were pickled in huge wooden vats. Large ones were soaked in brine that would change them to dill pickles. Smaller ones were soaked in a sugary, spicy solution to become sweet pickle gherkins. In adjacent buildings, huge pots of ketchup and tomato sauce were cooked, sending clouds of delicious aromas over the town. After only a week, the owner of the company asked me to take a permanent job as a foreman. I was flattered, but I had already found a higher-paying job.

My next job was at the lime plant in nearby Gibsonburg. There I worked from 7:00 p.m. until 7:00 a.m., helping to refurbish a massive lime-cooking kiln. Like my father who had worked in a lime plant more than thirty years earlier, I found the skin under my shirt cuffs dissolving. My sweat activated the lime dust and created ulcerated, bleeding rings around my wrists. I was relieved when the emergency repair work was finished and I could quit that job after a week of well-paid work. Having lined my pockets with cash, I headed back to Indianapolis on the bus for a longer visit with Darlene.

I had to buy a set of wheels to take me back to Los Angeles, so I searched the newspaper ads and found a car priced at $250. A friend took me to see the car. It seemed roadworthy enough, so I offered $200 cash and drove away in a ten-year-old pale-blue 1960 Ford station wagon. It was a humble but practical vehicle, but it would not have lent itself to picking up new girlfriends. Fortunately I had a practical-minded girlfriend who didn't care what kind of car I drove.

Late that summer Darlene and I spent several evenings together, but her daytime hours were consumed by medical studies. When it was time for me to return to Los Angeles, we were on a more secure footing with each other. We made no promises to each other except to be in touch, which meant by mail or occasional phone calls.

We kept our promises to each other that fall and winter. We wrote letters and talked on the phone regularly. She made plans to come to Los Angeles in January 1971. As part of her medical training, she would work until May in some clinics in Los Angeles. She would also visit the medical centers where she was applying for a residency in pediatrics.

Darlene had always been attracted to children, so pediatrics was a natural choice. It wasn't the highest-paid specialty, but it was one in which she could feel emotionally engaged. She also told me she had chosen pediatrics partly because kids have shorter medical histories to collect at the beginning of treatment. In medical school she had found that the histories of adults could go on at great length. She didn't feel she had the patience to listen that long.

Darlene's top choice for her residency was the University of California Los Angeles (UCLA) Medical Center, on the same campus where I was studying.

But she had applied at others in Southern California and in the San Francisco area as well. She would not know until "Match Day" in March 1971 where she would spend the next three years. We didn't know how we would manage our relationship if she matched with a hospital other than UCLA, especially if she matched with one in the San Francisco area. We had kept in close contact by letters and phone calls for four years, but it would be difficult to continue that way for three more years. I blithely assumed she would be accepted at UCLA where I was.

When Darlene arrived in Los Angeles, her first order of business was to find a place to live. Her first attempt was humorous. She called a place in Hollywood where a woman had advertised rooms for rent in her home, but the woman seemed to have forgotten her ad or perhaps couldn't understand Darlene.

"What is this?" the woman demanded on the phone. "Is this a 'hoe-axe'?"

Darlene carefully repeated her questions about the rental. This time the woman understood and said to come on over. I drove her to a palm-lined street in Hollywood in my glamorous station wagon. The house with rooms for rent was large, old, and unkempt. The front door was open, and only a screen door kept out bugs and intruders. I watched from the car while Darlene approached and rang the doorbell. She rang again. No answer. Without waiting another second, she nearly ran back to the car and jumped in.

"Hurry! Let's go! Let's get out of here!" she urged in a loud whisper. "That place is creepy!"

Darlene eventually found rooms to rent in a more conventional home, but we remembered the "hoe-axe" lady and continued to pronounce the word that way. Our roads had converged once again, and I began to think more seriously about our future together.

14

First Tent Camping Trip

Through my occasional attendance at Westwood Presbyterian Church near the UCLA campus, I had met Glenda Gay, wife of fellow economics graduate student Bob Gay. Both were from Kansas, and both were genial people who made friends quickly. Shortly after Darlene arrived in LA, Glenda and Bob invited Darlene and me to their apartment for dinner. We talked about plans for spring break. They were avid tent campers and were planning to take their tent to Joshua Tree National Park on a long weekend. They invited us to go along.

Darlene and I had very little camping experience. She and another girl had camped in a tent at the Anderson Camp Meeting one especially rainy June week when she was in high school. They stayed through two nights of heavy rain until Darlene's dad, under pressure from Darlene's mother, drove to Anderson to rescue the two campers. I had never slept in a real tent. My camping experience was limited to sleeping outside under old carpets slung over my mother's clothesline in my family's yard in Ohio.

The call of the desert was strong, and we would be with experienced campers. The time together, away from the pressures of our career studies, was appealing. We eagerly accepted their invitation.

On a Thursday morning, the four of us headed east on Interstate 10 after the morning rush. An infinite number of two-story apartment buildings and taller office buildings lined the highway, softened somewhat by palm and eucalyptus trees and blossoming red and purple bougainvillea vines. The highway department had placed raised discs on the lines between traffic lanes, and Bob delighted in driving on those "buttons" to make the car bump and shake. Darlene and I laughed. Glenda chided Bob. Bob laughed through a devilish grin.

At Joshua Tree, Bob drove us through several campgrounds, and we learned how campers find a campsite. As we cruised slowly, Bob and Glenda conferred on the merits of several sites. Darlene and I listened in, not realizing at the time how much this tutorial would help us on future camping trips. At last our guides chose a cozy place in Hidden Valley Campground that had just enough level sand for their 8×10 cabin tent. The site was sheltered from afternoon sun and winds by high rock formations that looked like a backdrop for a Western movie. The morning sun would warm our little haven, and the rocks behind the tent sloped up gently and could be climbed easily. A long desert valley dotted by Joshua trees stretched miles to our west and became one of our favorite mental images of that place.

On that first camping weekend, Darlene and I learned how to cook on a Coleman white gas stove, wash dishes with minimal water, bathe discreetly in the tent, and use each hour of the day well. We all hiked to the top of Ryan Mountain, and we explored abandoned mines. Some mine shafts were horizontal, and we walked in as far as we could without flashlights. Other mine shafts had been driven straight down into granite and were left uncovered, open to the sky. At one of these vertical shafts, we took turns dropping eight-inch boulders into the darkness below. We could hear the rocks moaning through the stale air below, accelerating until they hit a side of the shaft a hundred feet or more below. They then ricocheted off the sides the rest of the way down, banging the sides again and again, booming like distant thunder or cannon fire.

The highlight of our second day was when Bob drove his powerful old Plymouth Belvedere sedan off the park road and up the grassy shoulder of a mountain. He followed the narrow ridge with the mountain on our left and a steep escarpment on our right. The landscape to our right stretched far away to the horizon. Bob made one attempt on a line of attack that was too steep, backed away, and took a slightly shallower route. The car roared up the ridge so steeply that we felt we were becoming vertical. When the tires began to spin helplessly, the car started to slide backward. Darlene and Glenda screamed. Bob laughed. I gritted my teeth and laughed with him. The day's adventure was over. Even for a four-wheel drive vehicle, the ridge would have been dangerously steep. We had attempted it in a rear-wheel drive Plymouth sedan from the 1960s.

More surprises were ahead before that first camping trip ended, but our time in Joshua Tree had created a pattern of adventuring for Darlene and me that would continue throughout our married life. From that one weekend tutorial, we acquired an appetite for camping and the skills needed to plan a trip, enjoy it, and return home safely. From that weekend on, tent camping became our main recreational activity, and our camping trips were treasured bonding times for both of us.

15

Engaged on Interstate 10

A camping trip might seem like an unusual prelude to an engagement. The back seat of a car on the way to LA might seem even more unusual. But to us it was logical. The circumstances of our engagement fit our history, our relationship, Darlene's decisiveness, and the opportunity before us. Our first camping experience in Joshua Tree set the stage for what was about to happen.

Back in our first year of dating while we were both still living in Indiana, I had wanted to marry Darlene as soon as possible, regardless of our lack of money and our incompatible study plans. At least once I had urged her to marry me and wanted to ask her parents' permission immediately. She had resolutely refused, and it became clear to me there would be no possibility of marriage until she finished medical school.

When Darlene began to apply for internships in California, I thought it was simply a good and sensible plan for her. She would be close enough that we could date regularly while we pursued our professional studies. I had become accustomed to our long-distance, intermittent relationship, and I wasn't even sure I still wanted to be married. Still, we both could see that a future together was becoming more likely. She might have had more serious thoughts, but I didn't ask about her intentions.

The camping trip to Joshua Tree was a refreshing step back from the pressures of medical school and graduate school. The long, clear views across the desert energized us and gave us a longer view of life than we had in the city. It was good to be far from the tensions of my academic work and the anxiety of Darlene's internship placement. Spending Match Day together while we were on this camping trip out in the desert was providential.

Match Day is a day of high tension for thousands of young doctors. It is the day when the pairings of requests from medical centers across the country with new medical doctors applying for internship and residency programs are revealed. Doctors and hospitals must rank their choices, and those choices are reconciled by a nationwide computerized sorting system. When the pairings are revealed, the new doctors are required to accept the location of their highest-ranked pairing. The alternative is to wait a year to reapply and seek a different placement. Only under rare circumstances can a doctor request a location other than the Match Day pairing.

Darlene had applied for internships at several California medical centers. On the morning of Match Day 1971, she and I had breakfast at the campsite with Bob and Glenda and then borrowed their car to go to the ranger station. Darlene would use the pay phone there to call the Med Center in Indianapolis about her match. We went armed with a pocketful of quarters for the phone, but the call didn't take long. She was connected immediately and asked the person in Indianapolis where she had matched. She then asked for the result to be repeated to her before she calmly hung up. It was like her to absorb this great news in that way, slowly letting it simmer through her mind before she spoke.

"I matched with UCLA!" she exclaimed triumphantly.

"Great!" I said, hugging her. "Congratulations! Now you can move out here!"

"Yes, and we can do more camping!"

I hugged her again, and we returned to the campsite to tell Bob and Glenda.

Darlene understood how extraordinary it was that she had matched at UCLA, exactly as she had hoped. Many years later, I learned the long odds of her placement, an outcome so wonderful that some would call it a miracle. On the other hand, UCLA was fortunate to have attracted Darlene. Few new doctors had her good heart as well as her superb preparation. Being a female physician probably helped her chances, too, since those were the days of relatively few female physicians. Her good looks probably didn't matter to UCLA, but they mattered to me.

At first I didn't realize the profound change that had come over our lives, but Darlene did. She had clearer plans than my vague expectation that we would resume regular dating. I would learn her thoughts during the trip back to LA at the end of the weekend.

Dusk had fallen by the time Bob merged the Plymouth onto westbound I-10 on Saturday evening. He and Glenda in the front seat talked about the weekend and the trips they were planning for the future. Darlene and I were in the back seat, and I was gazing absently at the traffic outside and the rows of palm trees. We must have made small talk. All I remember is that Darlene suddenly turned to me.

"When are we getting married?"

I was stunned. Her question struck like lightning. We had talked of marriage ever since we met six years earlier, and our letters had been laced with suggestions that we might marry eventually, but we hadn't talked of marriage that weekend. We had only celebrated her placement at UCLA. Yet there she was, confronting me with the reality of what we had written and talked about and what she had made possible by getting her residency at UCLA, right where I was studying.

My mind whirled. Deep down I knew she was the woman for me, and I didn't want to spoil the moment. I hadn't planned it, but I knew I needed to be decisive. She had just asked *when*, and I had to say *something*.

"June!" I blurted out.

I put my arm around her, and we kissed. We were engaged!

"Let's tell Bob and Glenda," she urged me.

My head was spinning, but I think Darlene knew exactly what she was doing and what we needed to do next.

"Guess what!" I called loudly over the highway noise. "We just got engaged!"

"What?" Glenda shouted. "Really?"

"Yes! We're getting married in June!" I yelled.

"Are you sure?" Bob asked sarcastically. "Have you given this enough thought?"

"Yes!" Darlene and I yelled in unison and laughed. We had been dating for six years. "We're sure!"

Back at Bob and Glenda's apartment, we called Darlene's parents. It must have been very late in Indiana by then. I don't remember their reaction, but I assume it was positive. We then called my parents, and they were happy with the news. The wedding date we agreed on was June 12, 1971—a spring wedding in Indiana.

16

Wedding Day

*D*arlene and I had a very short engagement. Modern engagements can last a year or two or even longer, but ours was not a modern one, and we would not have a modern wedding. We were engaged on March 20, and we chose June 12 as our wedding date in Indianapolis, only eighty-five days later. We were two thousand miles away, and we needed to finish the school year, plan our wedding, and make as many arrangements as possible from that distance.

The wedding we planned for Saturday, June 12, 1971, was mostly in keeping with the traditions of that time, but we added a few flourishes of our own. Those free-spirited days of the early 1970s led us to plan our own ceremony and write our own vows. We wanted to preserve the spirit of the traditional vows while freshening the wording. I wrote a draft, and the two of us revised it several times. I clearly remember typing out drafts of the vows in my apartment in Los Angeles and checking them with Darlene until we had them right for us.

We also wanted to be creative with the wedding music and the invitations. We asked a quintet of our musical Indiana friends to sing the bridal chorus from the opera *Lohengrin*, a song known to school children as "Here Comes the Bride." The invitations were written in a playful script by Vivian Lowe, an artist friend using our wording. (Many copies of those unconventional brown invitations with hand lettering still exist.)

Another important task to be completed while we were in Los Angeles was finding our first home for when we would return after the wedding. We looked at apartments near UCLA and found one at 1616½ Veteran Avenue, a little more than a mile from the Med Center. We immediately fell in love with the apartment's old-fashioned charm. Nearly everything was out of date, even for 1971, and we loved it. It had two bedrooms, a kitchen that must have been modern in the 1920s, a tiny dining room, and a spacious living room. The bathroom had a tub and a separate shower, both with ancient plumbing. It was perfect for us. What was not out of date was the "wheat field" of deep, golden shag carpet in the living room. It looked beautiful back then.

We contemplated having the wedding ceremony outdoors in a picnic setting, but that would have been too outlandish for Indiana in those days, especially for Darlene's mother. We agreed that the wedding would be in the Garfield Park Church of God, the home church of Darlene's family. Darlene's dad contacted Rev. Larry Reynolds, the pastor, and asked if he would perform our ceremony. He agreed to consider our script but reserved editorial rights in case we had something wild in mind.

The wedding dress was a critical choice for Darlene, and she quickly found what she wanted in one of the small cities that make up Los Angeles. I was unaware of the superstition about the groom not seeing the bride in her gown before the wedding, and I remember driving her to a strange, distant part of that vast city and waiting excitedly while she was fitted for the dress she had chosen. It was an elegantly simple white gown, and she looked stunning in it. We returned for the altered dress a week later and paid nearly $100 for it. To us, that was a lot of money.

As our planning gained momentum, the wedding took on a splendid, traditional feel. The bridesmaids were to wear floor-length pink floral dresses that we felt had a nineteenth-century look. The groomsmen would wear tuxes. The kids in the wedding would be miniatures of the adults. It didn't register with me during our planning, but I was to be in a tuxedo too. Darlene's dad would escort her down the aisle in one of his own blue dress suits. Her mother would choose an elegant dress that fit her taste and sense of economy.

Upon our arrival in Indianapolis ten days before the wedding, we would have to deal with the collision between Darlene's medical school graduation on Friday evening, June 11, and our wedding on June 12. It couldn't be helped. We threw ourselves into the frenzy of preparing for both momentous events. Darlene needed only to show up for her graduation, but for the wedding we had to have blood tests, get a marriage license, meet the pastor who would perform the wedding ceremony, and buy wedding rings.

Our meeting with Pastor Larry Reynolds was light-hearted, hardly the serious premarital counseling we might have had if we had married five years earlier. We joked and talked about the special music we had in mind. Darlene warned Pastor Reynolds that I was the kind of person who might wear a red choir robe if the other choir members were in blue robes.

Applying for our marriage license and having blood drawn had an "otherworldly" feel to me—something like being inducted into the Army—but the moment passed quickly.

Downtown Indianapolis at that time looked like something left over from World War II: old department stores were dark with smoke stains, the streets were dirty and rutted, and newspapers blew in little cyclones in the streets. We came upon Goodman's Jewelers and described what we wanted: plain gold bands for both of us. We were shown two rings that exactly met our desire and fit our budget—the price was two rings for $25. The price of gold was still controlled near the Depression Era price of $35 per ounce, but it was deregulated two months later and began to soar. We bought low, but we never sold our gold.

Darlene's graduation from the Indiana University School of Medicine in Clowes Hall at Butler University on June 11 was the first of two major life milestones for us that weekend. The second milestone would be our wedding less than twenty-four hours later.

One thing was certain from the very beginning: Ours would be a "true Christian wedding," the only kind of wedding either of us had seen. A true Christian wedding, in my telling of it, was conducted in the bride's church by the local minister. A respectable number of parishioners and relatives would come to witness the great event. The ceremony would be brief and straightforward, and afterward the bride and groom would stand at the sanctuary exit to shake hands with the crowd. A few assertive individuals might insist on kissing the bride, but not many.

After passing through the receiving line, the crowd would migrate to the church fellowship hall for the reception, followed by the bride and groom. Pink punch, multi-colored mints, mixed nuts, and cake would be on the tables. At a true Christian wedding, no meal was served, nor was there dancing. No champagne or wine would be served and no toasts proposed, even with the pink punch.

And so it was on our wedding day, except Darlene's mother had ordered a small, multi-layered wedding cake in addition to the sheet cakes for the crowd. We hadn't wanted a wedding cake, but there it was, so we went ahead with the traditional cake-eating ritual. As was the standard, in that kind of Christian wedding, we opened our gifts in front of everyone and were photographed in the act.

After what seemed like six hours but was probably barely over an hour, the reception was over. Darlene and I changed into street clothes for our honeymoon trip and left the church in one of Grada's cars, headed for a brief honeymoon.

17

"Missing the Boat"

Our brief honeymoon was evidence of our youthful euphoria and our limited time. Unlike the extensive and expensive "destination" honeymoons of the twenty-first century, ours included a road trip to Cincinnati for two nights.

I had suggested Cincinnati as our destination largely because I had listened to classical music on Cincinnati radio station WLW while I was in college. Based on little else, I had formed a mental image of Cincinnati as a beautiful, romantic place. It was only a two-hour drive from the church, and it was far enough that any would-be pranksters were unlikely to find us. Thankfully, no one had adorned our car with "Just Married" signs and strings of tin cans on the back bumper.

Call it spontaneity or naïveté, but we drove off to Cincinnati without a hotel reservation. I somehow found the way to a Hilton and sheepishly booked a room, thinking the desk clerk might be suspicious of our marital status. Such things mattered in those days. We had dinner in a small German restaurant downstairs before our first night of married bliss.

In the morning, as we had breakfast in the hotel dining room on the top floor, we talked about our plans. The waiter told us about a river cruise, and it sounded like the right way to celebrate our first full day of marriage. I checked my watch and saw that we had just enough time to reach the dock to board the boat for the 10 a.m. cruise.

At the riverside, we saw no crowd and no evidence of a boat, just a ticket office. At the ticket office, we learned the boat had already left. My watch said 9:45, but that was Indiana time. We had missed the boat!

After recovering from mild disappointment, we spent the day at the Coney Island Amusement Park. We rode the thrilling, antique roller coasters, but the episode on the dock would become a favorite memory. We would often joke that we had "missed the boat" on our honeymoon.

18

Migration to California

After our weekend honeymoon, we returned to Darlene's parents' home in Indianapolis to prepare for the trip back to Los Angeles. Grada had given us a blue-green 1964 Chevrolet sedan for our road trip, and it had to be packed with Darlene's clothes, my luggage, and our wedding gifts. The shortest route possible from Indianapolis to Los Angeles was 2,086 miles. We stretched it with modifications to 2,400 miles of farmland, prairies, cities, rivers, mountains, and deserts to make it more adventuresome.

Darlene had to take medical licensing exams in Indianapolis three days after we returned from Cincinnati. While she studied for her exams, I packed the Chevrolet "to the gunnels." I filled every small and large space of the trunk and back seat with gifts and luggage, and I set out alone for Los Angeles early Wednesday morning, leaving behind my bride of four days. I took the standard route through Effingham, St. Louis, and Kansas City, spending the first night at a motel in Topeka, Kansas. By the second night, I was in Denver, ready for Darlene's arrival the next day.

On Friday morning at the airport, Darlene leaped into my arms at the end of the jetway at the Denver airport. We spun around, hugging and kissing like the honeymooners we were. She had completed her exams, and we were finally free of plans, family, and friends until the following Wednesday, when her internship would begin. Ahead of us lay more than a thousand miles of our favorite scenery: mountains, canyons, clear mountain streams, and deserts. This trip would be our real honeymoon.

West of Denver, U.S. Route 6 took us to an elevation of almost 12,000 feet at Loveland Pass. We stopped there to throw snowballs at each other and take pictures. We thought "Love-land" was well-named for the start of our journey. From there our southwesterly route took us to Ouray and then past the Four Corners—that unique place where Utah, Colorado, New Mexico, and Arizona meet. We journeyed on to the South Rim of the Grand Canyon.

Darlene took the wheel as we left the Grand Canyon, and I curled up in the front seat to sleep. It was after midnight when she stopped for gasoline.

"Can you drive now?" she asked.

I blinked in the glaring lights of the gas station. "Sure. I think I can," I said. "Where are we?"

"I guess this is Needles," she said. "We crossed the Colorado River, so we must be in California. How much farther?"

"We should be there in five or six hours," I guessed. "Good thing the sun will be at our backs when it comes up. Are you ready for some sleep?"

"I hope I can sleep," she said. "I'm tired, but I'm excited about getting there."

She curled up on the passenger side, and I took the wheel. The car had been built without air conditioning, but a small air conditioner had been added. It kept us comfortable enough, but we were glad to be making this desert crossing by night. She was still sleeping when the eastern sky behind us began to lighten and we descended into the Los Angeles basin. I had become enough of an Angeleno to see the copper-colored air as a welcome sign of home. We were making excellent time, and we were ahead of the morning rush.

The air was fresh and cool when we arrived at the apartment at 7:30 on Monday morning. The small frame building exuded hominess. All the trees, flowers, and lawns radiated newness and color. Unknown tropical scents filled the air.

"We're here!" I said, patting Darlene's shoulder. She sat up, blinked, and clapped her hands.

"Yay! Yay! Let's go in!" she said, uncurling herself and climbing from the car.

We were excited, and our weariness from the long road trip vanished. I unlocked the front door and Darlene bounded in ahead of me. At the top of the stairs, she laughed.

"Hey! What's this?" she yelled.

The apartment was buried in wadded newspapers. Bob and Glenda must have saved the *Los Angeles Times* for two weeks to "decorate" for us. Someone had played a wedding prank on us after all. We called them to say we'd arrived, enjoyed a laugh, and then stuffed newspapers into garbage bags so we could move in.

For two days, we worked to set up the apartment for living. We already had a bed and other furniture we had agreed to keep for a graduate school family who were in Europe that year. By Tuesday evening, we were ready for Darlene to begin her internship at the UCLA Medical Center a few blocks away the next morning.

The rapid pace of our married life continued for the next three years. Darlene was on call at the hospital every third night, and her days were long. My economics studies were intense but leisurely, compared to her schedule. We joked in later years that we survived those three first years together because we so seldom saw each other.

We loved our life in that first apartment, and we formed some habits of our married life there. An electric percolator from our wedding inaugurated the morning coffee routine that would be a daily celebration for as long as Darlene lived. An economist friend had given us a cast iron hibachi as a gift, and we used it to grill steaks and burgers on our tiny patio many times, glorying in the California sunsets. Life was good.

19

Children of "Troubles"

Darlene started her internship at UCLA on June 23, 1971. We had been married just eleven days. The next day, I started a part-time job. It was a welcome addition to our income. That short-lived employment brought us a surprise that lasted for years.

Don Norman, a graduate school friend, had arranged for me to work with him on a temporary job with the Red Devil Fireworks Company. We were to deliver "safe and sane" fireworks to retail stands all over the LA area. "Safe and sane" meant the fireworks were manufactured to merely flare and sparkle; they didn't explode or fly, or at least they weren't supposed to. The fireworks stands were operated by organizations such as Job's Daughters, Kiwanis, and Rotary. Three stands were run by members of the John Birch Society. I began delivering fireworks in a panel truck to parts of the city I hadn't heard of.

On my first day, at one of my delivery stops, a cat came ambling out to the fireworks stand from a house that sat at the back of the lot behind the stand. A young girl came from the house and picked up the cat. Two rows of tiny nipples showed clearly on the cat's tummy, surrounded by matted, damp fur.

"Her name is Troubles," the girl explained. "She has babies."

"I can see that," I said. "She must have been feeding them just now. What's your name?"

"Wendy Huddleston."

"How old are you, Wendy?"

"I'm nine. My mom is thirty."

"Could I see the baby kitties the next time I come here?"

"Sure! I'll bring them out next time!"

At the apartment that evening, I told Darlene about the kittens and asked what she thought about bringing two of them home. She liked the idea. We thought we would enjoy the cats' companionship, and they would be our first "children." We agree that we wanted the most ordinary two from the litter.

On my next visit to that stop, Wendy was watching. She brought seven squirming little kittens in a large cardboard box. Their eyes were just beginning to open, and they whined in a high-pitched, chirping sound. I focused on two black and gray tiger-striped kittens, the most unremarkable pair in the litter, just as Darlene and I had agreed.

"Are you going to sell some of your kitties?" I asked.

"Yes, but we haven't sold any yet," Wendy confided.

"Do you think I could buy these two?"

"I think so. I'll go ask my mom."

Wendy hurried back up the driveway with the box of kittens. When she returned, she announced, "My mom says you can have those two kittens. And you don't have to pay for them. She said you can have more of the kittens too."

"I think we can only take two of them," I said. "When can I pick them up?"

"My mom says they are too little now. They need to be with Troubles about a month more. You could get them then."

A month later, Darlene and I became parents to two kittens, the children of Troubles. We picked them up on a Saturday in early August and took them home in a shoe box. They squeaked and cried for a few minutes before they settled down for a nap, and we felt like good parents.

20

How the Kittens Got Their Names

We didn't immediately name our kittens, but inspiration came soon. How they got their names is as humorous as the names themselves.

On the first Saturday after we brought the kittens home, Darlene was on call at the hospital, and I went to the UCLA swimming pool. After a quick swim, I spread my towel on a lawn next to families with young kids. An especially sociable little girl talked with me, and I began to entertain her by making faces and funny sounds. I stood on my head for her and flopped to the ground. She squealed with delight.

"I think I love you!" she whispered in my ear.

I was bowled over. "I love you too. What's your name?"

"Lixie," she said.

It was a name I had never heard, but it was easy to remember. When Darlene came off call on Sunday, I told her about meeting Lixie and how she had said, "I think I love you." Just then, the white-faced female of our two kittens came into the room.

"Let's name her Lixie!" Darlene exclaimed, and it was done. Lixie was her name.

The other kitten went unnamed for another week until a graduate school friend, Bob Helms, came for a visit accompanied by his loquacious, eighteen-month-old daughter. She was learning words and phrases and how to count, and we loved hearing her experiment with language. She was fascinated by the kittens and petted them confidently.

"What should we name the kitties?" I said on an impulse.

"One kitty!" she said as she pointed to Lixie. She then pointed at the unnamed kitten and said, "Two kitty!"

And that's how Two got his name. Besides being the little girl's choice, it was the name of a person in a frontier history I had just read. "Two Johnson" was the second of fourteen children in a nineteenth-century Johnson family that simply numbered all their children.

At that first apartment, Lixie and Two were free to roam inside and outside wherever they chose. Our ancient apartment was equipped with a milk door, a small door through which milk had been delivered at the landing at the top of our back stairs. The milk door became the cats' door to the outside. The milk door opened into a broom closet, and we kept the closet door open for the cats to enter the living area.

When Lixie and Two were a few months old, they became avid hunters. More than once Darlene and I were awakened in the night to chirping in our bathroom. Each time it was because the cats had caught a young bird, brought it through the milk door and closet door, and put it in the bathtub to use as something like a hockey puck. They batted the bird from one end of the tub to the other until we rescued it and put it outside again.

Our two cats completed our "family" until our human children began to arrive. They kept us entertained, but we were never tempted to adopt more. Two and Lixie were enough. They lived with us in Los Angeles for three years. When we moved to Wisconsin, they lived with us for another six years before they were adopted by my cousins Tom and Marlyne Bruce in Anderson, Indiana. Two and Lixie both lived beyond fifteen years of age, and only in the end did they seem to be "children of Troubles."

21

The Cat Named "Eight"

*O*ur cats Two and Lixie were social creatures, and they provided hospitality for a number of their "peers and colleagues" from the larger cat world outside. They could invite their friends to come inside for snacks at their feeding dishes. Some of these friends came only at night for a midnight snack. Others were bold enough for daytime visits. They had so many friends that Darlene and I began to number them. Since Lixie and Two were ours, their visitors became known to us as "Three," "Four," and so on. Three was a grey and black tiger like Two. Four, Five, and Six were Siamese.

Not all the visiting cats were welcomed in as friends. At least twice we were awakened to a low, rumbling growl when Two warned and threatened an unwelcome visitor. One night Darlene and I crept into the utility room and found Two crouching menacingly with hairs on his back bristling. A new cat we hadn't met before was there, stealing some food. Two's growl became louder. We watched as he screamed and lunged for the intruder, who spun around, darted into the broom closet, and sped out the milk door. We named that cat "Seven," but he left in such a hurry that we didn't get a detailed description aside from his wooly coat.

The night that "Eight" came started like Seven's visit. It was 3:00 a.m. We had been sleeping soundly when I heard Two growl at an intruder. Thinking

I wouldn't awaken Darlene, I turned on my flashlight and tiptoed out to the cat food bowls. At first I thought I saw Two hungrily eating the dry food. Another angry growl came from the dark, and I noticed Two in his attack crouch, menacing this cat that looked like his twin. Two gave his final warning growl and lunged in a screaming attack that sent the unwanted visitor leaping for cover. In his panic, the intruder slammed the broom closet door shut, locking himself inside the utility room. He had blocked his way of escape. Two and I faced a strange, angry cat locked in our apartment.

The intruder surprised me by whirling around in the utility room and running straight past me, through the little hall, and into the bedroom. By this time, Darlene had awakened. I shone my flashlight into the bedroom just in time to see Eight leap onto the foot of the bed and spring up to one of the cornice boxes above the windows. He perched there a moment and then crept from one cornice to the next, taking an L-shaped route right above Darlene's head.

Darlene looked up and screamed, and Eight jumped over her to the foot of the bed and raced past me back to the feeding station in the utility room. I opened the door from our bedroom to the patio outside. When I returned to the utility room, Eight slammed himself against the broom closet door again and then zoomed past me, across the hall, and into the bedroom again. I ran after him to protect Darlene, but he bounded and ricocheted through the bedroom and finally out the patio door, over the wall of our patio, onto the roof below, and across the roof, where he made a great leap into space to somewhere on the street below. Eight was "out of sight," to use an expression from those days.

22

Yosemite and the Road to the Sea

*I*n November 1971, Darlene's parents came to visit us in Los Angeles, and we took them to more than our usual cycle of tourist spots. As we usually did with visitors, we saw Grauman's Chinese Theater, the stars on the sidewalk on Hollywood Boulevard, and the carousel on the Santa Monica pier. We all went to a taping of *The Johnny Carson Show,* and Darlene took them to a recording of *The Carol Burnett Show.* After a few days, we were to drive them to San Francisco to see a former pastor and his wife. Grada and Virginia would fly home to Indianapolis from there. Darlene and I decided to visit Yosemite National Park and drive back to Los Angeles after dropping her parents off at the San Francisco airport.

On the way to San Francisco, my desire for adventure led me to take the four of us on Route 101 rather than Interstate 5, which might have been faster. Route 101 took us through orange groves and along the Pacific Ocean at Santa Barbara. From there the highway went inland through less-picturesque farm country. I wanted to find a way back down to the ocean, so I veered off to the west on a small and unmarked road that kept narrowing as we traveled. Going by dead reckoning, we eventually found ourselves on a narrow gravel farm road.

The road had looked innocent enough at first. Parched pastures dotted with scrubby oak trees, decaying abandoned barns and houses, and rusting farm machinery told us of an optimistic past, but then the road ahead dropped off so steeply that all we could see ahead was the sky. I slowed the car to a walking pace to be sure we weren't heading for a cliff. The road took a steep, zigzag path downward, clinging to the mountainside. It was really just a logging road, not intended for travelers. It was so narrow that it would have been perilous to meet another car. I put the car in low gear, wishing we had a standard transmission that would have provided more braking power than our automatic transmission. The Pacific Ocean stretched out to the horizon below, so far below we had the sensation of flying.

The road twisted, writhed, and became even steeper on its downward path. Every time we smelled the smoke from the hot brakes, I stopped to let them cool. At one of the stops, Grada got out and looked down the winding road and to the distant ocean. He said nothing, and he was not smiling when I took his picture. Darlene jumped out of the car and clowned for the camera, flipping her hair to form wings on both sides of her head as though she were flying. Virginia remained in the car, no doubt trembling. I hadn't intended to frighten Darlene's parents, but I *had* hoped for an adventure. By the third stop to cool the brakes, I wondered if I had taken matters too far.

Only when we had descended so far that we could practically smell the ocean did our road straighten and flatten and make us feel secure. We gained a little speed and struck the paved Pacific Coast Highway somewhere south of Big Sur. Once again on stable ground, we glided past the roaring surf at Big Sur and past the luscious-sounding towns of Carmel-by-the-Sea and Monterey. Night had fallen when we came over a rise and saw the glittering lights of San Jose, a sight more welcome to Grada and Virginia than all the natural beauty of that day.

"Now that looks like *civilization* to me!" Grada exclaimed.

After we visited their friends and saw some sights in San Francisco, it was time for Grada and Virginia to catch their flight home to Indianapolis. Darlene and I asked them to change their return flight and continue on with us to Yosemite National Park. But the terrifying trip down the mountainside plus grim memories of rural Kentucky must have flashed before them, and they firmly declined our invitation. I tried to persuade them with visions of trees, mountains, rivers, and waterfalls, but Grada declined. His reply became memorable.

"Once you've seen one tree or one mountain, you've seen them all!" he said.

Darlene and I took them to meet their plane, and we were off to Yosemite.

Even though it was the off-season at the park, too late to see the springtime snow melt thundering over the waterfalls and too early for winter snows, Darlene and I loved our first visit to Yosemite. We hiked to Vernal Falls and on to the top of 594-foot Nevada Falls, farther up the same trail. Darlene posed for a risky-looking picture at the brink of Nevada Falls, mainly to scare her mother and impress her family later. Sitting on a flat rock at the lip of the falls and smiling over her shoulder, she looked impish and beautiful in her red bandanna, jeans, and hiking boots.

Upper Yosemite Falls, on the other side of the valley, was reduced to a small stream. Only a trickle of water reached the base where it had thundered down earlier in springtime. The base of the silent falls was a jumble of enormous boulders and a series of quiet pools. It was there that I had one of my most memorable drinks of water.

We spied an especially large, deep pool that had been formed by the hammering falls but now lay perfectly still. Its surface was like a sheet of glass, and we could look down twenty feet to rocks at the bottom. A boulder beside the pool offered a smooth surface, sloping down to the water's edge. I handed Darlene the camera and my hat, and I slid on my stomach to the water's edge. Peering to the depths below, I pressed my lips to the perfectly calm surface and began to drink. It was like drinking from an enormous, uncut diamond.

Darlene wisely did not imitate me. She knew too much about the possibility of intestinal parasites in that beautiful water, and she needed to remain healthy for her hospital work and to care for me if I fell ill. I didn't get sick, so I didn't learn the lesson I could have that day.

Two years later, Darlene and I returned to Yosemite. I remember little of that October trip except one adventure. Since we had no idea how to "get off the ground" in the sport of climbing, we signed up for a beginner's rock climbing class.

"The Valley," as Yosemite is known among technical rock climbers, is one of the world's centers for that esthetic and potentially dangerous sport.

Half Dome and El Capitan are the best-known climbing sites, but there are hundreds more.

Our instructor, Wayne Merry, was a famous climber who had established several routes on the vertical granite walls around the valley. He took us to a large boulder near the climbing shop and introduced us to the rudiments of "reading the rock" and finding foot placements and handholds while climbing. We learned to put our weight on our feet and use our hands mainly for balance. The lesson didn't take us more than four feet above the sand, and we often slipped off. That was enough climbing for Darlene, but it whetted my appetite for more. A few months later, I began climbing more seriously and did so until 1976.

Yosemite and the road to the sea remained in our memories as places of beauty and excitement during our early years of marriage.

23

Internship and Residency

Darlene's internship and residency at the UCLA Medical Center was a seemingly seamless series of assignments over the three years from 1971 to 1974. Most of her days were a blur of early rising, long days at the hospital, and frequent night calls. She was on call every third night, a frequency no longer allowed in medical centers. She was so tired one morning that she threw her Mickey Mouse watch into the hospital laundry in the pocket of her white coat, and the watch was lost forever. She was tired much of the time but cheerful nearly all the time as she adjusted to the traumas of death and life in a medical center. I, on the other hand, was deep in my economics studies at UCLA and nearing the time when I would begin my doctoral dissertation. Despite the challenges, we managed to have some fun times.

One Saturday after she had been on call the previous night, Darlene came home about 8 a.m. and said she was ready for the excursion we had planned. She had read in the *LA Times* of Circus Vargas, a traveling Mexican circus that had set up camp somewhere in the San Fernando Valley just north of the Los Angeles basin, and she wanted to go. The weather was sunny and warm, and the circus turned out to be colorful and traditional: red, orange, green, and black banners; tents that looked as though they could have dated from the 1890s; side shows; and carnival rides for kids. For the show in the Big Top tent, we had seats in the third row of bleachers.

It was an exciting and old-fashioned circus show with an entry parade, trained animals, and aerialists swinging high above the ring. The performing humans and animals did their best to hold our attention, but every time I looked at Darlene, she was falling asleep, slumping forward and in danger of falling off the bleachers. She would awaken repeatedly, catch a glimpse of the next act, and then drift off again. In my memory, the hazy dust inside the tent blurred the brilliant circus colors into an impressionistic canvas, and Darlene was the beautiful center of the scene.

We often had dinner together in the hospital dining room when she was on call, but the interior of the cavernous UCLA Medical Center was mostly unknown to me. At the time it was said to be the largest building in the United States except the Pentagon in Washington. The Newborn Intensive Care Unit, or NICU, was one of the few clinics I visited with her. She showed me the tiny babies that she and a battalion of other doctors and nurses kept supplied with oxygen, nutrients, and liquids through myriad tubes.

During one visit, she showed me a baby who had been born without a brain, with only an empty chamber where a brain would have been. In God's mercy, that baby died a few days later. Darlene was sad but resolute about his death. She understood the mercy of death when nothing more could be done. Her calm, resolute handling of those early medical challenges began to train me to face them calmly as well.

One very dark night in February 1972 while Darlene was on call, I was a bundle of nerves at home in the apartment. My last PhD qualifying exam was the next day, and I was studying during those final hours. That exam was a do-or-die one for my career as an economist. A poor score would send me off in another career direction, and I was fearful of what that might be.

About nightfall, neighbors in the next building, barely ten feet from our bedroom, began playing loud, violent music. I shook with anger and anxiety, unable to concentrate. When the music ended at last, I calmed myself and returned to my notes. A little later, I heard Darlene coming up the outdoor stairs to our back door. I hurried to open the door for her, and she burst in, crying and shaking. I hugged her, and she continued sobbing until she could catch her breath.

"What's wrong? Are you hurt? What's wrong?" I asked.

"My patient died!" she said, crying hard again. "I left the car at the hospital. I forgot it was there. I took the bus and walked the rest of the way home. Oh! My patient died!"

The patient, I learned when she was able to talk, was another baby born with a severe birth defect. This one had a chance for survival. She had cared for the infant boy for several days and had become attached to him, and his death had crashed down on her emotional defenses. We talked while I warmed up dinner for her, and we simply went to bed to end that awful day.

That dark night was the beginning of better days for us both. My PhD exam was behind me, and there was nothing to do but wait for the results. Darlene had a three-day break from the hospital, and we decided to drive to Palm Springs, a hundred miles to the east in the healing heat of the desert. At breakfast the next morning in Palm Springs, orange slices and the scent of coffee perfumed the air. We felt especially young among the white-haired retirees around us.

The highlight of the weekend was our ride to the top of Mount San Jacinto on the famous aerial tramway. When we boarded at the bottom, the weather was warm. At the top, we shivered in the cold air and had to purchase matching yellow windbreakers to fend off the chill. We hiked to a nearby rock outcropping where we both used our skills: She made drawings on an artist's sketch pad while I stretched out for a nap, precariously balanced on top of a boulder beside her.

When we returned to Los Angeles, Darlene's emotions had calmed, and I learned I had passed my last required exam. She still had two more years of residency ahead, and I faced the task of choosing a dissertation topic and beginning the research and writing. During the rest of her internship and residency, we enjoyed many good times, and we faced no more nights of crisis as dark as the one before our trip to Palm Springs.

24

Saved by an Apple Pie

*I*n the first three years of our marriage, we were happy with our daily routines, intense as they were. Sometimes we felt we were "playing house" together, living out some of the things we had seen our parents do in their marriages. I had more time, so I did more cooking than Darlene, but we took turns whenever possible. In that first apartment, we ate our meals in the small dining room next to the kitchen. Those two rooms and everything about the apartment were in a style that would now be called "retro." At one point in our first year there, we had become so energized in our marriage and home life that we decided to wallpaper our dining room, unaware that wallpapering was stressful and could threaten a harmonious marriage.

The dining room wallpaper had pictures of parrots that looked like vicious carnivores, so we decided to paper it over with something less menacing. We covered the vicious parrots with sedate, maroon-striped paper. The work was easy, and it turned out so well that we repeatedly congratulated each other on our work.

Our bedroom wallpaper must have offended Darlene, because she wanted to paper it next. The room was larger than the dining room and had two doors and four sets of windows, making it a bigger challenge than the one we'd already conquered. As we'd done for the dining room, we prepared the bedroom walls and began applying beige, faintly decorated wallpaper. To our dismay, we discovered that the well-aged building had shifted and settled, leaving not even one wall straight. Each strip of paper we applied had to be trimmed, re-set, trimmed again, and re-glued before it could be put in place.

As we worked, we became angrier by the hour. We were angry at the room, the wallpaper, the catawampus and out-of-alignment room, and each other. By the time our friends Bob and Glenda banged on our back door unexpectedly, we were in a high state of exasperation. Unaware of our state of mind, they came bustling in with a freshly-baked apple pie. All work stopped, and the four of us ate the whole apple pie. As we ate and talked, our anger and frustration subsided. Bob and Glenda helped us finish papering that night, and Darlene and I put away our papering tools forever.

25

"Visiting" Presbyterians

*B*efore Darlene moved to Los Angeles, I sampled several churches near UCLA. One was the Bel Air Presbyterian Church, where I sat one Sunday next to California Governor Ronald Reagan and Nancy Reagan. Another was the Brentwood Presbyterian Church, where I heard legendary UCLA basketball coach John Wooden give a sermon called "Make Each Day a Masterpiece." Neither of those became our church of choice as a couple. Instead, Darlene and I found a church home at Westwood Presbyterian Church.

The sermons at Westwood were excellent, if rather cerebral, and the music was inspiring. We learned to sing the hymn "Immortal Invisible" there because it was a favorite of Pastor Charles Orr, and we sang it often at home the rest of our lives together. That hymn alone would have made our time at Westwood Pres worthwhile, but we also especially enjoyed the coffee and cookies reception on the church's porch after worship. It was easy to meet long-standing church members and other newcomers there.

The sermon we remembered best was a children's sermon that our intellectual pastor gave for the kids one Sunday. He stepped down to the floor in front of the platform and invited the children to gather around him on the carpet. To introduce his story, he asked the children to think about especially happy times they had shared with their "little peers and colleagues." The rest of his story was lost on us. Only the "little peers and colleagues" phrase remained lodged in our memories.

Darlene and I both sang in the choir. Actually, she sang and I simulated singing. The music was challenging for both of us. The congregation was small, so we were a welcome addition to the choir.

We did not join Westwood Presbyterian Church, and I don't remember our being asked to do so. We would have declined, though, because formal church membership was outside our previous experience. Even so, at some point in our time as "visiting" Presbyterians, Darlene volunteered for me to teach a small class of very small Presbyterians, the three-year-olds.

The Sunday school supervisor, a middle-aged lady, was fond of me and liked my teaching style. One Easter Sunday morning, she gave me two brightly colored Easter eggs, which I absentmindedly slipped into a pocket of my suitcoat. About three weeks later, my clothing began to smell bad. Soon the entire closet smelled bad. An especially reeking sleeve of my suitcoat led us to the problem. The Easter eggs were still in my suitcoat pocket, where I had placed them on Easter Sunday and had promptly forgotten them.

There may have been a theological point in that mishap, but in my limited knowledge of Presbyterian theology, I didn't get it. Still, we remained visiting Presbyterians until we left Los Angeles in 1974.

26

Our Mostly Quiet Second Apartment

Our first apartment experience on Veteran Avenue had started well, but we soon found that its antique charm came with a nearly total lack of sound insulation. We could hear people talking normally downstairs, and we heard more than we should have when a cohabiting couple had arguments. We could trace the path of any woman clomping through the apartment in high heels. Our nerves were on edge because of our intense study and workloads, so it was time to move.

In July 1973, we moved to an apartment a few miles farther south from UCLA. That second apartment was at 3715 Kelton Avenue in Los Angeles, just a long block north of Venice Boulevard. It was about three miles straight south of our first apartment. The Kelton Avenue apartment was on the second floor of a newer, four-unit building with a layer of concrete under the carpets to protect us from noises below. When the breeze was from the west, we could hear the traffic on the San Diego Freeway, buzzing softly in the near distance. The place was like an idyllic, serene island in a vast city for us. Best of all, it was a mostly quiet place to spend the next year while Darlene completed her residency and I worked on my dissertation.

This second apartment was as spacious as our first one but far more modern. We had two bedrooms, two full baths, a den, a living room, a dining area, and a compact kitchen. We even had a gas log fireplace and avocado-green shag carpet in the living room. That carpet seemed beautiful then, even if Darlene shuddered at the thought of it in later years.

During the time we lived there, we commuted the six miles to UCLA. Darlene usually took the car while I worked on research at home or took the city bus to campus. Her income was our main support, but I had part-time teaching assignments three times while I continued my dissertation work.

We had moved primarily to avoid the noise of our first apartment, but on the very first afternoon while Darlene was at work and I was moving furniture, I heard an especially loud noise coming from the next building a few feet below our bedroom window. The neighbor man seemed to be working in an outdoor woodshop behind his apartment, and his radio was blaring. I panicked and wondered if the move had been a mistake. Crumbling to the floor, I prayed for peace. Suddenly the noise ended, and it never happened again. For me, that was a lesson in the power of prayer.

Some pet noise was unavoidable there. A Cuban family lived in an apartment on one side of our building. A solid wooden fence separated their yard from our entry walkway. As we approached our building, their huge German shepherd, Duke, often crashed against the fence not two feet from us, barking wildly. His Cuban owner was even louder, yelling, "Dukie! Dukie!" We never met Dukie or his owner, and we didn't miss them when we moved to Wisconsin a year later.

Another noise incident happened while we were living in that apartment. When Darlene was on call one Saturday morning soon after we moved in, despite the concrete floor, I heard extremely loud shouts, curses, and banging furniture in the apartment below ours. The next sound I heard was loud banging at the door below and a man's voice.

"Police! Open the door!"

A man and woman inside were arguing, and the man went raging out of the apartment after the police entered. I learned later that the two of them were unmarried law students who thought they could live economically together though they were not romantically involved and had little in common except the apartment. Their arrangement had broken down, and it was not long before they both moved out. A wonderful young married couple, Gil and Shelly, moved in with their peaceable dog, Bosco. Life was better than ever.

The remainder of our year in that second apartment was uneventful, even though we had a neighbor across the street who sat on his porch all night to watch for flying saucers. He explained to me one day that the flying saucers were spinning at about 300,000 revolutions per minute, which made them invisible to most people. He mentioned casually that he once had elicited a visit from the Secret Service after he sent a threatening letter to President Nixon. Needless to say, we kept our distance from him as well as from Dukie.

27

The Big Tent

In 1972, after Darlene's first year of residency, we rented a medium-sized tent for a camping trip that took us all the way to Crater Lake in southern Oregon. Having tasted camping with Bob and Glenda on the weekend we became engaged, we invested in new sleeping bags and camping cookware to go with the gas camp stove I had brought into our marriage. Darlene had happily adopted the stove as her own, and she plunged into camping as though she had been raised as a camper. It seemed to come naturally to her.

One of the more memorable stops on the trip to Oregon was at something called "Trees of Mystery" in Northern California. The place was relentlessly advertised on billboards and on signs on the front bumpers of cars that were headed south after visiting the place. As we drove north along the California coast, it seemed that half the southbound cars had garish "Trees of Mystery" signs wired to their front bumpers. We couldn't resist stopping, and we found a collection of trees and plants there that almost made it worthwhile. When we left, we carried the Trees of Mystery message farther north on our own front bumper.

The hardware store where we had rented the tent in 1972 burned to the ground a few months later, so we began shopping for a tent of our own in anticipation of future camping trips. We had promised Darlene's sister Evelyn and her daughter Lisa a camping trip, and they were coming in July 1973.

Bob and Glenda, assiduous shoppers, had narrowed the world of tents before buying theirs. We decided to buy a tent like theirs, and Bob told me where to find one. While Darlene was on duty one day, I ventured to "The Famous," the camping supply store in downtown Los Angeles that Bob had told me about. It wasn't famous *for* anything; it was just named "The Famous."

The store occupied the third and fourth floors of a creaking old warehouse building, and customers could reach it only by way of the freight elevator. Bob and Glenda's tent measured 8 x10 feet; Darlene and I chose the next size up, 9x12 feet. With it we would have space for guests and for the family we hoped to have in the future. I bought the tent for $120 and lugged it back to the car via the freight elevator. It was a significant investment. Twenty years later, the price for the same tent was more than $800.

Back at our apartment, I unpacked the tent and spread it out on the living room floor in front of the fireplace. When I had verified that all the pieces were there and had learned how to set it up, I repacked it for its first trip. We took it to Zion National Park that weekend, and I wrote the place and the date on the main entry flap. That entry was the first of many on a tent that would become one of the most prized possessions of our life together. The tent flap became a record of some of our best times.

We spent two nights at Zion on that first trip. A brisk, warm wind was blowing that first night, but we were so excited about camping that we unwisely lit a campfire. A fire was not against the rules, but the ranger drove through the campground throughout the evening to make sure all fires were well contained. When the ranger told us of the danger of a forest fire, we doused our campfire and went to our sleeping bags. We drove to Bryce Canyon National Park the next day and returned to sleep again in Zion.

From that weekend on, I wrote the location and date on the tent flap every time we camped with it. The first five entries were from July 1973 to the first week of October 1973.

1. Zion National Park, Utah — 7/13–14/73
2. Quaking Aspen Campground — 9/27/73
3. Sequoia National Park — 9/28–29/73
4. Kings Canyon National Park — 9/30/73
5. Yosemite National Park — 10/1–4/73

The listing continued over the years, and the final entries were as follows:

59. West Dolores Campground, San Juan National Forest, Colorado, #13, 7/2/03 (Small tent)
60. West Dolores Campground, San Juan National Forest, Colorado, #9, 7/3,4,5/03
61. Black Canyon of the Gunnison National Park, Site C-31 (Small tent), 7/6/03
62. Blue Mountain Camp, Site #13, Lake George, Colorado, 7/7–8/2003

Darlene and I camped throughout our marriage, and we did most of our camping in the West. We especially welcomed the cool, dry air in the mountains and the dry heat in desert afternoons. The West always seemed adventuresome and romantic to us because of its dramatic scenery and historic past and also because it was on our first desert camping trip that our roads had converged permanently.

Until five months before Darlene's death, she and I continued our camping adventures. We used the big tent for the last time in summer 2003, two months before Darlene's first cancer diagnosis. In 2000, we bought a smaller tent just for the two of us. We took the small tent to Death Valley in 2000 and to California in 2010.

The big tent is still in the attic above the garage, and I bring it down every year or two to check its condition. When I occasionally set up the tent in the back yard, I write that place and date on the tent flap. I'm always amazed that the tent is still in excellent condition for camping, whether I am or not.

28

Burnt Sugar Cake

Darlene worked hard to please me despite the challenges we faced in our first few years of marriage. On Thursday evening, October 18, 1973, the day before my birthday, she began work on a burnt sugar cake in our Kelton Avenue apartment. At the time, she had a killing schedule as a third-year resident at the UCLA Medical Center. She was on call every third night, and she rarely reached home before dark on non-call days. But she was determined to make a burnt sugar cake for my birthday because she knew it was my favorite. She planned to serve the cake on October 20 after dinner with our friends Bob and Glenda.

A burnt sugar cake is like a caramel cake, except it's more flavorful due to the burnt sugar. In concept, the procedure is simple: Put some sugar in a sauce pan and roast it until it smokes and nearly burns. Add boiling water to dissolve the burnt sugar, stir, and remove from the heat. For this cake, Darlene used a Teflon-coated sauce pan to prevent the roasting sugar from sticking. That was a mistake. She heated the sugar, but it didn't turn brown as nicely as she had hoped. Far worse, the burning sugar stuck to the Teflon and formed big, black flakes in the mixture.

She was not pleased. Instead of a smooth and dark tan color, her product was pale and appeared to have large black ants swimming in it. She picked out the larger black pieces and set the syrup aside until Saturday, when she would finish the cake.

On Saturday morning, she began work in earnest on the cake itself. She combined cake flour, eggs, baking powder, and the burnt sugar syrup. When the cake layers came out of the oven, they felt ominously heavy. When they were cool, she proceeded to ice them. As she spread icing on the bottom layer, she noticed how thin it was. When she added the top layer, the icing between the layers served as a lubricant, and the top layer started to slide off.

She called for help, and I held the top layer in place while she inserted toothpicks to hold the two layers together. She put more icing on, and the cake began to look pretty good. The toothpicks were well concealed, but the cake was *camel*-colored rather than *caramel*-colored.

Bob and Glenda came, and whatever we had for dinner that night was not as memorable as the dessert. After dinner, the four of us went to the living room. Darlene cut the cake in the kitchen, being careful to avoid the portions where the toothpicks were lodged. She brought the servings to the living room without comment, but I could tell she was burning with embarrassment about the fiasco the cake had become. No one else noticed. We chatted awhile, and all of us ate cake. Three of us enjoyed it.

When Bob and Glenda left, Darlene listened for them to reach the bottom of the stairs. She then marched to the kitchen, picked up the cake in both hands, raised it over her head, and slammed it into the wastebasket with a resounding thud that shook the floor.

"What are you *doing?*" I said.

"I'm not just *doing* it, I *did* it!" she said. "I got rid of that cake!"

I laughed and inspected the wreckage in the wastebasket. "I didn't think it was that bad," I said to console her.

"I did! It was *awful!*"

We cleaned up the kitchen quietly and went on to other things.

The next day, I saw Glenda at church and told her what Darlene had done with the cake.

"She threw it out?" Glenda exclaimed. "Bob and I really liked it!"

I don't think Darlene ever made another burnt sugar cake. She put up with my telling the burnt sugar cake story for the rest of her life, hopefully knowing I told the story not only as comical episode in our early lives together but also because of her loving desire to please me on my birthday.

29

Taking Off Our Wedding Rings

One day in July 1974, we went to a rock climbing practice area in the San Fernando Valley called Stoney Point. I had begun to develop some skill in technical, top-roped climbing, even though at thirty-three I might have been old for the sport. Darlene had chosen not to pursue rock climbing after the lesson she and I had in the Yosemite Valley in 1973, but she came along to watch me practice. That day of practice would remain in our memories for the sentimental moment it became, not for any great rock-climbing adventure.

My climbing partners at Stoney Point that summer were a former roommate and graduate mathematics student, Carl Richards, and a fellow economist, Steve Cauley. Carl and I already had made several trips to Stoney Point and had done one of the taller top-roped routes there. Steve had taught me a lot at Stoney Point and later would take me on a higher climb at Tahquitz Rock and Suicide Rock near Idyllwild, east of Los Angeles.

On this particular day, Steve was coaching me on bouldering, practicing hand holds and footing on some large boulders in the sandy parking lot at Stoney Point. It was low-level climbing without rope protection. We would simply jump or fall onto sand if we fell. I prepared to climb the face of a twelve-foot-tall boulder studded with sharp, pointed protrusions. I chalked my hands and was about to begin my climb.

"You better take off that ring," Steve said. "You don't want your finger ripped off if it gets hung up in a fall."

I looked again at the face of the rock. I knew he was right. I had nearly lost a finger many years earlier in a farm accident in Oklahoma when my high school class ring caught on a nail in the sideboard of a grain truck as I jumped down. But this was my wedding ring! How could I take *it* off?

I glanced at Darlene. Neither of us had taken off our rings since our wedding, and we intended never to take them off. I could tell she was thinking the same thing. She didn't want me to take off my ring, but she knew I should. She wanted me to make the climb safely.

"Let's both take our rings off at the same time!" she announced.

Darlene started twisting her ring, and I did the same. I handed my ring to her and hugged her. I don't remember how well I climbed that day. All I remember was that moment when Darlene took off her ring and led me to do the same for my own safety.

Aside from a few other climbing times and in the face of other hazards, neither of us took off our rings until the end of her life. On her last day of consciousness, I crossed our left hands on her stomach as she lay in the hospital bed. One of our children took a picture of our hands and rings together.

30

Hitting the Job Market

*O*ur three years in California were momentous, and we enjoyed our life together there. We were charmed by the smell of eucalyptus and the sight of distant, snowcapped mountains framed in palm trees. We had friends over for dinner often, enjoyed movies together in the nearby Palms Theater, and experienced the joy of being together after six long years of courtship. Many years later, we asked ourselves why we left California if we had liked it so much, but we had our reasons.

Darlene might have enjoyed the balmy Los Angeles weather for a few more years, but I had begun to feel a strange claustrophobia in a city so large that it could take forty-five minutes or longer to drive to the countryside under the best conditions. I longed for the snow, ice, and thunderstorms of the Midwest. With my dissertation topic approved and my initial research completed, I could continue my research and writing while living and working elsewhere. I needed only to make an oral presentation of my research plan before leaving UCLA. Darlene could use her medical skills anywhere, so she was free to go wherever. I focused my job search in the Midwest.

Another reason that prompted our move was that it seemed to us that our parents were getting old, and we wanted to be nearer them in their later years. That part of our reasoning would seem almost funny when we ourselves became older. In 1974, Darlene's parents were both sixty-five years old and were living active lives in Indianapolis. My father was sixty-three and my mother was only sixty. None were "old" as we might think of their ages now. Still, we sensed the call to be nearer to them.

In the winter of 1974, the American Economic Association held its annual meeting between Christmas and New Year's in New York City, and I attended. While there, I submitted my curriculum vitae for the job seekers' pool and garnered a few interviews. The most attractive one was with Dr. Richard Trestrail from Marquette University in Milwaukee. I met him in his smoke-filled hotel room, and we chatted socially for thirty minutes or more while he alternated between cigarettes and a pipe. At the end, he said he would have to persuade his colleagues back in Milwaukee, but he would like for me to come there for an interview. I said I would await his call.

After my trip to New York, Darlene and I spent the rest of that January in Indianapolis. She worked in several pediatrics clinics in Indianapolis as part of her UCLA residency while I continued to work on my dissertation. We stayed with Darlene's parents, and Darlene's sister Evelyn lived only a block away. I used Evelyn's house as a quiet place for my research and writing in the daytime while Evelyn was away teaching school. When I had a question or message for my mother-in-law back at the house, I called on the phone and sometimes started my conversation with a faked voice and a bogus message before getting to the real topic. I might claim to be selling insurance or home repair service, or I might say I was from an important university. It was all meant to be fun for us both of us; at least it was fun for me.

Late one morning, the phone at Evelyn's house rang. When I answered, the voice at the other end was at first garbled by laughter. *Was it Virginia calling?* I wondered. I quickly realized it was Professor Trestrail, calling from Marquette University.

"I guess I must have talked to your mother-in-law just now," he said, still laughing. "She wasn't expecting my call, but she gave me this number."

After his laughter subsided, we set a date for my interview at Marquette. In my excitement about his call, I forgot to ask why he had been laughing. When I went back to the Sayers' house for lunch, Darlene's mother was miffed. She told me what had happened.

"You got me into trouble with some professor that called!" she began. "You had just called me and pretended to be a professor. Then the phone rang again and I said, 'I know that's you calling me again! Stop calling with those silly voices!' The man didn't talk right away. He was real quiet. Then he did start talking, and I could tell he was a real professor. I said, 'Oh, sir! I'm terribly sorry! I thought you were my son-in-law calling and faking a professor's voice!'"

She paused to let what she'd said sink in before continuing.

"The man laughed and laughed, and then he said, 'Your son-in-law sounds like the kind of man I'm looking for!'"

That incident was the beginning of a beautiful friendship with Dick Trestrail. Like a surprising number of economists, Dick was a character too. He had dropped out of high school and lied about his age to get into the Army during World War II. After the war, he spent a couple of years as a lumberjack in the Northwest and often talked wistfully of his desire to become a Wyoming sheepherder. Earning his PhD in economics from the University of Washington diverted him from that dream, but he lived and breathed those Northwest memories as freely as he inhaled the smoke from his endless chain of cigarettes. He was intrigued by my own eccentric path into economics, perhaps partly because I had been a Future Farmer of America in high school.

Darlene and I were both pleased with the news that I would soon have an interview at Marquette University. She had held herself to a fierce discipline from the time she decided on medical school and was now finishing her residency, had focused intently on her medical studies and fallen in love with pediatrics. She had been our main income provider while I finished my PhD exams and worked on my dissertation. She needed a break from the grueling schedules, medical crises, and sleepless nights that had at times exhausted her. She needed a chance simply to *live*. It was my turn to be our main financial support.

31

A Glimpse into the Future

Dick Trestrail had persuaded the Economics Department at Marquette University to invite me for an interview while we were still visiting in Indiana. After he shared the news with me, he arranged a flight and lodging for Darlene and me. We were giddy with excitement. We felt this trip would be a turning point in our lives and careers.

On the day of the arranged flight, we hurried to the Indianapolis airport. It was in the middle of February, and it was already becoming late in the University's hiring season. The weather could have prevented the trip, but there happened to be a midwinter thaw. We had "missed the boat" on our honeymoon, and we nearly missed the plane to Milwaukee. The plane's door was closing as we ran up to the gate, but we were allowed to enter, out of breath as we were.

At the stop at Chicago's O'Hare Field, we were told that our flight to Milwaukee was canceled due to fog there, but we would be ferried by bus to Milwaukee's Mitchell Field. It was a gloomy 90-minute trip, but to us it was our entry to a mystical place we hoped would be our new state. We held hands until the bus deposited us in the open parking lot that served Milwaukee's Mitchell Field. Once inside, we rented a car and headed for Brookfield, a western suburb, partly because we liked the name. The fog had partially lifted, and it did not prevent us from scouting a few residential neighborhoods. When we slowed in front of a modest gray house with a "For Sale" sign in the lawn, a friendly dog scampered out to greet us. We took it as an omen, a sign that we would find a good place to live if we were to move to Milwaukee.

At dinner that evening, we were served an appetizer tray of yeast rolls and what appeared to be three scoops of ice cream or sherbet. Darlene sampled the lightest-colored scoop, smiled, and rolled her eyes.

"Yum! It's cheese!" she declared.

We had arrived in the land of plenty, and especially so for cheese. The tray held shredded Swiss, soft cheddar, and a rose-colored cheese laced with walnuts and raspberries. We tried all three and were happy with our introduction to "America's Dairyland," as the Wisconsin license plates proclaimed.

Darlene visited the Medical College of Wisconsin and another hospital and a private clinic that Marquette people had arranged for her on the day of my interviews. I met everyone in the Economics Department and several from other departments in the College of Business. The experience was not unlike the fog at the airport that had clouded our physical vision. We weren't quite sure about what we were seeing, but it looked promising.

We were back in Los Angeles when Dr. Trestrail called two weeks later from Marquette to offer me a position as Assistant Professor, to start in August 1974. I agreed to the terms he offered and said I would await the contract. Darlene was on call that night, so she and I celebrated my job and our new direction with an inspiring meal in the UCLA hospital cafeteria.

32

Leaving California

Goodbye, Old Paint, I'm leavin' Cheyenne,
Goodbye, Old Paint, I'm bound for Montan'.

—Credited to cowboy Charlie Willis, a former slave

With my new job and a momentous move on the horizon, Darlene and I were intent on making the most of our final weeks in California. We enjoyed three more camping trips before leaving the western states.

On May 1, we set out for our beloved Joshua Tree National Park, where we had first camped three years earlier. Darlene had worked that day, and I picked her up at the Med Center at the end of her day. We took a circuitous route north across the San Fernando Valley to Palmdale, Pearblossom, Apple Valley, and the town of Joshua Tree just north of the park. We searched for the Hidden Valley Campground and finally found it at about 11:00 p.m. Our former site was occupied. We drove around the rock outcropping next to it and found an empty site that faced the open desert to the west.

It was too late to hammer in our tent stakes and put up the tent—our hammering would have awakened nearby campers—so by flashlight we spread our heavy canvas tarp on a smooth, sandy place and slipped into our sleeping bags. The night was brilliantly clear, and the stars seemed to pierce the canopy of desert sky. The sun was just coming up when Darlene felt a cold, wet object on her nose.

"Oh! Good morning! Did you come to see me?" I heard her say.

A large German shepherd dog had come to investigate the open-air sleepers and had sniffed her nose. He next came and sniffed my nose and mouth.

"Come here," Darlene called to the dog, and she read the name tag around his neck. "His name is Lobo," she reported. "Lobo! Doesn't that mean wolf?"

It does, and after our wolf greeter went on his way, we were awake enough to start our day. In years to come, Darlene would treasure the memory of that night under the stars and the cold, wet greeting from a dog named Lobo.

After four days in Joshua Tree, we continued to the South Rim of the Grand Canyon. We pitched our tent near a group of hippies that had set up what looked like a permanent camp. Within their circle of tents, they had lawn chairs, cooking equipment, and laundry hanging on ropes strung between pine trees. These modern gypsies were far enough from us that we felt safe, but their camping style was far different from ours. Tribes of hippies like this one were not uncommon in the early '70s, but they presented some unwelcome hazards to conservative Midwesterners like Darlene and me. Had we been any closer, the aroma of marijuana might have drifted into our camp. Even so, the location was near perfect for us.

We hiked a short distance into the canyon on the Kaibab and Bright Angel trails before we moved on for one more night, choosing to spend it in Oak Creek Canyon, just north of Sedona. There we camped beside a stream that roared so loudly that we couldn't have heard approaching soldiers if there had been any.

Our next camping trip was just three days later. We returned to Los Angeles to check our mail and wash clothes before setting out for Yosemite to the north. We traveled to Yosemite this time with one of Darlene's colleagues, Ken Rich, and his family. Ken and Ann had a baby daughter and a dog named Kochoko, an African name meaning "Little One." Even though Kochoko peed into my sleeping bag with me in it, the trip itself was memorable.

Darlene, Ken, and I hiked to the top of Yosemite Falls, 2,425 feet above the valley floor. The hike was during the height of the spring snowmelt, and the lower, middle, and upper falls thundered down in three separate vaults beside our trail as we climbed. It was a strenuous hike for Darlene and me, and we celebrated at the top with a luxurious picnic lunch from our backpack: boiled eggs, ham, cheese, apples, and rye crackers.

Our final California camping trip in 1974 was to Mount San Jacinto State Park near Idyllwild, an unincorporated community about 120 miles east of Los Angeles. We camped two nights there while I did technical rock climbing with my economist climbing friend, Steve Cauley. An experienced climber, Steve led the way on a multi-pitch roped climb on Tahquitz Rock the first day.

Multi-pitch meant Steve would lead the way up the face of the rock, placing protection points where our rope would be looped through carabiners. I would follow him and be prepared to catch him on the rope that connected us if he should fall. After he was at the top of a pitch, I would remove the protection points as I climbed, and he would belay me in case I fell. Then I would protect him as he went up the next pitch.

Steve didn't take any falls that day, and for that he was grateful because I was so new to roped climbing and wasn't to be completely trusted. On the second day, lightning drove us off Suicide Rock after we had climbed only thirty feet from the base. My California climbing career ended that day.

Worth noting is what happened in California during our final five months of living there. Los Angeles police had a shootout with a terrorist group that called themselves the Symbionese Liberation Army. They had robbed banks, murdered two people, and kidnapped (or had been joined by) nineteen-year-old Patty Hearst, heiress to the Hearst publishing fortune. The group had moved from San Francisco and was hiding in a home in a Los Angeles suburb. Darlene was working at the Medical Center that night, and I had gone into Westwood Village for dinner. A TV in the window of an appliance store showed a house in flames. I watched as the gunfight continued and the house burned. Television news later reported that six members of the Symbionese Liberation Army had died in the siege.

During our three years of life together in California, people in the Midwest often teased us about living in Los Angeles with its smog, traffic, violence, and famous nut cases. We usually replied, "Yes, but think of it: Los Angeles has earthquakes, fires, flash floods, and mudslides in addition to traffic, smog, crime, and nut cases. With so much going against it, Southern California must really be wonderful if ten million people choose to live there!" For us, at least, it was.

PART THREE

Summertime Years in Wisconsin: 1974 to 1992

33

Milwaukee Migration

Darlene's residency at UCLA ended on June 30, 1974. By then, most of my data-gathering for my dissertation was finished and my research plan had been approved. We were free to skip town together and head to the Midwest, where I would begin my new job as an assistant professor of economics at Marquette University. We spent the first three weeks of July sorting our belongings, getting rid of things and preparing for the move to Milwaukee.

Marquette University had granted us some moving money, and we were determined to make the most of it, maybe even moving ourselves. We put up notices on UCLA bulletin boards and ran an ad in the Santa Monica paper listing things we wanted to sell. We began to sell off furniture that wouldn't fit into a 12-foot U-Haul trailer that our 1970 Buick LeSabre could pull. The weirdest thing we jettisoned was a low, black cedar chest we called "the coffin." It looked like a coffin and could have held the corpse of a small adult. It had housed a couple of our tablecloths, some books, and a few odd things that had no other home in the apartment.

On departure day, July 25, the trailer and our Buick were tightly packed with everything we still owned. I was eager to get going, but as we were about to leave, Darlene had second thoughts about a box we had left in the apartment as trash. She insisted we return and open the cardboard box that had stood next to my desk as a piece of furniture. I had cut a slot in the top so we could deposit papers we didn't want to deal with but didn't want to discard permanently. When we cut it open and examined its contents, we found important papers mingled with trash, papers we would need when we arrived in Wisconsin. We scooped up what we needed and left the rest in our trash bin.

At last we were ready to depart. Aiming to cross some of the desert at night, we left our apartment in the early evening. I drove our Buick and pulled the trailer, and Darlene drove the 1964 Chevrolet we had received as a wedding gift from her father. In Riverside we stopped at the home of Bonnie Sutton, one of Darlene's childhood friends from Indianapolis. As we'd planned in advance, we delivered the Chevrolet to her, having agreed on a modest price earlier. We were free to travel together to Wisconsin.

We headed into the deep desert late that night and were in Arizona by the time the sun rose. The beige desert sand was punctuated by red rock outcroppings. Thin, high clouds added drama to the otherwise clear blue sky. We had crossed the Colorado River in the night, and our route took us to Phoenix and then to Albuquerque and Santa Fe in New Mexico. We traveled past Wagon Mound and then through the Oklahoma panhandle to Alva and on to the tiny village of Dacoma, where my Bruner relatives could get their first look at Darlene. She dazzled them, of course. We spent two nights in the home of my elderly aunt Ethel Bruner in Dacoma and had a rollicking evening with my uncle Arthur and aunt Alice. We laughed especially hard when Arthur, who was about six-feet-four-inches tall compared to Alice's five-feet tall on a good day, said mournfully, "I'm just so *beat down* by Alice."

Even in the center of town, Dacoma seemed rural, a far cry from the vast expanse of Los Angeles. The sparsely settled western Oklahoma land was parched as always at that time of year. We were ready to head for greener pastures.

In Iowa, we turned on our radio and found a whole afternoon of country music by the velvet-voiced singer, Jim Reeves. It happened to be the tenth anniversary of his death in a private plane crash in 1964. When I was in Uganda in 1968, Reeves was the most popular American singer among the Africans. They especially liked his hauntingly sad "Am I Losing You?" Darlene and I sang along with him when we heard "I Love You Because," "Welcome to My World," and "He'll Have to Go."

In drizzling rain, we listened to Reeves' mellow voice as the hours and green hills of Iowa slipped by. We rounded Des Moines and reached the end of our day's energy at Cedar Rapids, where we settled down for the night after a quick call to Dick Trestrail to confirm our arrival in Milwaukee the next day.

The morning drive from Cedar Rapids toward Milwaukee was green and inviting. We crossed the Mississippi at Dubuque and entered the scenic hills of southwestern Wisconsin by late morning. It was new territory for us and so different from the sandy deserts in the West and the flatlands of central Indiana. We pulled our U-Haul trailer on winding, hilly roads, past quaint white-frame churches nestled in narrow valleys, and in sight of large dairy barns with silos that looked like castle turrets. Surely cheese must be nearby, we felt.

In Milwaukee, Dick Trestrail and his wife, Polly, took us into their home like members of the family. They insisted that I back the loaded trailer into their garage for security, even though it seemed an unnecessary precaution in their tidy Good Hope Road neighborhood. We spent the night at their home, and Darlene flew to Indianapolis the next day. I stayed another night so I could spend the day meeting my new colleagues at Marquette. The next morning, I made my first drive from Milwaukee to Indianapolis to join Darlene. We visited with her parents and sisters and their children until it was time to return to Wisconsin to settle into our townhouse apartment and begin our new life there.

It was exhilarating for both of us to be in the Midwest again, within driving distance of family and the places where we had grown up. Chicago beckoned from the south, and beyond it were Indianapolis and Anderson. Toledo and Elmore were only a few hours to the east. We rejoiced to have warm and humid weather once again, with fresh tomatoes, corn on the cob, and large family dinners. We were at home again in the Midwest.

Though we both had been raised in the Midwest, the region felt different to us. We were adults, and we were entering our professional lives in a new state. I had a great job as an assistant professor, and Darlene was excited to explore her opportunities in Milwaukee's medical community. Best of all, we could begin to dream of having children and raising a family.

34

First Autumn in Wisconsin

Our first Wisconsin home was a rented townhouse on Sierra Drive in what was then the eastern edge of Waukesha but is now in the city of Brookfield. The townhouse was just below the crest of a hill overlooking a farm, a Wonder Bread bakery, and a Holiday Inn on Interstate 94 just a half-mile to the south. The place was simple but spacious: three bedrooms upstairs, a living room and kitchen on the first floor, one and a half baths, and a finished walk-out basement. It was ample for us and our two cats, Lixie and Two, but it lacked the amenities of a typical professor's home.

On the day our townhouse was available, my officemate from Marquette, Gene Smiley, and his wife, Carol, came to help us move in. We made short work of unloading the trailer and had a pizza dinner. Darlene and I put our foam pads on our bedroom floor and had our first night of "camping" in our new home.

We had sold most of our furnishings back in Los Angeles and would have to rely on one paycheck for a while. We had enough money for rent and food with my income, but not enough to furnish our apartment right away. For the first year, we slept on the foam pads and ate our meals seated in lawn chairs at a rummage-sale table in the kitchen. By Christmas, we felt wealthy enough to buy a sleeper sofa and a fake leather recliner. We were ready for guests.

To furnish our apartment in Los Angeles, we had shopped at garage and apartment sales and found some wonderful bargains. One was a delicate antique couch with a feather tick seat that we bought for $10 from a young man who was eager to leave the Golden State. Another prize we brought from Los Angeles was a small, solid oak stand we bought for $6. The city was filled with excellent buys at secondhand stores, possibly because people had migrated west for the charms of Los Angeles and then either changed their minds or fell upon hard times.

In Milwaukee and its suburbs, we discovered quite the opposite. When we first saw signs announcing rummage sales, we were optimistic, imagining them to be like the garage and apartment sales in Los Angeles. It took several Saturday mornings of slogging through damp grass to garages and basements around Milwaukee and its suburbs before we learned what was being sold at Wisconsin rummage sales: They were selling actual *rummage!* Oddball dishes, pans, sporting goods, damaged furniture, and out-of-fashion clothing dominated the sales. The stable, frugal population of Wisconsin was evident in the things offered for sale. We were no longer among the migratory dreamers of Los Angeles.

Our lives were slightly complicated by the fact that we had only one car. Wisconsin Coach Lines made frequent stops at the commuter parking lot on I-94 near our townhouse, so if Darlene needed the car for the day, she had to take me to the bus stop and meet me again there in the evening. Even though we lived in the middle of farms and marshes, commuting by bus made us feel like true urbanites.

During my first semester of teaching economics at Marquette University, we did make one major household purchase: a Litton microwave oven, one of the best on the market at that time. The thing was monstrously big but low-powered by current standards. It came with a probe that would shut off the oven when food reached the desired temperature. The price was burned into my memory: $479. That amount would translate to about $2,349 in today's marketplace.

Cooler days and chilly nights brought colorful leaves in late September. We had heard of Door County, a scenic peninsula that juts into Lake Michigan, forming the northeastern point of Wisconsin. People had told us it was scenic, somewhat like New England, so we naively decided to drive there on a Saturday afternoon to see the fall color. Darlene picked me up at my Marquette office in midafternoon, and we headed north along the Lake Michigan shore. We saw a "Vacancy" sign at a motel near Sheboygan and continued north. It was getting dark when we reached Kewaunee at the lower edge of the peninsula. All of the motels there displayed "No Vacancy" signs. All the way to Algoma, we saw only "No Vacancy" signs. We finally stopped at a gas station.

"Are we likely to find a motel room up in Door County?" we asked.

The astounded man answered politely. "No, there won't be any. Everybody's here to see the fall leaves."

We had our tent and sleeping bags in the trunk, so I asked, "What about campsites?"

"No, sorry. I know for sure they're all taken."

We thanked the man and looked at our map. Hope seemed nearby. Green Bay was only forty miles way. It was a larger city. Surely we would find a motel room there.

As we entered Green Bay, we were again greeted by "No Vacancy" signs. We stopped at the second motel we found. I went in and asked the desk clerk.

"I see you're booked for the night. Do you know of a motel here with openings?"

Like the man at the gas station, the woman at the desk was polite. "Oh, no! There won't be any rooms tonight. The Packers are playing here tomorrow."

That did it. We knew there would be no lodging for miles around.

"Should we just drive back home?" I asked Darlene.

She thought about it and looked at the map. "Let's go down to Lake Winnebago. There might be rooms at Appleton or Oshkosh. If not, we can still drive home."

It was dark by this time, and we hurried south as fast as the traffic would allow. At Appleton, we saw a "Vacancy" sign and quickly pulled in.

"Do you have a room for two?" I asked.

"Yep. That's my last one!" the clerk said, pushing the registration book to me.

I began to fill in our names and address. The door opened behind me.

"Got any more rooms?" a man asked.

"Sorry, just gave out the last one. Better turn on the "No Vacancy" sign. Might find something farther south. The Packers are in Green Bay."

"I know!" said the disappointed traveler.

The next morning, Darlene and I continued along the west side of Lake Winnebago. She saw the Horicon Marsh National Wildlife Refuge on the map.

"Let's at least go to Horicon as long as we're this close," she said.

We drove through the marsh and saw many migrating Canada geese circling, landing, and taking off in the tall marsh grass. It was late afternoon when we stepped into our townhouse. We had picked the worst possible time to go to Door County, and we never found another good time to try. That was as close as we ever got to Door County.

That fall we were so excited to be in the Midwest for Halloween that we bought two pumpkins and carved friendly faces in them. Darlene didn't approve of the ghoulish jack-o'-lanterns and costumes of Halloween. We placed the carved pumpkins in front of an upstairs bedroom window on top of stacks of cardboard banker's boxes containing our files of medical and economics notes. To make sure passersby could see them, we placed 60-watt light bulbs in each pumpkin and plugged them in. They radiated happy smiles that were easily visible from the street. Three days later, we would regret that decision.

"Oh, no! Come here! Quick!" Darlene yelled. "Look at our pumpkins!"

I ran upstairs and found her attempting to extract the light bulbs from partially collapsed pumpkins. The heat of the lights had stimulated mold and rot, and the pumpkins had begun to melt. Their sides had begun to cave in, and green, purple, gray, and orange mold lined the interiors. Juice was running over the tops and down the sides of the cardboard file boxes. One moisture-weakened lid had partially collapsed.

We gently lifted the rotted pumpkins onto stacks of the *Milwaukee Journal* and took them to the trash bin. We learned an important lesson: Do not put electric lights in jack-o'-lanterns. It was more excitement than our pumpkins could handle.

A near-tragedy happened that first fall. Our cats, Two and Lixie, were free to roam around the lawns and tree rows when we were at home. They always showed up for meals and bedtime. But one Tuesday night, Two did not return for his supper. We called from the front door and from the walk-out basement door to no avail. The next day while I was at Marquette, Darlene walked the neighborhood and called his name, but no Two showed up. On Thursday when I took Darlene to board a bus for a trip to Indianapolis, Two was still truant. By Friday, our hearts sank. Two might never return.

On Saturday, I called Darlene in Indianapolis. While we were talking and worrying about Two, I heard scratching at the front door. I cautiously opened it, and there he was, skinny and haggard. Without hesitation, he burst in and did the strange sideways prancing walk he used whenever he scolded me. He went straight to his food dish.

"It's Two! It's Two!" I yelled on the phone to Darlene.

She screamed for joy, and we both shed a tear or two as we talked and marveled at his return. He may have been trapped in someone's garage while the owners were away on a trip and got out only when they returned. In any case, our "prodigal cat" had come home! When Darlene returned home, she was almost as eager to see Two as me. From then on, we kept both cats especially well fed, and they bulked up to about fourteen pounds each, bigger than some breeds of tiny dogs. Still, they were allowed to roam the neighborhood.

Having been born and raised as Angelenos, Two and Lixie had never seen snow. When the first snow arrived in late November, we wondered how they would react. Darlene opened the front door as usual, and the cats scampered out. Halfway across the lawn, they stopped suddenly. Turning around, they headed slowly back to the house doing a funny little dance, carefully lifting each paw, shaking it in the air, and taking the next step. We were convulsed with laughter, but the cats were not. Two cursed us in his special cat language when he was back in the house, and neither cat was eager to venture out in the snow again. Unlike us, they would not become true Milwaukee Badgers.

35

Wisconsin Snows

As winter approached, Darlene and I became more and more excited about winter weather. We eagerly watched the weather forecasts every evening on our tiny nine-inch black-and-white television, hoping for a winter storm watch. November and December were disappointing, but we did have a warm and slushy snow just after Christmas. January was cold and dry, with no snow at all. It seemed our visions of heavy snow and snowball fights might not happen.

One evening in early February, I had an unusually large bedtime snack: four bowls of Cheerios. That night I dreamed I was in one of those concrete-lined riverbeds that are the storm drains in Los Angeles. For some unknown reason, I had a large fish in my hand, gripping it just above the tail like a club, and I was chasing a pig that screamed and tried to escape. The pig lodged itself in a crack in the concrete wall, flailing its legs and screaming as pigs do when frightened. It screamed louder and louder as I closed in to club it with the fish, and I awakened to the sound of a snowplow scraping the pavement as it came up the road below our hill. The plow was scraping an inch or two of fresh snow off the otherwise dry pavement, and the scraping sounded like the screaming pig in my dream. In later years, whenever I had Cheerios at bedtime, Darlene warned me of pigs in the concrete rivers of LA and recommended temperance in Cheerios.

Like our first winter in Wisconsin, our second winter in 1975–76 brought very little snow. By February it seemed we would be slipping toward an early spring without any exciting winter weather. But on March 6, 1976, an unnatural calm came over Milwaukee. It was the prelude to our first major winter storm.

That night a steady drizzle began to coat the streets, lawns, trees, and power lines with ice. The glassy glaze made the trees especially beautiful, and Darlene and I took pictures. The power went out on the third evening of ice, so we snuggled down under heavy blankets on our sponge beds on the bedroom floor. We couldn't hear any wind outside, but the night was not quiet. The big oak trees twenty feet from our bedroom groaned and crackled with every breeze. Now and then a branch would make a "pop" noise followed by a sound like breaking glass as it fell to the ground.

Near midnight that night, we were awakened by an explosive "boom" in one of the oak trees. It sounded like a cannon shot. High in one tree, a big limb had snapped and had come crashing through the lower limbs and branches. Darlene grabbed my arm, and we waited for more noise. Instead the unnatural peace returned, broken only by smaller falling limbs.

Electric power was out for several days in southeastern Wisconsin. Trees and limbs had fallen on power lines in hundreds of places. Electrical crews came from neighboring states and from as far as Missouri to restore service. Tree trimming went on for months. It was a memorable Wisconsin winter, but we had yet to see a real Wisconsin blizzard.

Our hopes for extreme winters were rewarded in years to come by several fabulous blizzards, especially during the winters of 1978–79 and 1979–80. Snow was sometimes fifteen inches deep, and drifts could exceed ten feet in height. Schools were closed for nearly a week at a time, and it took days to shovel our driveway. We loved the excitement, but by March we became weary of snow and cold weather. In Wisconsin, warm weather sometimes didn't arrive to stay until June.

On the morning of May 9, 1990, during our sixteenth winter in Wisconsin, we awoke to an eerie silence outside. At first glance, it appeared to be a foggy morning, but a clearer view revealed that eleven inches of heavy, wet snow had fallen on trees that were already leafing out or in blossom. Tree trunks a foot or more in diameter were split from their tops to their roots. By that year we had enjoyed many wonderful Wisconsin snow storms, but that last one was too much of a good thing.

36

Accidental Methodists

We lived in the townhouse on Sierra Drive for two years, and during most of that time we shopped unsuccessfully for a church home. We first visited a congregation of the Church of God, the kind of church in which we had both grown up. Sadly, it was far away on the other side of the city. Our other church visits put us into unusual settings.

Once an economics colleague of mine at Marquette invited us to attend a Unitarian church, but the Unitarian Universalist service seemed like a political or environmentalist meeting. The Lutheran Church had been the faith of some of my ancestors, but we found its services formal and foreign to us. At the Wauwatosa Methodist Church, the pastor was Clarence Kelly, whose name was the same as that of the head of the FBI at that time. We liked Reverend Kelly's sermons, and the music was inspiring and traditional, so we began to attend there regularly.

It seemed important to us to know more about the beliefs of Methodists if we were going make Wauwatosa Methodist our church home, so we signed up for the Pastor's Class. The class was supposed to meet with Pastor Kelly for several weeks, and it would lead to membership in the church. We had no intention of becoming members because the Church of God congregations in which we both had grown up did not approve of formal church membership.

One's direct relationship with God was the only standard of membership it recognized. But Pastor Kelly's class seemed the best way to get in on the ground floor of Methodism, even if we were going to continue to be just regular attenders, not members.

After faithfully attending the first three of the six scheduled Sunday classes, we missed the fourth one. On the fifth Sunday, we decided we should tell Pastor Kelly that we appreciated his class but did not want formal membership in the church. But when we arrived at the classroom on the fifth Sunday, we were greeted by an ominous buzz of activity among class members. We learned that everyone in the class was going to be inducted into church membership that day, a week earlier than scheduled. Our names were already printed in the church bulletin.

Darlene and I looked at each other in mild panic. Surrounded by our fellow class members, we couldn't confer with each other privately about what to do. Neither of us was ready to create a scene or try to explain our theological background and reasoning to the others. What could we do?

Cowardice took over. We said nothing.

After the class, we sat nervously through the sermon, waiting for the moment when we would be paraded out in front of the sanctuary with the other class members and be introduced as new members of the Methodist Church. That Sunday we became Methodists by accident, or maybe simply out of cowardice.

I have wondered how long the Wauwatosa Methodist Church carried us on their books as members despite our chronic absenteeism. We assumed we ceased to be members when we went missing for a specific number of Sundays by default, but this time not by accident.

37

Discovering Elmbrook Church

As accidental Methodists we were no longer in an active search for a church, but in early 1976 we learned of a church that would lead us into some of the most important times of our lives in Wisconsin.

Darlene was working part-time at a clinic in downtown Milwaukee, and a doctor there, Steven Duck, told her about a church in our neighborhood called Elmbrook Church. It had been birthed from home prayer meetings in the 1950s and had grown to thousands attending every Sunday. Darlene caught his enthusiasm for the church, and we decided to check it out. We found that it was just on the other side of Interstate 94 from our townhouse. We drove past one day and saw an immense, new building in a sea of mud, awaiting landscaping. Surrounding it was a paved parking lot that seemed to cover acres.

Back at home, I looked up Elmbrook Church in the phone book and called to ask when services were held. I then asked what I later realized was a comical question for such an evangelical church: "Can just *anybody* attend your church?" Without a hint of a giggle, the person said that yes, anyone could attend.

The next weekend, the medical group from the clinic where Darlene was working held a large Saturday night social function for all the employees. It was a glittering event at a country club, and I met some of her colleagues. We both were so caught up in the excitement that it was after eleven when we left. On the way home, we stopped talking when a local radio station began playing Judy Collins's rendition of "Amazing Grace," a version in which she starts softly alone and is gradually joined by a choir that grows larger until the hymn's triumphant climax:

> *When we've been there ten thousand years,*
> *Bright, shining as the sun,*
> *We've no less days*
> *To sing God's praise*
> *Than when we'd first begun!*

We drove on in silence, hearing the song in our minds. Both of us were deeply moved. Despite the lateness of the night, we were up early the next morning to visit Elmbrook Church.

A seven-minute drive took us into the swirling traffic in the vast parking lot, and we were soon in the biggest church building either of us had ever entered. We were greeted warmly at the door, and we immediately sensed friendliness, energy, and enthusiasm in the people. The huge sanctuary reminded us of the Church of God camp meeting services we had attended in Indiana as children. The congregation's singing at the beginning of the service was strong and harmonious, and the songs were familiar. Then the senior pastor, Stuart Briscoe, took the platform. He was in his forties, slim, athletic, and well dressed. He paused for a moment to claim everyone's attention.

"Jimmy Carter has a goal!" he said in a clear, strong, tenor voice.

The year was 1976, and Jimmy Carter, an evangelical Christian, was running for president. Carter would be nominated that summer and would hold office until 1981. But Stuart's sermon was not about Jimmy Carter or politics. He must have expanded on some biblical principles about goal-setting, righteous living, and dependence on God, but I only remember his opening line from that day. Darlene and I were enthralled.

In those days, it wasn't unusual to have a Sunday evening service, so we returned that evening, full of expectancy. We weren't disappointed. The service was similar to that in the morning: strong congregational singing, prayer times, and Scripture reading. Stuart Briscoe's message was one of his characteristic

Bible studies. He taught the Bible in depth from the pulpit, something we had rarely experienced before.

Near the end of the service, Pastor Briscoe announced that a young couple, Bob and Jane Henley, had just returned from singing in a Billy Graham Crusade. He asked them to come to the platform to tell about the crusade and their experience there. He interviewed them and suggested they lead us in singing the hymn "Amazing Grace." It was the very song that had moved Darlene and me so deeply just the night before. The "coincidence" was unmistakable.

Darlene grabbed my hand as Jane began to sing. Bob joined Jane, and then he motioned for the congregation join in singing as well. Someone near the front stood, and then everyone stood, singing like the choir we had heard on the radio the night before. More than a thousand voices joined in the triumphant closing lines. After a closing a prayer, people began to leave. But Darlene and I just stared at the front of the church, unable to move for a few minutes. We had found our church home.

38

Our New Church Home

*I*n our first four years at Elmbrook Church, we were active mainly in attending morning and evening services and some special events. Week by week, we absorbed Scripture lessons from the pulpit. Since we found ourselves in the middle of large crowds on Sundays, Darlene began to attend women's Bible studies, and I volunteered to help align cars in an unpaved gravel portion of the parking lot. I called it my "parking lot ministry" to misguided cars.

Darlene bought a copy of the New International Version of the Bible, since that's what Stuart Briscoe used for his sermons. We shared that Bible at first, but Darlene gave me my own copy for Christmas 1980 (which I still have and use). We both were becoming far more disciplined Bible students than before, and we read our Bibles consistently. From the beginning, I wrote the date beside every chapter I read. Darlene did that less consistently until the last years of her life, but she read at least as consistently as I did.

We hadn't heard the term "megachurch" until we came to Elmbrook, but that's what it was. Josh McDowell, a prominent visiting speaker, once told the congregation that we were not a "non-denominational" church, as we described ourselves. He said that any church with more than two thousand members *is* a denomination. Attendance on the weekends was probably about four thousand when we started and about six thousand when we left in 1992. Later in the 1990s, attendance rose to about eight thousand.

Elmbrook was a mission-driven church, something we both appreciated. The church provided partial support for 150 missionaries in all parts of the world, and the Missions Festival in the fall was one of the biggest events of the year. The mission budget alone was over $2 million, and support for the local congregation's work was more than that. Giving was so strong that building expansions were typically paid off in three years or less.

At Elmbrook we were part of a very large church family that we gradually came to know in the first few years. Settling on a church and finding a house nearby set the stage for another momentous change: starting our family.

In time, all of our children attended Elmbrook Church. When Jenny, our firstborn, was only two weeks old, we began to take her with us to Sunday morning and evening services. We were older than most first-time parents of newborns, about a decade older than most, but our baby daughter helped us meet other parents of infants. As a result, we met many other people in that congregation of four thousand. Jenny opened many doors for us, as did Anna and Matthew later.

Jenny had been unwilling to go into the nursery, so we took her with us into Sunday morning church services. The first time we insisted Jenny stay in the nursery, at about age two, she screamed and cried as we left. When we returned to pick her up, she was calm, even happy. A pleasant, blond man about our age handed her back to us and told us she had been fine there with the other toddlers. After a couple of happy weeks, we learned that the man's full name was Don Trinkle, which sounded almost like *twinkle,* as in a star. He had befriended Jenny that first Sunday, and she knew him affectionately as "Trinkle-trinkle." His example made us want to help teach Sunday school so we could "go thou and do likewise."

When Darlene asked about teaching in the children's program, we learned we would have to become members of the congregation first. Membership was required before anyone could greet people at the door, teach, sing in the choir, or take on any other leadership role. I asked about being a greeter in the lobby, and Darlene asked about teaching in the children's program. Membership required a 12-week Sunday evening course on basic Christian theology, capped off by an evening in which class members would give their testimonies orally to the others in the class and the pastors and elders who might attend.

We trusted this church thoroughly, and we wanted to assist in its work. The requirements for church membership at Elmbrook didn't violate the non-membership position of the Church of God. The Elmbrook method merged the spiritual experiences in the Church of God with a more disciplined organizational structure than we had known before. So we took the membership class, gave our testimonies, and became church members—this time *on purpose.* We were no longer accidental Methodists.

To follow Don Trinkle's example, Darlene and I joined the team that taught the three-year-olds on Sunday mornings. We were part of a nine-person team that taught a class of fifty three-year-olds. We started teaching in 1980, and Darlene continued until we left Wisconsin in 1992. During that time, as a pediatrician and a somewhat older mom, Darlene became a mentor to many younger mothers.

The most profound change that happened to Darlene and me personally during our sixteen years at Elmbrook Church was our renewed and energized Christian lives. We attended church almost as regularly as we had as children, and we were more active, purposeful, and happy in prayer and Bible reading than ever before. The Sunday services were interesting, inspiring, and sometimes exciting: We looked forward to them. We found new energy and more maturity in our faith. The church prepared us for more mature parenting as well. Elmbrook Church and our experiences there were among the reasons Darlene said that our years in Wisconsin were the "summertime of our lives."

39

From Sierra to Summit

Not long after our move to Wisconsin, Darlene had begun to work full-time in a pediatric clinic, and our combined incomes positioned us to buy a house. In the spring of 1976, just when we began to attend Elmbrook Church, we discovered a house on Summit Drive on the hill overlooking the church. The name of the street, Summit Drive, stirred our memories of camping, hiking, and climbing in California. The fact that we found it while living on Sierra Drive gave it a sentimental tinge.

It was a brick ranch-style house that sat just below the crown of the hill. It had picture windows facing east and south, and the view extended to a ridge a mile to the south. We were stunned by the view, and everything about the house was perfect for us at that time: three bedrooms, a bath and a half, a semi-finished half basement, and a wood-burning fireplace. Cast-iron radiators supplied heat along the baseboards in all rooms, an especially even form of heating.

Our offer of $63,000 was quickly accepted by Rose Carrows, the widow who had lived alone in the house since her husband's sudden death two years earlier. Rose wasn't quite alone: She had a nervous, yippy little Chihuahua dog that raced around barking in its silly falsetto voice when we first toured the house. Rose was a slim, nervous redhead herself, so they must have been a congenial couple.

We giggled like children when we applied for a mortgage. We were thrilled to be buying our first house, and this particular house was exactly what we wanted. The loan officer at Great Midwest Savings and Loan calmly told us we should have bought a larger, more expensive house, but we just kept giggling and signing papers. A larger house would not have fit our limited means, and none was likely to have the splendid view that we would have at 1045 Summit Drive.

Darlene's dad came from Indianapolis to help with the move. Grada rented a truck, and the three of us loaded it. When we arrived with the first load, Grada recommended that I back the truck up onto the lawn until it was right at the front door for easy unloading. It was a brilliant and sensible decision, but some of neighbors must have scowled behind their window curtains. It wasn't the last time we would discomfit at least one set of neighbors.

By this time, we had enough furniture to make a house livable. We had a kitchen table and some mismatched dining chairs, all from garage sales, Goodwill, and the Salvation Army. We had a sleeper sofa, a recliner, and an antique Morris chair in need of restoration. We had purchased a used bedspring and mattress somewhere, so we were no longer sleeping on the floor on foam pads.

Our first night alone in the Summit Drive house was Wisconsin perfection: cool, dry air stirred by a stiff, western breeze. When we awoke the next morning, a cool, fresh wind was blowing through the house as though we had been camping. I discovered that the main garage doors under the house had been open all night. So had the door from the garage into the basement and the door at the top of the stairs next to our bedroom door, allowing the wind to race through the whole house. It was a glorious first morning. Our first child, Jenny, would be born nine months later.

We lived in that home for sixteen years. For us, it was a perfect place to start our family. The house was small and in excellent condition, so we didn't have to be preoccupied with its upkeep. It was large enough to accommodate Darlene and me and our eventual three children, yet small enough that we could keep track of the kids when they were little. The back yard had level space for play sets, two swing sets, and a sandbox. The front yard sloped steeply to the street for winter sledding or summer rides on the plastic Slip 'N Slide. The view from the living room was a continual joy in all seasons.

The Summit Drive house was comfortable and efficient, but it could have been better if we had made two improvements. The first would have been power garage-door openers. When we arrived home, we had to get out of the car, walk to the garage entry door, unlock it, go to the appropriate garage door, lift it, get back into the car, and pull it into the garage. When we left the house, we had to reverse that procedure. This routine happened in all kinds of weather: heavy rain, sub-zero temperatures, hurricane-force winds, ice, and snow that was sometimes more than a foot deep. We never made that improvement at the Summit Drive house.

The second "luxury" was one we denied ourselves for too many years: air conditioning. For the first twelve years, the reliable breezes at our hilltop cooled the house enough except on a few exceptionally hot days each summer. But the summer of 1988 was stiflingly hot. In desperation, I went to Best Buy one night just before closing and bought a window air conditioner. That night I modified one of our dining room windows with plywood to install the air conditioner. We hung sheets over the kitchen and living room entrances to trap the cool air, and we slept on the sleeper sofa and the floor that night and for a few nights after. This temporary solution caused Darlene and me to agree on central air before the next summer's heat. When we turned on our new central air in 1989, we wondered why we had waited so long.

40

New House, New Baby

Darlene and I both had wanted to be parents ever since we were children. We even talked about it when we were first dating. In spite of the time and effort we had expended on our professional lives up to this point, having a family was our primary ambition. We had a house and steady incomes, and neither of us felt nagged by unfulfilled educational or professional ambitions. Having waited so long, we were ready to turn our attention to children, knowing they would become the most important focus of our lives. Nine months after moving into our house on Summit Drive, we would know the full truth of Darlene's saying, "New house, new baby."

Darlene devised a poetic way to let me know our first child was on the way. We had a brown pottery coffee cup decorated with rounded scallops that seemed to resemble the rounded tummy of a pregnant woman. We had begun to call it the "pregnant mommy cup," looking hopefully toward the day when Darlene would actually be a pregnant mommy-to-be. And so it was on that one summer day in 1976, we were having morning coffee and Darlene said with a twinkle in her eye, "Do you see what cup I'm using today?"

I glanced up absently and said, "Yes."

"Look again," Darlene said. "What cup is it?"

"Hmm. Well, it's the pregnant mommy cup. PREGNANT MOMMY CUP! Is that what you are saying?" I yelled. I leaped across to her and hugged her. She laughed joyfully.

"I just found out for sure yesterday," she explained, tears brimming in her eyes. "Dr. Borkowf said it will be about the end of March or early April."

"Oh! That's wonderful!" I said.

"We are going to be parents!" Darlene said, enjoying the sound of those words, "and I'll keep using the pregnant mommy cup!"

During that first pregnancy, Darlene's mind was on the health of the baby. She ate carefully, monitored her weight, reduced her coffee consumption, and continued to drink from the pregnant mommy cup. Ultrasound technology at that time could detect some abnormalities in unborn babies but not the sex of the infant. Some very serious abnormalities could be detected by ultrasound by the mid-1970s. "Darlene the doctor" had been following these medical developments for personal and professional reasons.

"I have been thinking and praying about the possibility that our baby could have a congenital defect," she said to me one day.

I just listened as she continued in terms I could understand.

"Doctors can tell if the baby in the womb has an enlarged head or an exposed spinal cord or other defects." She took a deep breath and looked squarely at me. "If our baby has a defect, I don't want to have an abortion."

We sat quietly for a minute. I hadn't thought about this possibility. If the baby were born with one of the conditions she had named, we both knew what it could mean in terms of special care, expense, and time for treatment.

"Okay," I said simply, and we said no more about that topic. Her mind was made up, and so was mine. She never wavered, nor did I.

When our first child was born, Darlene was thirty-one, and I was thirty-seven. She didn't appreciate my comparing us to Abraham and Sarah in the Bible, but we were indeed relatively old first-time parents.

41

Jenny Elizabeth: March 30, 1977

I was more than ready for our first child's arrival. On March 25, 1977, about two inches of snow fell on the driveway on Summit Drive. As a hyper-conscientious expectant father, I hurried out to shovel the driveway in case the baby came that day. It was unnecessary, but I had to do *something* to prepare for the baby. No emergency arose that day, and the snow melted.

On Tuesday, March 29, the anxious waiting was about to end. I was at my office at Marquette University when Darlene called.

"Can you come and take me to County General?" she said matter-of-factly.

The question seemed to thunder in my head.

"Yes! Is this *it*?" I shouted.

"No, this may not be *it*," she replied, mimicking my emphasis, "but Harry wants to see me at County General for another test."

At her scheduled prenatal appointment that morning, Dr. Harold (Harry) Borkowf, her obstetrician from South Africa, had said she was overdue. He might want to induce labor that afternoon.

Trying to remain calm, I told a few colleagues where I was going and headed west out of the city in my 1964 Chevy. Speeding up the hill from

Milwaukee to the community of Brookfield felt like flying. It was a windy day, warm for that time of year. Little white clouds were scudding across a blue sky. I was flying toward them on my way home on an electrifying mission.

Darlene had packed her suitcase a few weeks earlier, so we were off immediately to the hospital. It wasn't an emergency, but our excitement would have matched most emergencies. At the hospital, she checked in while I parked. By the time I arrived at her room, Dr. Borkowf had decided to induce labor.

Darlene was given intravenous fluids to activate her labor. Labor began, but the process was slow. Contractions continued throughout the evening, but the baby didn't emerge. At about 10 p.m., the doctors ordered an X-ray to be sure of the baby's position in the womb. Darlene was transferred to a gurney, and I walked beside her to the elevator. We were taken to an X-ray exam room in the hospital's basement, and I stood in the hall outside the door while the X-ray was performed.

The door to a patient's room across the hall was open, and I could see a very frail, very old man propped up on pillows. He was sleeping or unconscious, with his mouth open wide and his head thrown back. A young doctor came to dial a call on the wall phone near where I stood. Someone answered on the other end, evidently a close family member.

"He's really very weak," the doctor said, "I don't think he has much more time. I think it would be good for you to come here to see him."

The doctor listened for a minute. "No, I don't think it would be wise to wait until morning. Couldn't you come now?"

He listened again. "I still believe it would be good for you to come, but I understand. We will do the best we can for him." The doctor hung up and returned to his patient.

Just then the door to the X-ray room opened, and Darlene was wheeled out. We returned to the elevator, and I never heard if a family member came that night to see the dying man. Birth and death were across the hall from each other that night.

Back in the hospital room, doctors and nurses continued to keep track of Darlene and the baby's condition. Wires leading to a fetal monitor had been attached to the baby's head. At about midnight, the baby's stress rose to an unacceptable level. A team of doctors and nurses suddenly appeared and surrounded Darlene.

"We're going to take the baby now," a doctor firmly informed me, and he escorted me to an intern's station nearby. Darlene was wheeled quickly past me into an operating room down the hall. Beyond a set of swinging doors, she was being prepped for an emergency C-section. I could only vaguely imagine what was happening.

I made small talk with the two interns who were on duty that night, and I listened for any sound from the operating room. It was farther away than I thought, and I heard nothing. At about 1:30 a.m., an older doctor appeared. He was holding a baby, and he turned so I could see.

"You have a healthy daughter," he said, "and your wife is doing fine. She's tired from the long labor, and she had general anesthesia for the C-section. She'll sleep for a while."

I looked into the face of the baby. Baby! It was *my* baby, *our* baby!

"I'll take her to the newborn nursery on the third floor to get her cleaned up," the doctor said. "You can come up there and see her. Your wife won't be ready to see you for a while."

When I reached the newborn nursery, the nurses directed me to a crying baby in a glass box. A note on the glass box said "Kardatzke." It was our baby! I peered into the box and watched her cry.

"Do you want to hold her?" a nurse asked.

I hadn't thought I could hold her so soon, since I thought babies were so fragile. *Of course, I want to hold her,* I thought.

"Yes, I'd like that," I said.

The nurse wrapped her in a couple of soft cotton blankets and put a tiny knit cap on her head. She was still covered with the waxy material that had protected her while she swam in the amniotic fluid in the womb.

"We'll clean her up better after you're done holding her," the nurse said.

She was still crying when the nurse handed her to me. Darlene and I had already decided that the name of a girl baby would be Jenny, so I talked to her and used her name. "Hello, Jenny. Welcome to the Earth. I'm your dad."

At the sound of her name, she stopped crying and looked up at me. I kept talking to her for nearly an hour and then gave her back to the nurses for a more complete cleaning. She was sleeping by then and didn't need me. They said my wife might be coming out of anesthesia soon, and I could go see her.

Darlene began to awaken sometime very early in the morning. She was still dopey from the anesthesia and pain medication, but she turned her head toward me and managed a faint smile.

"I was holding our baby just now," I told her. "She is beautiful. She stopped crying when I held her and talked to her."

Darlene smiled more broadly and said thoughtfully, "Baby Jenny. What should we name her?"

What should we name her? I thought. *Had Darlene changed her mind? Was she already thinking of some other names?*

While I was panicking silently over her question, she fell asleep again. It was time for me to go home where I could sleep for a few hours too.

Three inches of new snow had fallen that night. I had hoped for warm spring weather for the birth, but this was Wisconsin, and it was only March 30. I drove home in the snow sometime in the early hours before dawn.

When I was dressed again after a short sleep, I looked at myself in the bathroom mirror and said, "I'm Jenny Kardatzke's father."

It sounded wonderful, and I would use that sentence many times to introduce myself during Jenny's childhood when she was often better known than either Darlene or me. But that morning I wondered if her name would really be Jenny.

Darlene was fully awake when I arrived back at the hospital. "What did you mean when you asked what we should name Jenny?" I asked. She didn't remember the conversation at all, so I reconstructed it for her. "You said, 'Baby Jenny. What should we name her?'"

"That's funny!" Darlene said with a little laugh. "I must have been wondering about her middle name. I guess I couldn't remember it last night."

With that, the mild crisis over her name was resolved. She was Jenny Elizabeth. "Jenny" was the name of a beloved family member of mine who had died at age twenty on the Kansas frontier in 1892 shortly before she was to be married. "Elizabeth" was a name that appeared in both the Sayers and Kardatzke family histories.

Darlene was in the hospital about a week, and she shared the room with at least two other women. I wasn't allowed long visits, and little we said was really private. She was happy and relieved the day I brought her and Jenny home.

That first evening at home, Darlene sat in our living room in a rocking chair, holding baby Jenny and looking toward the hills to the south. I put on a recording of the Mormon Tabernacle Choir singing "Father in Heaven," and we both cried with joy.

> *Father in Heaven, in thy love abounding,*
> *Hear these thy children thru the world resounding,*
> *Loud in thy praises. Thanks for peace abiding,*
> *Ever abiding.*

42

Anna Katherine: February 15, 1980

We had always intended to have more than one child, if possible. Darlene the pediatrician preferred a three-year space between the births. True to her professional convictions, we became expectant parents for a second baby who would be born about three years after Jenny's birth.

We were both overjoyed and thankful when Darlene told me the news. She may have used the "Pregnant Mommy" cup again, but I don't remember.

As the day approached for the birth of our second baby, we considered the fact that this time might be the last time Darlene would be pregnant. Because of her age, she might not be able to get pregnant again. Also, the ordeal of birthing another child might make us decide against trying for more. With those thoughts in mind, I asked Darlene when she was about eight months pregnant if she would let me photograph her in her two-piece swimsuit. She was always shy about her body, and my suggestion might have seemed weird, but the scientist and historian in her took over and she allowed it. She posed in front of our south-facing windows, beautifully illuminated by the brilliant winter sun. We were both amazed later to see how her body had stretched to accommodate the baby. Without the pictures, we might have forgotten.

Anna Katherine: February 15, 1980

The months seemed to go by more quickly than they had during Darlene's first pregnancy. Her second C-section could have been scheduled for Valentine's Day, but she was glad when the doctor decided on February 15. She may have thought having a baby on Valentine's Day would seem trite, or perhaps that the joy of the baby's birthday would be diminished by the romantic holiday. On February 14, I bought her a bright red, heart-shaped box of chocolates to celebrate Valentine's Day and also the eve of the second baby's birth.

Snow had fallen, and roads were slushy in the morning. We took Jenny down the street to stay with our friend Rose Rand. Jenny was delighted to have a special day out, and she was excited that the baby would finally arrive. She had been hearing about the baby for a long time.

For this birth, I was to be with Darlene during every stage of the procedure. She was calm, knowing the nature of each step of surgery prep, since she had performed the same procedures during her medical training and had experienced them before. I, on the other hand, was less calm. The part of the prep that made me feel squeamish was the spinal block injection. I heard a little "pop" when the needle penetrated the spinal cord, but Darlene did not react. She was calm and tough and experienced. I followed her lead.

Jenny's birth had been an emergency C-section; this one was planned, so there was ample time for the hospital staff to put me into a surgical gown, paper shoe covers, and a surgeon's disposable paper cap before the actual delivery was to take place. They instructed me on scrubbing in and put me into a pair of latex gloves. It was my best masquerade, as a "real doctor" rather than an economist.

Darlene smiled as I came into the operating room, and we touched hands through my latex gloves. She was already receiving IV fluids and anesthetic, but she was conscious and aware of the preparations. She was covered in light green sheets from her chin down except for the area directly over her enormously pregnant belly. Dr. Borkowf showed me where to stand behind him. He would be next to Darlene's side, and I could see the whole operation. I looked around and counted eight people: Dr. Borkowf, an anesthesiologist, a pediatrician, three nurses, and three people I couldn't identify, possibly OB residents. The room was very chilly, so the nurses took care to keep Darlene covered in warm blankets.

I soon saw how hard doctors and nurses work. Dr. Borkowf took command, asked for a scalpel, and started the incision. He cut through the skin and then through layers of muscle and other tissue I didn't know were there. I watched every step intently. Darlene seemed to sleep during this part of the operation. When Dr. Borkowf exposed the baby's head, I could see a crown of matted, dark hair. He manipulated the baby to urge it out of the womb, but it was slow work.

"It's a big head!" he said.

Inside my surgical mask, I kept saying quietly, "Come on, baby! *Come on, baby!*" Suddenly the baby came surging out, covered with the protective coating.

"You have a girl!" Dr. Borkowf announced as she emerged.

Anna replied with strong greeting cries. Darlene smiled and took a deep breath. She would tell me later how relieved she was to be able to breathe more easily after this especially large baby was born. Anna weighed in at 8 pounds 4 ounces compared to Jenny, who was 6 pounds 10 ounces at birth. Anna was our largest baby.

By then I was probably numbed with shock at what I had just seen, by far the most dramatic medical experience I'd ever had. I watched blankly as baby Anna was handed to nurses at a warming table across the room. I could see that she was larger than Jenny had been at birth. She had a large, barrel chest, and she kept announcing her presence in a healthy voice. The attending pediatrician checked her quickly, and one of the attending staff must have cut the umbilical cord. A nurse then rolled the warming table with Anna on it to the newborn nursery. I remained, watching the surgeons work on Darlene.

Dr. Borkowf and his team began closing the incision, and it was a far more elaborate process than I had imagined. It was not as simple as just pulling the skin together and sewing it shut. There were layers and layers of tissue to be repaired, one after the other, starting from the inside layers. At each layer, the doctor pressed a small curved needle through tissue and drew the cord tight, again and again. Then the next layer was closed. The doctor and his team worked rapidly, but it was two hours later when Dr. Borkowf turned to me and said I could leave. Darlene had done very well, he said, but she would be sleeping for a few hours. The doctors continued until the suturing was completed.

The newborn nursery this time was chaotic, since it was midday, not the middle of the night. Baby Anna had been cleaned and wrapped in a couple of soft cotton blankets. She was in a warm plastic incubator and looked robust, rosy, and healthy. I was allowed to hold her a few minutes, but the nursery was not adequately staffed for long visits from adoring dads. She was sleeping comfortably, so I soon gave her back to the nurses and went to check on Darlene.

Darlene was in a private room this time, not a dorm-like ward as when Jenny was born. This was Milwaukee County General Hospital, the same hospital where Jenny had been born, but this time Darlene was given an upgrade. But in that old building, the narrow room seemed more like a prison cell than a modern hospital room. Her bed was beside a window, and her personal things were spread on the window ledge.

She was awake when I arrived, so we talked about the baby's name and confirmed that she would be Anna Katherine. We had decided on her name several weeks earlier, basing her first name on my Grandma Ann Bruner and Anna the prophetess in the Bible. Katherine was a name that appeared more than once in our family histories.

As we were talking, a nurse wheeled Anna in for her first attempted breast feeding. Darlene was alert and held out her arms to receive the precious package. I smiled when she glanced at me before giving her full attention to the hungry baby.

My mother came from Ohio by train to help with Jenny, Darlene, and baby Anna. Anna was my mother's seventh grandchild out of an eventual twenty-two. Darlene was happy to have such experienced help for a few days, and my mother told her she lived for times like that. She even cooked an ancient family recipe of a German dish we called "kraut kraupfa" and baked my favorite, a burnt sugar cake. She stayed several days, and she and Darlene talked happily of child rearing, cooking, and travel. They always had a close relationship.

From the beginning, there was something special about Anna's energy and the way she expressed it. Even from early childhood, her creativity made her legendary for "marching to a different drummer." I was the second of my parents' three older children, so for a few years I was in the middle until my younger three siblings were born. Anna was a middle child like me, and we both saw ourselves as a little "different" from our siblings.

43

Matthew August: July 22, 1983

Darlene and I delighted in being parents. Jenny and Anna were both healthy and active. They played together well but with differing styles and different temperaments. They learned to walk and talk differently as well. We took notes on the funny vocabularies each girl invented while learning to talk. Their differing personalities made us wonder what a third personality would be if we were to have another child.

In the first two years after Anna was born, Darlene hadn't wanted another baby, but in time she softened as she watched the girls grow and play together. We began to hope and try for a third child. In December 1982, she told me that she was pregnant. This was to be our third child, and her announcement was low-key but joyful.

We rejoiced privately and secretly. Darlene was always careful to avoid announcing private events too early, if ever. Pregnancy did not guarantee a live birth, and she may not have wanted her pregnancy to overshadow our otherwise normal life with two young girls. At home, however, we made elaborate plans. We were experienced parents, so we already had a crib, a car seat, and bedding. We knew which diapers we wanted and the commercial formula we would use if Darlene's milk were not adequate. The girls had trained us well.

Darlene was "beginning to show" in early 1983, so we decided to tell Jenny and Anna about their expected new sibling before the whole world figured out what was happening. One chilly March day, Darlene sat with the two girls on the couch in the living room holding the microphone of a cassette recorder while I held our state-of-the-art 8mm movie camera. When she told them about the baby, I would make a video of her conversation with the girls.

Darlene began by carefully explaining that we were going to have a new baby, that they would have a baby brother or sister, and that they would be the big sisters. Jenny, at age six, understood. An extreme grin strained her face, and she screamed in excitement. Anna, at three, didn't really understand why Jenny was so excited. She joined in and mimicked Jenny's excitement as best she could. I kept the camera rolling as Darlene laughed and recorded the girls' shouts as they ran in circles, yelling.

Darlene mentioned her pregnancy to Sherry Hall at church one day, wondering aloud if it would be difficult to manage three children. Sherry and her husband, Dave, had been missionaries in Nigeria and had taken their five children with them. They were active at Elmbrook Church in 1983.

"Don't worry!" Sherry said. "Once you have your third child, your house just becomes happy bedlam, no matter how many more kids you have!"

From then on, "happy bedlam" became one of Darlene's watchwords when the tumult of our home life seemed overwhelming.

Spring of 1983 was cold, and we did not have two consecutive warm days until mid-June. But the summer of 1983 was hot, and Darlene was miserable as she waited for her scheduled C-section. Her estimated due date was not until August 5, 1983. We moved the girls into the back bedroom. The baby's south-facing room was stocked with diapers, blankets, and baby clothes. The crib was made up, ready for its precious cargo, and a couch and rocking chair were there. The house was ready. We were ready.

As a precaution against an emergency C-section, Darlene's delivery date was set for July 29. When Dr. Borkowf decided to go on vacation at the end of July, the delivery date was moved up further to July 22. The change of date may have saved Matt's life.

On July 21, I took a picture of Darlene wearing a tan jumper and red blouse in the car just before we pulled away for the hospital. Her tummy nearly reached the dashboard, but she was radiant in spite of her discomfort in the heat and the lack of air conditioning in our home. Our neighbors, Rose and Roger Rand, had agreed to watch the girls. We dropped them off at the Rands' house on the way to the hospital.

This delivery would be at St. Mary's Hospital on Milwaukee's east side, a much newer building than Milwaukee County General. Darlene was to be admitted in the afternoon in preparation for an early-morning delivery. After she was settled into a room, I returned home to the girls and my evening time with them.

When I arrived at the hospital the next morning according to schedule, Darlene had already been prepared for surgery. A nurse put me into a surgical gown, a cap, and paper shoes just in time for me to see Darlene being slid onto a gurney. She smiled and said, "I'll see you in there" as they rolled her out.

In a few minutes, a nurse guided me to another floor and into the glare of the operating room. Darlene was fully draped in sheets, and I was directed to sit on a rolling stool next to her face. She smiled again as I took my place next to her. I would be in the operating room for the entire procedure again, but this time sheets formed a tent over the surgical site. Neither of us could see her body below her rib cage. I would be in the room, but I would not see the actual delivery.

When Dr. Borkowf began, I didn't see the incision or the deep cutting needed to extract the baby as I had when Anna was born. I only saw Darlene's face, and we watched each other's expressions as the surgeons' work proceeded behind the sheets. She felt no pain, only some motion and pressure as the doctors worked.

In a few minutes, Dr. Borkowf exclaimed, "Well! Look at this!"

I thought he was going to say we had the most beautiful baby he had ever seen. Instead, he held up the umbilical cord so we could see it. It was tied in a knot. He then explained its significance with all the caution and tenderness of a surgeon.

"See that? If he had stepped on that, it would have been 'Bye, bye, baby!'"

I stared blankly at the knotted umbilical cord; Darlene, however, knew exactly what the doctor meant. The baby had been swimming in circles in her womb and had looped the cord. If the knot had been under the baby's foot during one of its stretches, the oxygen supply would have been cut off. In a minute, the baby would have had brain damage. A little longer, and our third child would have been stillborn. The longer he remained in the womb, growing, swimming, and stretching, the greater this danger became. The two-week change to the earlier delivery date may have prevented a disaster.

"You have a boy!" Dr. Borkowf announced at last.

Our third baby had come into the world, and Darlene and I were surprised by the news that we had a son. She was one of three sisters, and we already had two daughters. We had assumed we would have a third daughter, so it was a thrill to also have a son. A wave of completion and fulfillment swept over both of us. We had three children, as we had hoped. Our family was complete, and we were thankful and joyful.

A nurse brought the baby next to Darlene's face so we could both see his ruddy face and hear his healthy cry. She placed him on a brightly lit table in a corner, and I started the movie camera just as the nurse folded a cloth over the umbilical cord and unceremoniously cut it off. I took a picture of the ominous knot. After a few minutes, I was directed out of what had been aptly called an "operating theater," a place of real drama.

That afternoon, I left Darlene dozing at the hospital while I hurried to pick up Jenny and Anna for their last swimming lesson of the summer at the Waukesha YMCA.

"You have a baby brother, girls!" I yelled as they ran out of the Rands' house.

Jenny and Anna ran in circles in the front yard, screaming and clapping. Two of the Rands' children joined them, and Rose and Roger shook my hand and we all hugged. It was a happy little party, and there would be more, but it was time for the last swimming lesson of the summer.

I was dazed as I watched the girls swim at the Waukesha YMCA, trying to comprehend what this day meant. When we left the steamy heat of the indoor pool, I told the girls to stay in their swimsuits so we could go to Minooka Park on the outskirts of Waukesha for a swim in the lake. I swam with them there, and then I sat on the beach and watched them frolic in the cloudy, warm water. The lowering sun cast an unusually beautiful light on the water, trees, and sand, and on the little girls who were now big sisters. They were silhouetted in the setting sun like a scene in a Romantic-era painting. I was proud to be the patriarch of a family of five.

Meanwhile back at the hospital, Darlene was thinking about a new dilemma: What should we name this baby boy? Had the baby been a girl, her name would have been Mary Sayers Kardatzke. We had considered several boys' names. We rejected Nicholas because the nickname "Nick" ended in a hard "k" that would collide with the same sound in "Kardatzke." "Nick Kardatzke" would be hard to say.

After settling the girls in at our house with Rose Rand, I returned to the hospital. Darlene and I talked about all the names we had been considering, and we settled on William, a name with a long history in both of our families and the name of some men we admired. We agreed to tell everyone that the baby's name was William, or Bill. For two or three days, he was William to us. Our neighbor, "Grandpa Bud," even made a large banner for us that proclaimed "Welcome home, Mom and Little Bill!"

But Darlene and I both became uneasy about the name we had chosen. Something bothered us. It didn't feel right. Darlene began studying her book of baby names again. I was only a little surprised when I came to see her on July 25.

"I want us to think about a different name for our baby," she said.

"Okay," I replied, "do you have a name in mind?"

"Last night I read in this book that 'Matthew' means 'gift from God.' When I thought about his knotted umbilical cord and what might have happened, I thought, 'Yes! That's right! He's a gift from God!'"

"Right!" I said, thinking too of that knotted umbilical cord. "That seems so right. But there is already a Matthew in the family."

Just four months earlier, my sister Sharon had given birth to a son and named him Matthew, and his last name was Benefield. What would Sharon think of our using the same first name? I didn't want to ask her directly, so I called my mother to ask her advice. She laughed and said she thought it would be no problem, so I called Sharon. She laughed, too, and said it was fine. After all, the two boys would have different last names and would live in different states. Their shared first names might form a bond between the two boys as they grew up.

After I shared the result of the phone calls with Darlene, we decided: our son's name would be Matthew August Kardatzke. His middle name had belonged to my great-great-grandfather, August Kardatzke. He was the first Kardatzke to come to the New World, arriving in May 1869.

When our neighbor Grandpa Bud heard the baby's new name, he pasted over the original first name so the banner he'd already made then read, "Welcome Home, Mom and Little Matt!"

Darlene and I delighted in telling people about the two cousins named Matthew. We told them, "They are First and Second Matthew, just like in the Bible."

Some people laughed knowingly. Others nodded as if to say, "Yes. That's a good idea. Just like in the Bible."

Jenny and Anna doted on Matt from the beginning, seeing him first while Darlene was still in the hospital. I took them there on Sunday afternoon, and they each sat on a couch and held him for a few minutes.

Not knowing what to call him, the girls cooed, "Hi, Little Mathy!"

In the years ahead, he would get so much good care from Darlene, Jenny, and Anna that the girls sometimes called him "the boy with three moms."

One chapter of our life had ended, the child-bearing chapter, and we were on the cusp of a new one, happy to be parents of three children.

44

Birthday Cakes and Parties

Darlene grew up in a family in which every birthday was a special celebration. Her mother always baked one of her specialty layer cakes, either a yellow cake with caramel frosting or a strawberry cake with pink frosting, and the family gathered around for the birthday dinner. Darlene's mother would say she had a dinner "on" the birthday person: "Next Tuesday we are going to have a birthday party *on* Doug." It sounded to me like a prank when I first heard her say it, but those dinners were one of her favorite family events.

Darlene inherited the love of birthday celebrations, and she planned cakes and parties like her mother's. By modern standards, our children's birthday parties were modest events. There were fewer gifts than is now common, and only close family members or nearby neighbors attended most of those parties. Darlene's birthday cakes, therefore, were the center of attention.

Darlene's cakes were works of art. The cake itself might be a simple white or chocolate sheet cake from a mix, but she made an artistic creation out of each one using a tiny cookbook that included designs for a dozen cakes shaped in the form of animals or people. She would cut the sheet cake into shapes that could be arranged to look like a face, a girl in a dress, a duck, a dog, or some other creation. One of her favorites was a bunny rabbit cake that she made for the girls' springtime birthdays more than once. She made cakes to especially delight each child, and I took pictures of them and the children as proof of her birthday artistry.

Each of our children had at least one birthday party each year but typically more. They would have a birthday party at home with Darlene's cake, then one with some of our Wisconsin neighbors, and then birthdays with both sets of grandparents if we were able to travel.

A few birthday celebrations strayed outside the usual bounds. Anna had a birthday at Skateland, a roller-skating emporium in Wisconsin, and she had a swimming party at an indoor pool another year. Jenny's birthday often came during spring break, and we once had her birthday dinner in a revolving restaurant at the top of a hotel in Cincinnati on our way south for the week. Matt had a bunch of friends over for a memorable sleepover. All of the kids remember lots of pizza, Coca-Cola, video games, and above all, Darlene's artistic birthday cakes.

She surprised me on my sixtieth birthday in 1999. She collected photos and mementos from my whole life and conspired with some of the office staff at Sycamore. When I arrived at school that day, there was a hallway banner thirty feet long on which she had placed photos, copies of diplomas, and some favorite objects of mine to illustrate my life. I was surprised, delighted, and overwhelmed. It was an act of love from one who loved birthdays.

For her own sixtieth birthday in November 2005, Darlene said she wanted to go sky-diving: jumping from an airplane with a parachute. The rest of the family suggested that would be extreme, and we feared for her. She didn't make the jump.

45

The Great Midwest Triangle

Our eighteen years in Milwaukee were punctuated by regular triangular trips from Milwaukee to Indianapolis to Elmore and back to Milwaukee. For variety, we might reverse the triangle and go to Ohio first. Sometimes we took a one-destination trip to see just one set of grandparents and the local relatives, but Midwest triangular trips were the most common.

An entire triangle trip covered over nine hundred miles, not counting local excursions at our destinations. We made those trips in all kinds of weather, sometimes in such dangerous winter weather that it might have been, in hindsight, a bit reckless. More than once we started for Indianapolis with an infant aboard when the outside temperature was near zero Fahrenheit and the wind chill was menacingly low. Twice we traveled back home before the snowplows had cleared the road. Beyond Chicago, we had to follow beaten-down tracks in one lane of I-94 all the way to our neighborhood. When we reached home, we carried the kids into the house and waited until morning to dig out the driveway.

Once we had a flat tire in the busiest interchange in downtown Chicago during a blizzard. I had to change the tire in the middle of traffic. A police car stopped behind us to protect us from oncoming cars, and we could hear other cars colliding at low speed farther up the ramp behind us. With a fresh tire on, we rejoined the traffic on snow-clogged I-94. We were intrepid travelers.

At Christmas one year, it was so cold that our full-size van wouldn't start; the engine wouldn't even turn over. So we packed all our luggage and Christmas gifts and ourselves into my 1984 Toyota Corolla hatchback. The Corolla was a small car that we rarely used for family trips, seldom even taking it to church a half-mile from home. This time we were taking it on a trip of about a thousand miles in potentially dangerous winter weather. We made the entire triangular trip from Milwaukee to Indianapolis, then Toledo, and then home, crammed into that tiny car. When we reached home, it seemed to take us three days to uncoil our bodies again. The best thing about that trip was that our 4-speed, stick transmission got over thirty miles to the gallon, a small joy in exchange for our misery.

The triangle trips took us past the Six Flags Great America amusement park north of Chicago, but when the kids were young, Darlene and I tried to distract them as we drove past. We would direct their attention to something inside the car or point out something on the opposite side of the interstate. When we finally gave in and went to Great America when they were older, we all had fun. All of us except Darlene became daredevils on the roller coasters.

When we were brave enough to drive through downtown Chicago, the kids enjoyed seeing the Sears Tower and other landmark buildings up close. When we passed the Sears Tower, we knew we had traveled our first hundred miles and were fully on our way.

When we took the Skyway southeast of downtown Chicago, the kids always shouted that they wanted to see "The Annie Bridge." It was a disused, rusting railway drawbridge that had been left in the "up" position for many years. To them it looked like the raised drawbridge that Little Orphan Annie climbed in the movie *Annie* to escape a villain. Anna especially identified with the bridge, seeing herself climbing that ladder of railroad ties away from a bad guy below.

Crossing the Wabash River on the way to Indianapolis and the Maumee River on the way to Elmore were milestones along the way. Otherwise the most exciting geographical features of the trips were the grandparents' houses. They were the gold at the end of the rainbow.

46

The Climbing Tree

A crabapple tree stood in the corner of our Wisconsin back yard that we affectionately called "the climbing tree." Unlike most crabapple trees, its lower branches spread horizontally a few feet above the lawn rather that jutting up vertically. A little pruning kept the center of the tree open for climbers, and the girls became expert climbers. When they were too short to reach the low branches, Darlene or I would lift them into the tree and stand guard while they explored several routes to higher branches. When they were tall enough to get into the tree alone, they learned how to hang by their knees in a couple of places.

Anna especially enjoyed being a tree climber. When she was about nine years old, Darlene heard her yelling from somewhere in the yard.

"Mom! Mom!" came Anna's voice from outside.

Darlene looked down into the yard from the kitchen window and then through the dining room windows, but no Anna appeared. Down she looked again out the picture window to the south and saw the distant ridge, the street winding down below our house, and the big maple tree by the driveway. Still no Anna.

"Mom! Mom! *Mom!* Look over *here!*"

Suddenly a hand waved from leaves high in the maple tree, straight out from Darlene at the window. Anna was high in the big maple tree. Darlene gasped.

"Stay there! Stay there, Anna! I'm coming!" she yelled. She ran out the back door and down to the tree.

"How did you get up there?"

"I just climbed up!" Anna said. "I used a chair."

A chair at the base of the tree showed how she had managed to reach the first big limb. From there on, she said it had been easy.

"Hang on tight!" Darlene said. "Can you get down from there?"

"I think so. I got up here, didn't I?" Anna replied confidently as she began picking her way down the tree.

After the descent, Darlene hugged Anna and told her not to climb that high alone. From then on, however, she enjoyed bragging about Anna's climbing ability.

The climbing tree produced gnarly green apples larger than most crabapples. They weren't edible, not even in applesauce, but they were fun to roast in our bonfires. We had a burning site just a little farther into that corner of the lot, and we had bonfires of my tree trimmings two or three times a year. When the fire was crackling, the kids liked to throw the apples into the flames. It was the best use we ever made of those apples.

Our bonfires were usually on Saturday mornings, and Darlene often called us in for pancakes and bacon when the fire could be left unattended. Those bonfires and pancake breakfasts were a magical tradition, and we continued to have pancakes and bacon on Saturday mornings long after we left Wisconsin, the maple tree, the burning pile, and the climbing tree.

Many years later, Anna chose a home for her family in Wisconsin with big maple trees in the yard. Her children would sometimes scare her with their daring climbs. When their young cousins visit and the trees are alive with the sounds of grandchildren, I think of Darlene. Surely she would have smiled and shaken her head. She might even have bragged a little.

47

The Tree Row

Our property on Summit Drive was separated from the neighbors behind us by a row of Chinese elm trees. The previous owners of our house must have planted them to create a barrier between our house and the neighbors. The tree row was populated with birds, bugs, and bunnies. Growing in among the trees were flowering shrubs, weeds, and vines. Between the trees and shrubs were trails just large enough for small kids to slip through. For our young kids, the tree row was a long, narrow, safe forest to explore.

One early spring day when Matt was a toddler, Darlene took him into the yard while the girls were in school. Fallen twigs, leaves, and other natural debris littered the melting snow. While Darlene picked up sticks, Matt wandered to the back of the yard to the edge of the tree row. Darlene saw him pick something up and put it in his mouth. He did it again before she reached him. He was smiling and chewing, and there were brown crumbs around his mouth.

"What are you eating?" Darlene demanded.

Matt opened his hand to reveal a clump of little round rabbit droppings.

"Oh! No! Don't eat that!" Darlene said.

After shaking the droppings from his hand, she wiped his face, took him into the house, and rinsed out his mouth. Later she would laugh when she told the story of Matt discovering tasty "rabbit candy" in our yard.

In summer 1984, when Matt was less than a year old, we had lots of rain. One storm went on nearly continuously for three days. The Chinese elms in the tree row soaked up so much water that they became waterlogged all the way up to their top branches. Inside the house, we heard snapping, crackling noises coming from the back yard. We looked out and saw sparks leaping from the power lines to the trees. Sparks and flame followed the trees to the ground in dancing lightning bolts.

Darlene shrieked and ran to the back bedroom where Matt was napping. Just as she scooped him up, she heard a loud "boom" from the back yard. A transformer in a corner of our yard had blown due to the overload of current through the trees. The lights in the entire house went out, and we were in the dark for two days. A few weeks after our power was restored, a crew came through and severely topped all the trees in the tree row. It was a futile gesture. The Chinese elm tree row soon returned to its old height and waited to defy new storms.

48

Tree Row Relatives

*B*ehind the tree row, we had a great treasure in two sets of neighbors. We were involved with them more than with the neighbors on our side of the tree row. One couple was "Grandpa Bud and Grandma Edna" and another was "Uncle Earl and Aunt Joanne." Bud and Edna Churchill were more than twenty years older than Darlene and me. Earl and Joanne Menick were ten years older than us. The four of them seemed like relatives of ours that matched their ages, so we gave them the honorific family titles. They became surrogate grandparents and relatives to our kids while our own families were so far away.

We first met Joanne soon after we moved in. She squeezed through the trees and bushes and climbed down the low stone retainer wall into our yard to introduce herself. She and Earl had thought it best to warn us.

"We have four teenagers!" Joanne announced after brief introductions.

I looked across into the Menicks' backyard. Sure enough, two high school girls in swimsuits were sunning there. The two boys appeared in their yard the next day. We had no cause for alarm. The teenagers were good neighbors and were soon grown and away from home.

It would be difficult to overstate how much we owed to our tree row relatives. They were good friends to us and helped us in many ways. Bud and

Earl loved home improvement projects and did some work on their houses together. When we had projects underway, they could answer all our questions and always offered to help. Bud was a plumber, among other things, and he helped me with our well and water softener until city water arrived. When our house was re-roofed, he supervised the roofers while I was at work. We could never match their neighborly helpfulness.

When Jenny was very young, Darlene felt she could do some part-time medical work to keep her pediatric skills current. She worked part-time for a private pediatrician in Brookfield, which meant we needed a part-time babysitter. Joanne Menick had been a preschool teacher but wasn't working just then, so Darlene asked if she would consider babysitting for Jenny. Joanne agreed, and her role as "Aunt Joanne" began in earnest. She came to our house to take charge of Jenny when Darlene needed to leave, and Jenny enjoyed playtimes in Joanne's toy-filled sunroom.

After Anna was born, Darlene needed even more help. Anna became one of Joanne's charges too, and Matt was added three years later. All three of our kids experienced Joanne's loving, expert attention while they were very young and benefited especially by her background as a preschool teacher.

Darlene had a break from her medical practice in the year before Matt was born, and I hired Joanne to teach a Pre-K class at Brookfield Academy. She continued to babysit for us on occasion, and the girls both knew her as "Aunt Joanne" or just "Joanne."

When Anna was old enough to go into a Pre-K class, she would have Joanne as her teacher, so I thought she needed a tutorial on adult names. I suggested to Anna that at school she should call her teacher "Mrs. Menick," not "Joanne." She understood that immediately. It probably seemed like the grown-up thing to do. Then I thought I should give her a pointer on what I was called at school.

"At school, people call me either "Dr. Kardatzke" or "Dr. K," I began. I thought a moment and said, "But I guess you would call me 'Dad' at school."

Anna thought for a second and then said, "I'll just call you 'Nyle!'"

I was flabbergasted. I had never heard her say my name before, and now she was ready to trot it out in public.

Bud and Edna Churchill were close friends of the Menick family, and we got to know them well too. They had lost a daughter named Cindy many years earlier, and their son lived in Maine with their two grandchildren. Bud and Edna happily adopted our kids as surrogate grandchildren.

Grandpa Bud was an engineer at Allis-Chalmers, the giant farm machinery company in Milwaukee. He oversaw the practical training program for young engineers, arranging and monitoring their hands-on engineering experiences in the company. Bud had a workshop in his basement that included carpentry, plumbing, and electrical tools; a large workbench; a drafting table; metal and wood-turning lathes; and gas and electric welding equipment. Bud could build almost anything in his basement. He took our kids to his shop for little projects of theirs, too, and once he helped Darlene build a bird feeder as a gift for her father.

When the kids were old enough, Bud built two swing sets for them. One was made from discarded galvanized well pipe we had salvaged when our well needed a new pump and pipes. Bud made detailed engineering drawings first, cut pipes to the right lengths, welded some, and bored holes for bolts to complete the job. The kids all rode the swings and hung upside-down on the crossbars at the ends of the structure for several years.

When the kids began to outgrow the metal swing set, Bud built a much taller swing of wood. He drew up the design on his drafting table, and he did most of the construction work. The swing was suspended between two 12-feet-tall, 4×4-inch wooden posts. Bud added stability to the vertical posts by installing angling legs on each side. The angling legs were bolted to the vertical posts, and the bolts passed through quarter-inch steel plates that he had cut with his gas cutting torch. He made the holes in the plates on his powerful drill press. To anchor the posts in the ground, Bud and I dug two parallel trenches in the lawn and poured concrete around the bases of the posts.

That swing was perfectly stable and secure. When riding it, the kids had a sensation of flying because the long pendulum of the swing at its highest point raised them to a height where they could look abroad at the neighborhood and down at the hills below.

When our years in Wisconsin were coming to an end, the swing had aged so much that Bud and I had to take it down. We dug down to the huge underground concrete bases and cut the wooden posts just above the concrete.

We left the concrete foundations in the lawn where they have remained to this very day. Our kids had aged, too, by the time we left, and they treasured their memories of their tree row relatives: Grandpa Bud, Grandma Edna, Aunt Joanne, and Uncle Earl.

49

From Professor to Headmaster

I had started teaching economics at Marquette University in 1974 while completing my dissertation, a statistical test of a theory in the economics of information. More specifically, it examined the fact that gasoline price wars in the 1960s were far more common in some cities than in others. In June of 1977, two months before I mailed the final draft to my Los Angeles typist, I received a phone call that would change my life and Darlene's forever.

The call was from Bill Law, a businessman I had met two years earlier when I helped him organize an economics conference in Milwaukee. I was aware that he served on the Board of Directors of a private school. When he called, he came quickly to the point.

"Kardatzke, have you ever thought of running a private school?"

I was taken aback. "No, Bill, I have never thought of that."

I had been preparing for ten years to be a full-time economics professor, I was about to receive the PhD degree, and I was enjoying my university teaching as an assistant professor. I had never even entertained the thought of running a private school, and I told him so. I greatly admired Bill Law, a successful leather tanner and a principled fan of free-market economics, so I thanked him and agreed to hear him out, but only after my dissertation was in the mail.

Two months later, Bill took me on a tour of one of his tanneries. At lunch, he described Brookfield Academy and its history in detail. He explained that he and the other Board members were looking for a new headmaster, and he thought I might have the qualities they were looking for. I agreed to consider it, and I also agreed to teach a Principles of Economics class to high school juniors and seniors at Brookfield Academy that year while still teaching full-time at Marquette. I taught Tuesdays and Thursdays at Marquette and the other days at Brookfield.

Teaching at Brookfield that fall acquainted me well with the school, and I enjoyed it more than I had thought I would. My teaching was part of the interview process for my eventual position as headmaster. I had met the other three members of the Board of Directors, and I recognized them as principled men I could trust.

In February 1978, after one semester of teaching there, the Brookfield Board offered me the position with the title "Executive Director." I had a week to decide, and I agonized over it. To make the decision, I tried to envision what might happened in each of the two jobs in five years, depending on whether things went well or badly in each. I created a 4x4 grid on a sheet of paper. The grid contained two columns with two rows under each column. At the top of the columns, I wrote "Brookfield" and "Marquette." In the two rows, I wrote out what might happen in five years.

I could see the future rather clearly if I remained at Marquette. I would immediately plunge into research based on my dissertation study of gas wars, and I would push for tenure. If that went well, my job would be secure at Marquette; but I might be tempted to go to an even more competitive university and do more of the same kind of research. If I didn't achieve tenure, I would have to leave and look for another position, probably in a lesser institution.

I couldn't see the future as clearly if I were to take the Brookfield job. There was a happy possibility, and there was a possibility that it wouldn't go well and I would be looking for a new job in five years or fewer. But the fact that I *couldn't* see the future at Brookfield attracted me. I was drawn to the adventure and the responsibility I could have.

Brookfield Academy offered an entirely new challenge and much greater variety: I would deal with people of all ages from young children and young adults to parents and grandparents. I would have an opportunity to be a leader within the faculty and to help shape what might become an even more outstanding institution. I might to some small degree emulate the president of Anderson College, Robert Reardon, who had done so much there. I couldn't turn my back on this opportunity, and I accepted the new role and the career change.

Darlene completely supported my decision and probably supported me in prayer more than I knew. The job had risks for both of us. A headmaster's wife could sometimes be like a pastor's wife, who often was expected to play the piano, teach Sunday school, and patch up the diplomatic foibles of her husband. Many wives of headmasters became actively involved in entertaining, fundraising, marketing, and student recruitment in the schools. Darlene was not designed for that kind of public activity. Her maternal duties and her part-time medical career kept her out of the spotlight, and she liked it that way. I was happy to have her as my personal counselor, strategist, and adviser.

While there were long-term risks for me personally, there were short-term gains. My income increased immediately, which in turn reduced financial pressure Darlene might have felt to do more medical work outside our home. She was able to stay out of the workforce for long stretches when Anna and Matt were born, and she limited herself to part-time work when she re-entered the workforce. She was thankful that my income allowed her to be at home with the kids when they were young.

Besides the increase in income, my career change also made it possible for Darlene and me to give our children private schooling. At Brookfield, I could see them in their classes, during recesses, and in school activities.

It was a shock at first to leave my comfortable existence as a professor. When I informed my friend and department chairman Dick Trestrail of my decision, he asked that I write a letter of resignation so he could begin the search for my replacement. I sat down at my typewriter at the university and watched my words take shape on the page. I could see myself from somewhere near the ceiling of that little office, bent over my typewriter, clicking and clacking out my resignation from an excellent university position and a promising future. It felt as if I were was writing my own death sentence, yet it was actually my declaration of independence, my charter for a new course in life. In spite of the risks, I was confident I was doing the right thing.

Soon after I agreed to accept the new position, I looked back over the major episodes in my life. I could see a pattern I hadn't seen before. All of the major events in my life had been pointing to something like Brookfield Academy, not to being a tenured professor of economics. It was the first time I had seen that God had been shaping my life, unbeknownst to me. God had put together an improbable series of experiences that had prepared me for a career I hadn't intended.

My unexpected invitation into campus politics as a student at Anderson College and my later role in managing student activities as a staff member there would fit at Brookfield better than in teaching economics at Marquette. The Peace Corps adventure in Ethiopia that had widened my view of the world would be useful at Brookfield as well. From my years of part-time professorship, I had earned a credible record as a teacher that would count for something with the Brookfield faculty. Even my academic and social challenges in high school would contribute to my understanding of students at Brookfield. God had prepared me for the action, politics, and uncertainty of heading a private school.

Life in a private school can be intense. Crises abound despite the best proactive plans, and teachers and headmasters can make wrong decisions with the best of intentions. When I began my work at Brookfield, I learned to pray each morning, usually on my knees. I learned, perhaps for the first time, that many matters in the school were out of my control, and only God could bring me through the stormy seas and into green pastures. I prayed for help, and I gave thanks that I had been given this new life.

50

Mothering and Doctoring

Darlene's determination had carried her through college, medical school, internship, residency, and into her career as a doctor. Pediatrics would remain a professional commitment for the rest of her life, but her deepest calling and commitment was to be a mother. Her professional life as a pediatric doctor was an outgrowth of her deep, maternal desires. When the children arrived, they became her highest priority. For Darlene, mothering and doctoring meant expressing her professional expertise in raising our kids, all the while keeping her hand in the world of doctoring. She took only part-time medical work while the children were young, and she avoided being on night and weekend call to preserve our home life.

Throughout her medical career, Darlene extended herself to other mothers from her positions in the medical centers where she worked. Twice during Darlene's residency, high school classmates of hers had children in the UCLA hospital. She found her friends and saw their children, though they were not directly under her care. She did the same at the Medical College of Wisconsin and later, in Indianapolis, she visited the children of her childhood friends and children of my distant relatives in the vast Riley Hospital for Children.

Darlene's mothering of our children included actual doctoring at home when the kids had earaches or the flu or minor injuries. She could not only take their temperatures and give them cough syrup, but she also could take out her stethoscope and listen to their lungs or peer into a painful ear with her otoscope. She could write prescriptions and send me off to get them filled, but she consulted with our family pediatrician for anything more serious. I sometimes wondered how other parents could raise children without having a fully-trained pediatrician in the house.

Medical school and her internship and residency, plus our move from California to Wisconsin, had left Darlene tired and in need of a break from her demanding professional life. She didn't want to go into full-time practice, so she investigated agencies and clinics where she could work part-time. She was especially drawn to the inner city, and for a time she worked in a program for infant and toddler development in Milwaukee. She was the pediatrician for a government-funded inner-city clinic, and a large part of that job was to try to persuade people to use the government-funded services that were available to them. People were sometimes unaware of the aid programs they could use, and they sometimes were so overwhelmed with their troubled lives that they needed coaching on how to get help.

Darlene also worked with Dr. Frederick Blodgett, a respected older pediatrician, on a lead paint awareness program. Many of the older inner-city houses still had peeling and curling lead-based paint that had been applied many decades earlier. Kids sometimes chewed painted porch rails, and sometimes paint chips fell into their food. Darlene and Dr. Blodgett worked to make parents aware of this hazard, and they lobbied to have lead-based paint removed or covered.

Child psychology had been included in Darlene's training, and it grew into her lifetime professional passion. As she listened to the interactions between mothers and children in the clinics where she worked part-time, she could see vast differences between happy, healthy children and their mothers compared to sulking or depressed or disruptive children and their mothers. The unhappy children of inattentive mothers often were physically less healthy and slower to recover from illnesses. Sometimes they failed to thrive and gain weight as expected. They very often had school troubles.

From her earliest days in part-time pediatrics, Darlene coached young mothers on how to care for their kids emotionally as well as physically. It was often like spitting into the wind: The young moms were busy and harried, and their kids often kept them off balance. Darlene's advice probably flew out of some of their minds the moment they left the office to pick up their antibiotic prescriptions and inhalers, but she had done what she could.

Darlene used to quote another pediatrician by saying, "There is no such thing as a baby." What she meant was that a baby can't survive on its own; it requires support from someone, usually the mother. A baby and its mother *together* was the reality of early childhood. When she worked in general pediatrics clinics, infant mental health was an important element in her doctoring in the midst of sore throats, diarrhea, and ear infections.

For a couple of years, Darlene covered the private practice of Dr. Ralph Olsen near the Ruby Isle Shopping Center in Brookfield. She later worked two or three days a week in the Waukesha Pediatrics Group, led by Dr. John Guy. Most of this work was well-baby work: checking on the progress of healthy babies, a relatively low-stress version of her later developmental pediatrics career in Indianapolis.

While working in the well-baby clinic in Waukesha, Darlene often worried about the possibility that one of the babies she examined might have a rare disease or a neurological issue that would need immediate, specialized care. She was fearful that she might misdiagnose one of these rare cases. Ironically, her medical career culminated in developmental pediatrics at the Indiana University Medical Center with patients who had serious or unusual conditions such as spina bifida, Down syndrome, autism, and birth injuries. There are no immediate cures for these conditions, and the parents often needed as much care from her as their children. Her patience and compassion were better fitted for treating these long-term conditions than for the acute care and emergencies that sometimes cropped up in general medicine.

She loved her role as a mother, mother-in-law, and grandmother. When our own kids were young, Darlene had a keen ear for interpreting kid noises. She could tell if a child was injured, frightened, or merely having a tantrum. She handled tantrums skillfully, mainly by denying the child what it wanted. She developed positive-sounding ways of setting limits. Rather than saying, "Sit down in your chair!" she would sometimes say, "You may now sit down quietly." It generally worked.

Years later, our daughters and our daughter-in-law often called Darlene for advice when their children were babies. Those conversations sometimes went on for nearly an hour. I usually heard only her side of the conversation while I did other things around the house. Sometimes I was on the line when one of the young moms called, and I listened in. I remember lying on the bed upstairs listening while she talked on a phone in the kitchen. Her wisdom and her joy in talking about parenting said more about her loves than anything else could have.

Darlene earned the support and affirmations of her medical colleagues during our Wisconsin years. When we left Wisconsin in 1992, the staff at Waukesha Pediatrics took out a huge, adulatory ad in her honor in the *Waukesha Freeman*.

PART FOUR

Autumn: 1992 to 2009

51

Wichita Calls

We were charmed by Wisconsin from the very beginning of our time in the state. We moved to Waukesha in August 1974, and we stayed until 1992. After two years in the rented hilltop townhouse and sixteen years in our lovely little house on Summit Drive, events and inner urges led us far away from our settled life in Wisconsin, away from the summertime of our lives.

I had served as Headmaster at Brookfield Academy for twelve years when I began to feel that my time there might be coming to an end. During those years under my leadership, the school had prospered academically, athletically, and in enrollment. We built a new elementary school building and a new gym, but the high school students shared a building with their middle school brothers and sisters—hardly an arrangement conducive to student recruitment. Our inability to reach an enrollment of one hundred students in the high school despite excellent academic, athletic, and drama programs frustrated me. I began to feel that I would like work in a different school and live in another part of the country if an opportunity should arise.

By this time Darlene was working two or three days a week at Waukesha Pediatrics, a large pediatrics group on the other side of our city of Waukesha. She enjoyed her colleagues there, and the work kept her mind focused on her great professional love: pediatric medicine and the well-being of very young kids. Her deep love for infants and children found expression as she conducted well-baby visits with their young mothers. Our three kids were all enrolled at Brookfield Academy and commuted there with me daily. It was a happy arrangement.

In the spring of 1991, I received a letter from a management search company in Kansas City about an opening for Headmaster of Wichita Collegiate School in Wichita, Kansas. That letter set off alarm bells in my mind. I was familiar with Wichita Collegiate, and I had even taken my Brookfield administrators there in 1980 to learn from the Wichita faculty and administration. I had known the founding headmaster and his successor whose leaving had precipitated the search. The founders of Wichita Collegiate and the founders of Brookfield Academy were like-minded, but Wichita Collegiate was larger and more sophisticated than Brookfield Academy at the time. Becoming Headmaster of Wichita Collegiate would be a promotion for me.

Besides the kinship between the two schools, the city of Wichita itself held personal appeal. Family travels had taken us to Kansas many times to visit relatives of both of my parents. My mother's childhood home was near Alva, Oklahoma, and we had gone there several times for family reunions. After those reunions, we had gone tent camping in New Mexico and Colorado.

The opening at Wichita Collegiate would be a chance to move to lands we loved to visit. If we moved there, we would be living "way out West" and within a shorter drive of our favorite camping areas in the mountains. The job opening was an exciting prospect.

After in-depth interviews, I was offered the position in Wichita. I accepted, but I soon was wracked with "seller's remorse," wishing I hadn't. The decision to leave Brookfield Academy was more painful than I had anticipated. It was as painful as my decision to go there in the first place, leaving my position as an economics professor at Marquette University. After three agonizing weeks, my emotions settled. I could see that it was the right choice despite the effort and uncertainty it would mean.

The remainder of that school year was overwhelmingly busy. I was still Head of School, and I continued to teach two sections of economics in Brookfield's high school. Darlene kept up her part-time work at Waukesha Pediatrics. The kids were busy with school, and we attended many events with them. I oversaw hiring new faculty for the next school year, including my own replacement in the economics classroom. As is standard in private schools, I was not involved in the selection of my successor at Brookfield. We made two all-family trips to Wichita, and I made three trips alone to initiate my involvement in the school. We put our house on the market and bought a larger house in Wichita. Brookfield held several farewell events, including a party at a country club for parents and teachers. I called that country club party "my funeral." We left town two days later.

52

The Kansas Detour

As it turned out, our move to Wichita was a short but eventful detour that lasted only for the 1992–93 school year. Without that detour, Darlene might not have found her way into her ultimate career in developmental pediatrics. In an unintended way, it gave me the chance to head a third school, one with a distinct mission and personality. And as a family, the move to Indianapolis offered us opportunities we couldn't have guessed in advance.

We arrived in Wichita in June 1992. We were "way out West," but this was the urban West, not the stuff of covered wagons, homesteaders, and cowboys. Wichita was a modern, fast-paced city in the '90s, seeming to seethe with ambition and imagination. Some local people dubbed it "an entrepreneurial city," since half the people there longed to strike it rich with another version of Pizza Hut, Learjet, White Castle, Coleman camping equipment, or another of the many companies that got their start in Wichita.

Wichita Collegiate School held welcoming parties for us, and the school staff was especially gracious. I was immediately caught up in the cycle of summer meetings and staff retreats before the opening of school. It seemed that I could have been in any city in the country, and my workdays would have looked the same: commuting to the school in the morning; spending the day in meetings, conversations, and writing; and then heading home for a late dinner or maybe out to a school event.

Darlene's life that summer may have been more varied than mine, since she was busy with the kids and getting our house in shape before school began. Our air conditioning went out, some appliances needed work, and the house badly needed a deep, general cleaning. Darlene managed all of it.

As our household became more settled, Darlene began to volunteer as a consulting pediatrician for Rainbows United, a nonprofit organization that provides services for families of children with special needs. It "happened" that this experience led naturally but unexpectedly into her subspecialty in developmental pediatrics the next year. She also joined the choir at Central Community Church on the west side of Wichita, where we commuted two or three times a week. Her days were full and varied.

Central Community Church was an obvious choice for us in Wichita, even though it was on the west side, seventeen miles from our home on the east side. My uncle Elmer had pastored a tiny, early version starting in 1941. He had led it from a small, modest congregation into one of nearly two thousand in a huge, well-designed building. Many of my family members were active there in 1992. On our first Sunday there, Bill Koch's beautiful sailboat, America 3, was in one of the lobbies celebrating his recent victory in the America's Cup race. The church that year was vibrant and full of life. Some of our best sanctuary worship experiences were there.

We were eager to capitalize on our new location. We took a camping trip to Colorado in July and were looking forward to more camping adventures during the coming years. We pitched our tent just north of Buena Vista, Colorado—a mountain town that is called "Bee-yuna Vista" by the locals. Our outing that day was a fishing trip to a quiet mountain stream a few miles from the campground. When we returned from fishing, we decided to drive past the campground to admire our tent from the road. We could see the place where our tent *had been*, but the tent was gone!

At the campground, we found our precious tent on the ground and our belongings strewn over a path across other campsites and into a ravine. Other campers had gathered some of our stuff and had piled some rocks on the flattened tent to hold it down. We learned that an extremely strong straight wind had blown through the campground, and we were hardest hit of all the campers.

When I inspected the tent, I saw that one corner was ripped open and part of the base was torn loose. It seemed beyond repair. We packed up all our gear and the damaged tent and headed for Wichita. By that time, it was almost sundown. The few motels along the way that we found that night were booked, but we saw a sign for a tourist home as we entered Salida, and we found a room for the night. Back in Wichita, I stored the damaged tent in our garage, unwilling to part with it but never imagining we could repair it and use it again in future years.

Our Wichita home was an attractive, two-story house that was much larger than our house on Summit Drive in Wisconsin. We bought it instead of renting for a year while we looked for the best place to live, partly to show how committed we were to Wichita and to Collegiate School. In a few months, we learned it had been a mistake. We failed to heed the warning words in an old hymn, "The future lies unseen ahead, it holds we know not what."

In 1972, Wichita Collegiate was the leading private independent school in Wichita. Collegiate had nearly twice as many students as Brookfield Academy, and it had more contact with other schools because of its membership in an accrediting association. It was the northernmost school of an accrediting association that included schools in Louisiana, Texas, Oklahoma, New Mexico, and Arizona, and it was the only member school in all of Kansas. Besides academic and artistic programs, Collegiate was an athletic powerhouse. That year it had a star football player who seemed likely to carry the team to a conference championship, and the basketball team was one of the best in our conference.

From the very beginning, I knew my tenure at Wichita Collegiate might be short. Although I had asked the right questions about the headmaster's relationship with the Board of Directors and had heard the right answers while still living in Wisconsin, it became obvious that some Board members and influential parents were in the habit of intervening in school life in ways that could compromise the professional integrity of the teachers and administrators. I knew it would be difficult to manage those patterns of behavior and maintain the necessary boundary lines. Even before we moved, my attempts to influence action in the school were rebuffed by Board members. I tried to smooth matters diplomatically but didn't succeed. In retrospect, I could see that I did several things that offended, irritated, or alarmed some of the Board members while pleasing others.

The underlying frictions at Wichita Collegiate School came to a head in January 1993 when the man who was the Upper School (high school) administrator asked me if he could return to the teaching post he had previously held in the Upper School. He was under pressure from a few Board members and parents who felt their children in that part of the school might better be served under different leadership. The administrator and I hoped the pressure would subside if he was replaced, but we knew there was also a chance that the change he had asked for would precipitate a crisis with the Board. We discussed the possible course of events confidentially for a couple of weeks, and I finally decided to offer him the teaching position he wanted.

Trouble was not long in coming. One Board member quickly informed me that he and a committee of Board members, not I, would select the next Head of Upper School. This action would have violated principles of private school management and the standards for our accreditation as an independent school. I also knew that such action would undermine my position as Head of School. For several weeks, the conflict simmered behind closed doors. I sought confidential advice from other school heads and from the school's accrediting association. I also contacted private school consultants I had used in the past. All of the professionals I consulted emphatically supported my insistence on my being the one to hire the next Head of Upper School.

When I shared those professional opinions with the Board, I was told that the separation of power between the Board and the Head of School was not relevant to the special mode of operation the Board had in mind. At that point, I informed the Board Chair that I couldn't function under the conditions he and a majority of the Board had in mind. I said I would resign as of June 30, at the end of the school year.

The Board took great umbrage at my offer to resign. At a climactic meeting in early March, the Board decided to "accept my resignation" that same night, not at the end of the school year as I had proposed. It seemed, in effect, that they were firing me for insisting on the primacy of the headmaster's role in hiring and offering to resign rather than accept their preferred mode of operation. I was out of the school, and it was March 2.

Some Board members resigned that night, as did the Associate Head of School and the Admissions Director. By the end of the next day, the matter was in the news, including the local newspaper, the *Wichita Eagle,* and the local TV station. That night, Darlene sent a fax to our friends at Brookfield Academy: "There has been an explosion here in Wichita, and the pieces are still on the way up."

Several large, dramatic meetings were held on campus in the next days and weeks. Behind closed doors, the remaining Board members and I looked for ways to resolve the conflict and calm the uproar, at least until the end of the school year. After several unsuccessful attempts at reconciliation, the Board gave up on me. I was glad to be free. By then it was April.

When I left the school, Darlene and I did not know what to do next with our lives. I might have found other employment in Wichita, but my conflict with some of the city's leading citizens might have limited my opportunities. The former Associate Head of School and I discussed starting a new private school, but I declined the offer to join him in what has become an excellent school, founded in 1994. Other opportunities in another place, unbeknownst to us at the time, would carry us far away from Wichita.

In April, Darlene began talking about professional interests that she might want to pursue under these new conditions. She had always had an interest in the psychological and emotional aspects of pediatrics, especially as these affected babies and toddlers. One of our conversations was on April 15, while we waited in line in our car at the post office to mail our income tax return. She described her interest in psychiatry and the post-doctoral work that it would entail. She was hesitant, though, because she thought psychiatry was becoming a mainly pharmaceutical profession. She didn't want to become only a "pill pusher," as she might if she went into psychiatry. She hoped to have more involvement with patients than she thought modern psychiatry would allow.

In that same conversation in the post office line, she mentioned developmental and behavioral pediatrics and explained how they were situated professionally somewhere between general pediatrics and psychiatry. She explained that developmental pediatrics focused on prenatal and neonatal problems such as Down syndrome, spina bifida, autism, and birth injuries. In contrast, behavioral pediatrics addressed behavioral and emotional issues in childhood and adolescence. She felt especially drawn to those two subspecialties of pediatrics.

At about the same time, she learned of a conference on developmental and behavior pediatrics to be held in May in Indianapolis at the Omni Hotel on Shadeland Avenue. Her former mentor, Dr. Morris Green, would be there as one of the conference speakers. It seemed important to us both that she go.

That conference became a watershed moment in her career and in our lives as a family. While she was there, she heard from Dr. Green that she could have a fellowship in developmental and behavioral pediatrics at the Indiana School of Medicine in Indianapolis starting in September that year. The fellowship would pay a modest stipend that she could supplement with part-time work as a hospital pediatrician. By the end of May, Darlene had accepted Indiana University's offer of a fellowship in developmental-behavioral pediatrics.

This new opportunity for her was an answer to prayer. Her income would tide us over until I found a new job in the Indianapolis area, and she would be entering the subspecialty of pediatrics in which she could develop her special passion for the well-being of infants and toddlers. Her mother, sisters, and other relatives were living in Indianapolis. My parents were still living at my childhood home near Toledo, and I had a plenitude of other relatives all over the eastern Midwest. We set our sails for Indiana.

53

Home Again in Indiana

"For my thoughts are not your thoughts, neither are your ways my ways," declares the LORD. "As the heavens are higher than the earth, so are my ways higher than your ways and my thoughts than your thoughts."

—Isaiah 55:8–9

I never would have chosen to move to Indianapolis on my own. I doubt Darlene would have chosen it either, under other circumstances. It was her hometown, and it seemed too familiar to be interesting or exciting. Besides, it didn't have and *still* doesn't have the mountains, deserts, and ocean we both loved. Indianapolis lacked the excitement of being out West in Wichita, the Old World flavor of Wisconsin, and the drama of West Coast California. But Indianapolis proved to be better for our family than any of those settings at the time we washed up on the shores of the White River in August 1993.

In June, we made a road trip to Wisconsin and Indiana in our brown 1989 Dodge Grand Caravan. In Wisconsin we found Brookfield Academy thriving under the new headmaster, Bob Solsrud. He had already been in the school for twenty-three years in a variety of teaching, coaching, and administrative roles, and he was the ideal person to lead the school at that time. We drove past the huge new sanctuary at Elmbrook Church. "The 'City of God!'" I gasped when I saw it.

In Indianapolis we visited friends and relatives, including Darlene's mother, who was in assisted living on the far south side of the city. We felt comfortable and at home in Indianapolis, and even the city's familiarity felt welcome. We thought we could be secure and at peace living there. We looked at public and private schools and applied to have our children admitted at Heritage Christian School in the northeast corner of the city. We had heard of Heritage through Darlene's nephew Doug Guffy, and it was a great gift to us.

When we returned to Wichita, we showed our house to many potential buyers. Darlene and I were not inherently tidy people, but we and the kids tidied the house for every showing. We also popped popcorn and made fresh coffee, having heard that those cozy smells could induce a sale. We even baked fresh bread one time. None of our tricks worked, and we left for another visit to Indianapolis in July with no offer on the house.

Darlene had a far keener sense of urgency than I concerning the logistics of the move. At her insistence, we made a last-minute deposit on a townhouse apartment on a steamy day just before we left again for Wichita. We left Indianapolis on Matt's birthday, July 22, not knowing of the dramatic meeting that had taken place at Indianapolis' Sycamore School the day before. In fact, we had never heard of Sycamore School.

We arrived home in Wichita late that night. There was a message for me on our phone's answering machine from Dr. John Rau, a man I knew to be one of Darlene's future colleagues at the hospital. He said I should call him, and I thought it must be a mistake. *Maybe he had intended to call Darlene*, I thought.

When I called Dr. Rau on Friday morning, he told me he had been pleased to meet Darlene during her interviews at Riley Hospital, and he had learned from her that I had experience as a private school headmaster. His son, he said, was enrolled at Sycamore School, a private-independent school in Indianapolis that would be looking for a new head. The school was for gifted kids, preschool through eighth grade. There had been a conflict between the Head of School and the Board of Directors. Following a big meeting of parents and teachers at the school on Wednesday night, the headmistress had resigned, left the meeting, and boarded a plane for Florida. Classes would be starting in a month; they clearly needed a new Head of School soon.

Where have I heard this before? I asked myself silently.

I asked Dr. Rau some key questions and learned the names of the Board President and the Chairman of the Search Committee. The opportunity was clearly something I should act on promptly. I was excited about the possibility of finding employment, and I thought I had something to offer. I called the Board President, told him about my fifteen-year background in private schools, and faxed my resume. A series of phone calls, letters, and faxes ensued. I had phone interviews with staff and Board members, and they sent some print material about the school and about gifted education, an educational specialty that was new to me. We agreed that I would visit Sycamore School as soon as possible after we arrived in Indianapolis.

The tractor-trailer moving van was an even larger one than had been used when we left Wisconsin for Kansas. The truck was huge, and our stuff filled it completely. Some items were even tied to the back. It pulled away from our home at 2860 Wilderness Court in Wichita on August 13, and our family left a few minutes later in our two heavily loaded mini-vans. It was Friday the 13th, but to us it was an auspicious day, not ominous. We were heading toward a new and better home.

54

Autumn's Harvest

If our Wisconsin years were "the summertime" of our lives, our first years in Indiana were our "autumn time." They were years of fulfillment for Darlene, me, and our kids. While we would not have picked Indianapolis as our ideal city for romance, excitement, and vacationing, our lives had turned around in such a way that it became our ideal city of refuge, a place for a fresh start. I thanked God often for moving us there at the end of our trek from Wisconsin to Kansas and finally home again to Indiana. Darlene and I couldn't have imagined the challenges and blessings of that year of change, but we saw all of them as providential.

The two big moves, from Wisconsin to Kansas in 1992 and from Kansas to Indiana in 1993, had melded our family together more closely than we might have been without our migrations. Those moves were our family's personal Exodus. Only *we* had gone through those events together. Only *we* had a sense of being delivered to a new land, even if we hadn't seen in advance that it really was a "promised land." The identity of our little tribe of five was defined and deeply affected by the adventures we had shared during our migration.

It's true for some adolescents that moving to a new city during high school years can be traumatic, but that would not be the case for Jenny. When we left Wisconsin at the end of her freshman year, she was ready for an adventure, for new friends, and for new prospective boyfriends. When we left Wichita at the end of her sophomore year, she was ready for another adventure, more new friends, and more prospective boyfriends. In both of her new school and church settings, Jenny immediately became happily active and involved.

Anna's response to the moves was different, especially the move from Kansas. In Wisconsin Anna had established a niche for herself at Brookfield Academy. She was known for her lively and "innovative" ways. Her flare for the dramatic showed when she delivered an especially witty speech to the combined Middle and Upper Schools shortly before our departure for Kansas. She saw our move to Kansas as an adventure and was excited about it, at least initially. At Wichita Collegiate School she had a leading part in a school play and was finding her place among the students there and at church. Our move to Indianapolis disrupted the social success she had begun to enjoy in Wichita, and her merger into Indiana life took longer than for the other two.

Matt was philosophical and almost journalistic about the first move. He was in second grade when I told him the news about leaving Wisconsin, and he began a series of "last" pronouncements: "This is our last Thanksgiving here"; "This is our last Christmas here"; and then, "This will be our last Presentation Day here." He wasn't emotional about those lasts; he just wanted to reflect on them as part of our history. On the day when I told the kids about the conflict at Wichita Collegiate School and that we probably would be leaving Kansas after just a year, he took in the whole story and then said, "Well, if we are going to leave, it's good we are leaving now before we get too attached to anybody here."

For the kids, one of the benefits of this last move was that they would *not* be in a school where I was Head of School. They escaped the controversies and embarrassments they might have endured if I had remained at Brookfield Academy or Wichita Collegiate. Not only was I not an employee at Heritage Christian School, but I was so busy at Sycamore School that I didn't visit Heritage often. When I did visit, I always felt obliged to confess that I was a "derelict parent." Because of her work, Darlene was even more derelict about visiting than I was. As a result, our three kids had greater independence in their new school in Indiana than in their previous schools, and they thrived in that independence.

Because we would be living on the north side of Indianapolis, the Church at the Crossing was an obvious choice and excellent fit as our church home. We were accustomed to large churches, and this one was large enough to feel familiar even though not as large as our previous churches. The sermons were inspiring, and the music was varied and mostly traditional. Darlene was especially intent on our kids having an active church life, and the youth program was the best our kids experienced.

Darlene immediately joined the choir, and in our second year she volunteered for me to help teach Matt's class of fifth and sixth graders. Matt and some of his more congenial "peers and colleagues" were at my discussion table that first year, and it was so easy that I was persuaded to continue for another six years.

The move to Indiana allowed Darlene to complete her professional calling, something that couldn't have happened as well anywhere else. Her fellowship in developmental-behavioral pediatrics at the Indiana School of Medicine (Riley Hospital) led her to becoming Assistant Clinical Professor of Pediatrics.

Darlene was passionate about helping mothers learn how to raise mentally healthy infants, toddlers, and children. She was in her element as a developmental pediatrician at the Riley Hospital, a nationally prominent center for developmental pediatrics where infant mental health was a natural component of her work.

Developmental pediatrics allowed her to work with families whose children had serious and sometimes intractable medical issues. It also allowed her to focus on her real passion: infant mental health, which forms the emotional and psychological foundation for physical health and well-being in children and ultimately in the adults they become. She could see that healthy adults are usually the product of attentive parenting from birth onward.

Darlene and I worked with kids at opposite ends of the opportunity spectrum. The students in my schools had very great opportunities because they were bright, healthy, and usually from affluent homes. Her patients had intractable mental and physical limitations and were often from families with limited income.

Indianapolis allowed me to continue my work in the "headmastering racket," as I liked to call it. I considered several alternatives before we left Kansas and before I heard of Sycamore School. I discussed my employment dilemma with Richard Koenings, a Milwaukee attorney whose wife, Sharon, had been a colleague of mine at Brookfield Academy. Richard gave me some profound career advice. "Nyle," he said, "I think you should just decide what you really like to do and look for that."

I thought about Richard's advice and decided that what I liked best was what I had been doing: working with the people who work with the kids in a school. With that profound clarification in mind, I was ready when Sycamore called and the month of phone calls and faxes ensued. It wasn't until our moving van was unloaded at our Indianapolis townhouse that I first visited Sycamore School.

My visit at the school was only five days before classes were to begin, and the Board of Directors was to meet the next day. They asked me to become the Interim Headmaster, and I accepted but recommended that my title be "Head of School" instead of "Headmaster" in case the person who would succeed me would be a woman. I told them it seemed best not to set the stage for another "Headmistress," which sounded too much like "Head Mistress."

On August 23, 1993, I introduced myself to the Sycamore School faculty as Interim Head of School. To complete its due diligence, the Board completed a nationwide search, and in December they asked me to become the permanent Head of School. I was happy to accept.

Sycamore's sudden appearance in my life was nearly miraculous, although I started at Sycamore at a much lower salary than I had at Wichita Collegiate or at Brookfield Academy. Also, Sycamore's fringe benefits in 1993 were only "free coffee and free parking," as I liked to say, and I wasn't kidding. With Darlene's income, the financial situation of our family was stable, even though we had yet to sell our house back in Wichita.

On our June and July visits to Indianapolis, we had looked at popular neighborhoods on the north side of Indianapolis both inside and outside the I-465 loop. We found attractive houses in all areas, but some neighborhoods seemed overly upscale for our way of life. Traffic would have been an issue at most of those houses. We discovered an older neighborhood right behind Heritage Christian School, so close that the kids could walk to school if necessary. Most of the houses were built in the 1960s, and many were quite large. All of the houses had large yards as well. The neighborhood reminded us of Brookfield, Wisconsin, so we asked our realtor to focus on that neighborhood.

Meanwhile, our house in Wichita was on the market. Quite a few people looked at it, but none made an offer. Finally, a potential buyer contacted our realtor with a low-ball offer. We countered with an offer slightly below our asking price. The buyer slightly increased his low-ball offer, and he said it was his final offer. We decided not to accept it. The realtor then told us the buyer seemed to have had his feelings hurt when we withdrew, even though he had said it was his final offer. We resumed negotiations. After three more offers and counter-offers, we agreed on a price. Our Wichita house sold to the only person who had been willing to make an offer. We were free at last to buy a house in Indianapolis.

Almost immediately after we made that sale, our Indianapolis realtor called one Monday morning to report on a house on Colebrook Drive that seemed to meet our specifications. I went to see it that afternoon and realized, in the words of Brigham Young, "This is the place." Darlene went with me two days later and agreed it might well be our house, but she insisted that we see more houses. On Saturday, we visited five houses as fast as I could force us through them. I was convinced that the house on Colebrook Drive was the house for us, and I was afraid someone else might snatch it away from us.

We were back in the realtor's office before noon. We formulated an offer that was just a little under the asking price so the owners wouldn't feel they had asked too little. It was close enough to their price to be attractive and, we hoped, especially appealing since we had enough money from our Wichita home sale to make the financing easy. Late that same night, our realtor called to say the owners were at a wedding in Michigan but had accepted our offer. We were nearly delirious with the news.

The realtor had already scheduled an open house for the next day and couldn't cancel it, so our whole family went to see "our house." Many others came as well, including at least one neighbor who had been hoping for two years to buy it. Word got out that the house already had been sold, and our sheepish behavior gave us away as the buyers.

At Thanksgiving 1993, we moved into our house at 6215 Colebrook Drive. It felt as though we had boarded a wonderful ship that would carry us off into the future. Darlene and I had entered a golden autumn of our lives, and our children had entered a new springtime in theirs.

55

First Decade as Hoosiers

No one knows with certainty what a "Hoosier" is. Theories about the origin of the state's nickname range from admirable to derogatory. Our family had no strong convictions about what to call ourselves when we arrived. Darlene was born in the state, so she could call herself a Hoosier if she liked. The kids were all born in Wisconsin, so perhaps they were Badgers by birth. None of us had lived in Kansas long enough to think we were Jayhawks. I had been born in Ohio, and I valued memories of my childhood, but I hadn't lived in Ohio since 1957. Like it or not, we were becoming Hoosiers.

We had ten years of "normal life" after we moved to Indiana. Normal life does not make the news headlines even when fraught with arduous work, difficult decisions, and minor crises. Our first decade in Indiana was filled with family, work, church, and home life—the essence of the good life we had hoped for. When the decade began in 1993, all three of our children lived at home. Jenny was a junior in high school, Anna was in eighth grade, and Matt was in fourth grade. By 2003, all three had left home. Anna had married Greg Herman in May 2003 and moved to Bloomington, Indiana, where Greg was studying for his MBA. By September 2003, Jenny was in graduate school at Ball State University in Muncie and had met Chad Rasmussen. They would soon be engaged. Matt was a sophomore at Anderson University and, though he knew it not, was about to meet Kathryn Arrasmith.

In those first ten Hoosier years, Darlene and I had grown into our big house on Colebrook Drive, fully occupied it, and then had seen much of it begin to lie fallow as our children went on into their adult lives. We remained in close contact with them and found that the term "empty nest" was for us a false image of that phase of life. Instead, we found we had a "surging nest" to which our kids returned time and again to bring friends, furniture, other belongings, and eventually fiancés and spouses. We were happy to find that we were still parents to our children, but in a new way.

Darlene's time was dominated by her work as she finished her fellowship in developmental/behavioral pediatrics and became one of the first board-certified developmental pediatricians in the state of Indiana. On nearly all workday mornings, I took two cups of coffee upstairs for her and one for me. We would chat for a few minutes while we became fully awake and then have a minute of prayer before the race to leave on time for work. She often took a breakfast of yogurt, fruit, and Grape Nuts cereal that she could eat at her desk at the hospital while reviewing patient information online.

Our regular cycle of home, work, school, and church activities was punctuated by a few travels in our first decade as Hoosiers. In December 1994, I traveled alone to Eritrea, where I had taught in the Peace Corps thirty years earlier. Eritrea had fought a thirty years' war of independence, and I found that some of my students were in key government positions. Other students had died in the war or while trying to escape the violence by fleeing to the Sudan. Many former students were living in exile in Europe or the United States.

Since 1992, our camping tent had languished in the attic above our garage after its near-fatal encounter with that strong wind that had ended our 1992 trip to Utah. In 1996, Darlene and I decided to bring it down from the attic and examine it for mold or other decay. We thought we might just cut off the flap where we had recorded all our nights of camping and then throw the tent away. To our delight, the tent was in good condition except for the long rips on one side and a tear in the waterproof base. We decided we could repair it, and Darlene set up her sewing machine in our family room. For several days she worked to sew up the ripped tent wall, and I found a way to stitch the tear on the heavy waterproof base. We tested the tent for two nights in our back yard before deciding it was sturdy enough for another camping trip "way out West."

In 1996, we made a triumphal family camping trip to Colorado with our newly repaired tent. It required two tries to make that trip. On the first try, we packed everything into our 1990 Dodge Grand Caravan and headed west in early June. We went first to Wichita, where my uncle Elmer Kardatzke (nicknamed "Mit" because he had big hands) was said to be near death after a series of strokes. We planned to visit him and the relatives there for three days and then go on to Monument Valley in southeast Utah.

When we were ready to leave Wichita, word came that Uncle Elmer had died during the night. His funeral was scheduled for June 12 at Central Community Church, the same church we had attended during our year in Wichita and the church Elmer had pastored in the 1940s to 1960s. We changed our plans and stayed for the funeral.

June 12 was the twenty-fifth wedding anniversary for Darlene and me, as well as the day of Uncle Mit's funeral. We hadn't planned a big anniversary celebration, so our kids quietly ordered a cake from a local bakery and surprised us with it at the funeral dinner. Darlene was a very tolerant wife to have been happy with such a simple, ad hoc celebration. A photo shows her clowning and acting shocked while I kissed her on the cheek to celebrate our anniversary.

We were out of time for the camping trip we'd planned, so we headed back east right after the funeral dinner. We could tell that our tired old minivan was struggling to climb over interstate highway overpasses and would not have made it over the high passes in Colorado and Utah. We spent a night in Branson, Missouri, to see the dazzling Shoji Tabuchi musical show. We marveled that such a collection of entertainment and recreation had been created in the Ozarks, and we seemed to be among the last to discover it. We were thankful to limp back home to Hoosier territory with the van still barely intact.

Soon we traded in the Dodge minivan for a full-size white Chevrolet van. It was used, but it was luxurious to us. It allowed us to mount a second Western expedition later that summer, but we never made it then or later to Monument Valley in Utah. Instead, we took the repaired big tent and celebrated its new life in New Mexico and Colorado, including two nights at Campsite 13 in Lake George. It was a joy to use that old tent after it had been "resurrected."

In 1998 Darlene went with me to Santa Fe, New Mexico, for a meeting of private school headmasters at which Sycamore's accreditation was approved for the first time. It was an exciting time for both of us, punctuated not only by Sycamore's success but also by a visit to the Georgia O'Keeffe Museum and the crackling news about President Bill Clinton and Monica Lewinsky.

Darlene and I took Matt with us in 2000 on a spring break trip to Paris. Instead of dashing from city to city as we sometimes had in our domestic travels, we stayed in Paris, rode the Metro, and enjoyed museums, parks, and restaurants. A day trip on the train to Chartres was our only big excursion. It rained every day except during the cab ride to the airport on the day we left. Still, it was a fine trip.

A memorable event that Matt has yet to hear the last of happened on that trip. At a restaurant near the Louvre, an especially sociable waiter took orders from Darlene and me and then turned to our teenage son. "And what will it be for the baby boy?" he asked.

In June 2001 we celebrated my father's ninetieth birthday with a Kardatzke reunion in Ohio. Family members came from coast to coast, and we visited sites precious to our family's history, including the grave of August Kardatzke, the first of our ancestors to reach the New World. My dad made us laugh by jumping off the tour bus and nearly running to his great-grandfather's grave ahead of everyone. At the hotel gathering one evening, he sang a long-lost song called "I'm Lonesome Since I Left My Gal Way Down in Indianer."

On May 31, 2003, our daughter Anna married Greg Herman. Their wedding was a lovely event at the church they had helped start in a former warehouse. A good-sized crowd was seated in a semi-circle around the low stage. Two young pastors conducted the ceremony. It was reminiscent of the home weddings in Darlene's family and mine in the 1930s. Darlene was happy and radiant in all the pictures from that day.

Instead of throwing rice when Greg and Anna left the church, we all blew little siren whistles. One of Darlene's great-nieces asked, "Did Anna come up with that?" Indeed, she had. From this wedding I learned never to "count the cost" of one of my children's weddings or even be curious about it. I learned to let Darlene charge everything and pay the credit card bill. I advise other fathers of brides to do likewise.

The world did not come to an end on December 31, 1999, as some expected. Nor did all the clocks stop and all the computers that controlled the world go into paralysis. But the new millennium did seem fraught with more unexpected challenges for us.

56

Halcyon Days of Camping

Our first ten years living as Hoosiers included some mild adventures for Darlene and me. We capped off those first ten years with a 2003 camping trip to the West. Camping always gave us feelings of peace and calm, the very meaning of "halcyon," a word I learned in graduate school from an economics book.

This camping trip to Arizona began with a short stop in Joplin, Missouri, where I was to lead an accreditation visit at a private school in September. I visited with the headmaster and members of his staff in preparation for the three-day visit in the fall. Darlene and I then continued westward through familiar territory in Oklahoma, Texas, and New Mexico. Canyon de Chelly National Monument in eastern Arizona was the westernmost point in the trip. Red sandstone walls enclose a narrow canyon dotted with small farms tended by Navajo. We drove to several overlooks and peered down on the peaceful farm plots on the canyon floor where Native Americans seemed to be living in another century long ago.

Driving northeastward back into New Mexico, we had a close look at Shiprock, a 1,583-foot clump of rock thrusting from the desert floor. It had beckoned us four years earlier when we saw it in the hazy distance from Mesa Verde National Park in southwestern Colorado. Shiprock is considered sacred by the local Indians, so we couldn't drive close to it, but we weren't disappointed. It towers abruptly over the surrounding desert, and when viewed from the highway, it does look like the prow of a stranded ship. Shiprock was awe-inspiring, and it was easy to see why the Navajo interpret it in religious terms and manage access to it closely.

Heading for home, we glided peacefully into southwestern Colorado and passed through the town of Dolores. It was dark by the time we arrived at the West Dolores Campground, about thirty miles from town. It was July 3, and only one campsite remained. It was not a good one. The tent space was on a slope and was too small for our large cabin tent, but we found enough room under a bush for our small, two-person tent. By the light of our headlamps, we squeezed our tent under the bush and tossed in our sleeping bags and ground pads. The location reminded us of the story of Hagar and Ishmael in the desert, and with that biblical thought, we settled down for a chilly mountain night, snug in our temporary home.

When we registered, the genial campground host tipped me off that a large site next to the creek would be vacated the next day. At daybreak we were up and ready. As soon as the other campers left that site, I took an armload of our camping gear and walked across the campground to claim it. We registered for the bigger site and moved everything by mid-morning. Besides our two tents, we had brought a screen house for Darlene to use as a watercolor painting studio. I set up the screen house for her, and she got out her watercolors. I went to the creek for a short, futile fishing expedition. It was a day of happiness and tranquility for both of us. It was, especially for me, "halcyon."

On the next day, the Fourth of July, jubilant patriots celebrated across America, far from our mountain site in southwestern Colorado. Fire suppression rules kept our campground quiet, unmolested by the fireworks exploding elsewhere. Only birds overhead and the rumble of tires on the gravel forest road broke the peace that evening.

The next day at the Black Canyon of the Gunnison, we again dealt with a campsite too small for our big tent. The camping area, situated above the canyon and shrouded in bushes, was the haunt of porcupines and deer. It was called a "pygmy forest" because the pinyon pines and fragrant juniper bushes were abnormally short due to the climate. We nestled our tent among low pine trees and waited for the porcupines that never came.

The next day, we headed east through the towns of Cimarron and Gunnison and over Monarch Pass. Our destination was Campsite 13, a campsite in the Blue Mountain Campground two miles south of the village of Lake George and about an hour's drive west of Colorado Springs. Campsite 13 had become almost sacred to our family after many visits beginning in 1978. We originally chose the site because it was near the outhouse and was one of only three sites available that busy camping weekend. That night was the first time we camped with our daughter Jenny, who was seventeen months old. Years later Anna and Matt camped with us there too. Campsite 13 was a place of pleasant memories and stories. Though it is unremarkable in its own right, it had grown to mythical significance in our immediate family.

We did not suspect that this camping trip would be the last with our beloved old tent, a Eureka cabin tent. We had camped in it for thirty years, and I had written the name and date of every campsite on the door flap. By 2003 we had pitched that tent sixty-two places for about a hundred nights of camping, and we hoped to use it for another hundred nights.

57

Bad News Breaks In

In the last three days of September 2003, I was in Joplin, Missouri, as leader of the accreditation team at the Thomas Jefferson Independent Day School. The three-day accreditation visit went smoothly, and the team recommended renewal of the school's accreditation. I wrote the final report on October 1 and drove to Tulsa the next day for my flight home to Indianapolis. Darlene had been working in the hospital all week, and I was looking forward to seeing her.

During a change of planes in Memphis, I found a voicemail message from her on my cellphone. When I called, we greeted each other as usual. She asked about the accreditation visit. I told her I would arrive at Indianapolis at about 1:30 p.m. She asked if I would stop at the hospital on my way in from the airport. She said to come to the parking lot near the Emergency Room entrance, and she would come out to see me there. My flight was being announced, so we signed off with our usual: "I love you."

I was pleased that she had asked me to see her in the middle of her work day. It was a pleasant surprise, but then dark thoughts crossed my mind. *How had she sounded on the phone? Did it sound as though something was wrong? No. But then why did she want to see me this afternoon instead of this evening?*

My mind ran through several scenarios. *Had something happened to my elderly parents? But they had been in stable health despite my father's stroke two years earlier. What about our adult children?* I thought again about her tone of voice and put my questions aside. I would know soon enough.

While waiting for my checked luggage in Indianapolis, I called her again. She was cheerful and businesslike, as usual. She gave me directions to the hospital from the airport, and I said I'd let her know when I was near the Emergency Room parking lot. I did my best to cancel my earlier fearful thoughts as I made the short drive to the hospital.

Darlene came out quickly. She seemed pensive as she walked toward me, a stethoscope peeking from one pocket of her white lab coat. I jumped out of the van to meet her. We hugged and started to talk outside the van, but she said she was cold and wanted to get in. When we were in the van, she took a deep breath and stammered. I felt a sudden chill.

What was wrong? Had one of my parents died? Had something happened to one of our kids? I didn't think that anything might have happened to *her*.

"You have something to tell me, don't you?" I asked.

She nodded and blinked.

"What is it?" I persisted.

Her face reddened, and tears welled up in her eyes. "I have breast cancer," she said simply.

"Oh, honey!" I exclaimed. I stretched across the van and hugged her as well as I could. "Oh, honey!" I said again and again.

"It's okay," she said to comfort me.

"I found out on Tuesday," she continued. "I thought the lump in my breast had changed, and I went to see Dr. Goulet again."

Dr. Goulet was a surgeon, and she had consulted him earlier about a place in one of her breasts. Nothing had shown up on her mammograms. When he checked her again on Monday, he too thought her breast had changed. He did a needle biopsy and on Tuesday confirmed the cancer.

"I didn't call you about it because I knew there was nothing you could do while you were doing that accreditation," she said.

She had held this secret by herself until I returned, I thought to myself. *She must have felt so alone as the thought of cancer came to her again and again while she was seeing patients.*

I didn't understand the seriousness of breast cancer at the time. I had heard of women who had been successfully treated for it, so I thought of it as potentially serious but readily treated and probably only a temporary concern.

"This is a sneaky kind of cancer," she said. "It hides between the glands and doesn't form an obvious lump like other kinds of breast cancer. It may have been there a long time."

I thought back to the day several months earlier when she had felt a possible lump. I touched the place she indicated, and I thought I could feel some firmness at that spot too. She had gone for mammograms regularly, but they had shown nothing. *We may have felt the tumor that day, months earlier, but it hadn't grown enough to be biopsied.*

She told me what she knew of the next steps. First, she would have an appointment with an oncologist on Friday, the very next day, and I would need to be there. She had been given a choice of oncologists, and she thought she would be meeting with a woman at the Simon Cancer Center next to Riley Hospital where she worked. We prayed together, and then she hopped from the van. She still had work to do that day.

I sat silent and numb in the van, watching her walk briskly back into the hospital. She looked young, jaunty, and carefree. Her white lab coat shone in the sun. With her fast pace, she appeared to be healthy, confident, and even joyful. But as she walked away, I felt she and I both were leaving the secure, peaceful life we had known. Things would never be the same.

It was still early in the afternoon, and I needed to at least stop by Sycamore School. In the parking lot, I slumped over the steering wheel for a minute before gathering myself up to enter the building. My cell phone rang. It was the president of the accrediting association, asking me to participate in something or other. I mumbled a reply, and his call flew from my mind.

Inside the school, life was humming along happily. Those who saw me greeted me, and I said the trip had been good. Darlene had cautioned me not to tell *anyone*, not anyone at all, about her diagnosis. Nothing at the school required my attention, so I went home to prepare our dinner.

The next day, Friday, October 3, we met Dr. Anna Maria Storniolo, Darlene's oncologist. Dr. Storniolo had been highly recommended by other doctors, and we soon saw why. She fairly hopped into the examining room and shook our hands. She was confident, cheerful, assuring, and exuded competence. Perhaps in her mid-forties, she was slim, dark-haired, and wore plastic-framed glasses that accentuated her eyes. We talked a few minutes, and she began to take Darlene's history. Darlene herself had been healthy, even after three C-section babies. Her father, however, had died of pancreatic cancer; and the older of her two sisters had been successfully treated for breast cancer—a red flag for sure.

The doctor washed her hands and began to examine Darlene. She found the tumor in the left breast easily. It was small, and she said she understood why it had at first been overlooked. She then began to explain Darlene's diagnosis and plan of treatment. She pulled a marker from her lab coat and made notes on a whiteboard, diagramming the tumor's location and its connections in the breast. She explained the nature of this type of tumor and listed possible chemotherapies that were most likely to be effective.

She erased the board and wrote a timeline for treatment. There would be powerful chemotherapy in October and November. After a time of rest, the left breast would be removed, and her condition would be re-evaluated to determine what further treatment might be needed. Darlene asked a couple of medical questions, and I simply tried to take everything in. A few minutes later, we checked out of the Cancer Center and headed to our workplaces for the afternoon.

Back at my office at Sycamore School, everything had changed for me. The school hadn't changed: The halls were still filled with the hush of serious schoolwork and the occasional chirping of kids changing classes. But I had changed. I felt lonely. I called Darlene several times during her work at Riley Hospital that day, and we talked about how and when we would tell our kids the news.

58

Telling the Children

At the time Darlene's breast cancer was discovered, our children all lived within a ninety-minute drive of our home in Indianapolis. Jenny was in graduate school in Muncie. Anna and Greg were in Bloomington, where he was in the MBA program and she was commuting to Indianapolis for her bachelor's degree. Matt was a sophomore living on campus at Anderson University in Anderson, Indiana. All of them already were planning to see us on Saturday except Greg, who was going to stay in Bloomington to study for an exam. It was Homecoming weekend at Anderson University, and we had made plans for a family dinner several weeks earlier. Our children were expecting only the happy celebration we had been planning.

Darlene had decided she wanted to have all the kids together so she could tell them about her cancer in person. To make sure they would be with us by 6:00 p.m., I told Jenny that we needed a family meeting. Chad Rasmussen, Jenny's new boyfriend, was coming with her. Anna arrived in high spirits in late afternoon, but she was frightened when Jenny told her there was to be a family meeting.

Seeing Anna's response, Darlene asked me privately if we should call Greg and have him hurry to join us even though he was immersed in his studies in Bloomington. I said we could tell him later, not really understanding the seriousness of what was about to happen. Darlene later regretted accepting my recommendation, wishing we had urged Greg to come.

When Jenny, Chad, Anna, and Matt were all together on the family room couches, Darlene went in and sat in the middle to tell them the news. I watched from the kitchen and kept dinner moving along.

"I'm going to have some medical treatments," Darlene began. Their eyes were riveted on her. "I found out this week that I have breast cancer."

Our children all burst into tears. Jenny held her head in her arms and sobbed. Anna put her hands on her face and cried. Matt fixed his eyes on Darlene and cried. Chad tried to comfort Jenny. Darlene calmly elaborated on her diagnosis while they shuddered and wept. When Darlene was finished, I joined them and we all stood together in a circle. Everyone prayed, one by one.

Deep sighs and sniffles filled the air when Darlene sat down again with the kids and answered their questions. I went back to the kitchen to finish cooking, and Chad joined me to finish the cherry pie he had started to make.

Dinner conversation that evening was intense, and talk continued until bedtime. Our home had never felt this way. Always before whenever we had gathered for holidays, the place rocked with laughter and singing. In some family gatherings, Darlene had played the piano and had sung along with the rest of us. Jenny, Anna, and Darlene were especially good at harmonizing. We would laugh and sing at those times, but on this night our hearts were heavy, and our minds were clamoring for meaning. Darlene was the quiet center of the emotional storm, perfectly calm even though her life was in danger.

At church the next morning, the sermon title, "Facing Unexpected Difficulties," seemed as if it had been designed for Darlene. Senior Pastor Steve Rennick hadn't prepared the sermon specifically for Darlene, but I had called him on Saturday to ask that Darlene be prayed for at the altar in front of the congregation. After communion, Pastor Rennick announced that someone had requested prayer for healing. He didn't announce the reason for Darlene's request, but she went forward and knelt alone at the altar. Her purple blazer fixed itself in my mind as she knelt.

Our family joined her at the altar, and we placed our hands on her shoulders. Others from the congregation joined us and placed their hands on family members. Pastor Rennick prayed for healing and for faith in God's love and healing power. At the end, we stood and dried our eyes. Those who had joined us gasped when we told the reason for the prayer. Others approached us as we left, and when they learned Darlene had cancer, they promised to pray.

After a Sunday lunch of leftovers from our Saturday night feast, we talked together as a family more and cried again. Darlene and I then sent everyone on to their studies that afternoon. The house seemed suddenly too large and too quiet. Only the echo of our telling the children filled our minds.

59

Preparing for Treatment

Darlene and I both went to work on Monday morning. Sometime that day, she walked from Riley Hospital to the Cancer Center for a pre-op test in preparation for minor surgery the next day to install a port for infusing chemotherapy drugs. We were both acting almost as though nothing had happened, but we knew that heavy treatment and surgery lay ahead.

Darlene explained to me that the first step of chemotherapy was the installation of a port for infusing the chemotherapy drugs. The port would be a metal or plastic button about the size of a silver dollar that would be surgically implanted just under the skin high on the chest. From the port a catheter tube would lead to a large vein inside the chest. The port would be accessed by inserting a chemotherapy needle through the skin and through a membrane on the outer side of the port. Blood draws and repeated chemo treatments would be performed through the port rather than through veins in her arms, making the procedures less painful and less likely to lead to infection.

Darlene and I met in a waiting room in the basement in early afternoon. I wanted to be there with her for the pre-op test, which was a sentinel node biopsy to determine whether cancer had spread to her lymphatic system. She couldn't eat or drink anything that day because installation of the port would be under general anesthesia, but she insisted that I get lunch in the hospital cafeteria. When I returned, she was ashen and subdued. She had received more news.

The MRI the previous Thursday had shown a second tumor and swelling in the lymph nodes. Swelling in the lymph nodes told the doctors what they needed to know: The cancer had spread to the lymph nodes and possibly throughout her body. No sentinel node biopsy was needed.

Darlene was shaken. She teared up for a minute when she told me but quickly set her concerns aside. We settled in for a long wait in that little basement waiting room. We were fixed on each other as we waited.

At 4:30, we turned on the TV and watched the unfolding news of other troubles in the world. It was 7:15 by the time the surgeon was available, and Darlene was taken for surgery. I had dinner in the cafeteria and went to the surgery waiting room on third floor. I hadn't been in the waiting room long, and I wasn't prepared for what happened next.

Dr. Goulet strode across the lobby to me, I stood, and he said, "I'm very sorry."

My heart stopped, and my mind raced. *What could have gone wrong? Was there a new complication? Had she died?*

"I'm sorry to have kept you waiting so long," he continued. "She's out of surgery now, and everything went perfectly."

I breathed again, but my mind was still numb as he told me where to find the surgery recovery room.

Not long after, Darlene was wheeled down the hall and into a recovery room. I waited by her bed, and I was surprised by how quickly she recovered and was released to go home. By then it was the wee hours of Tuesday morning. Anna was at our house and stayed with Darlene while I went to an all-night Walgreens for pain medicine.

Darlene slept well, and she stayed at home the next day to recover. It was October 8, 2003. She had the port and was ready for treatment. We were a week into the cancer season of our lives.

60

Chemo Begins

October 13 was a Monday, less than two weeks after Darlene's cancer was first discovered. It was the day that her chemotherapy would begin.

"This is a big day," Darlene said when I handed her a cup of coffee that morning and sat down next to her bed. Coffee together at her bedside had been a standing ritual throughout our marriage. I watched as she sat on the edge of the bed with one leg folded under the knee of the other.

"I hope I don't have a bad reaction to the chemo."

"Me too," I mumbled. I had only the vaguest idea of what chemo would be like for her. Even she, a medical doctor, knew of chemo only through her training and the reading she had been doing since she was diagnosed. Her world of developmental pediatrics was a world away from adult cancer treatment.

"How long did they say it would take?" I asked.

"I think most of the day. We won't get home until mid-afternoon."

We reported at the Cancer Center at about 8:30 for the blood draw through her recently installed port. When the blood tests had been evaluated, a nurse took Darlene into a specially prepared room where she was seated in a large recliner chair. She sat upright while the nurse connected a bottle of saline solution to her port. To the saline solution, the nurse added an anti-nausea medicine, followed by red Adriamycin and then clear Cytoxan. These latter two chemicals would go on a "search and destroy" mission throughout her body, attacking all fast-growing cells including cancer cells.

When the chemotherapy nurses learned that Darlene worked at Riley Hospital as a pediatrician, one said, "I could never work with little kids! I would be in tears all the time."

Similarly, Darlene's pediatrics colleagues at Riley couldn't understand how the oncologists and nurses at the Cancer Center could do that kind of work.

We had been told that cells in the mouth, because they grow rapidly, would be affected, sometimes causing painful sores. Darlene dutifully sucked popsicles and ice cubes during the infusion to lower the temperature in her mouth to slow the growth of those cells and make sores less likely. The popsicles worked well for her: no mouth sores.

Three other women were receiving chemo in that little glass-walled room with Darlene. I watched from a chair outside the room. It was an out-of-body experience for both of us. Darlene seemed to be in a space capsule, heading for some new region of life. I was traveling with her outside the capsule. Where would it take us?

She had no trouble walking to the car after chemo, and we picked up chicken nuggets from McDonald's and chocolate shakes from Steak 'n Shake for a late lunch. Something mild and familiar seemed best when she didn't know what side effects she would have. It was a beautiful, warm fall day, our favorite kind of day. The beauty of the day was strangely comforting despite her cancer treatment that morning.

On the day after the first chemo, Darlene stayed at home and rested. I cooked the pork chops she requested for dinner, and we had a quiet evening. She went to work on Wednesday afternoon and all day Thursday. She said she wanted to live life as normally as possible, and that ideal of "normal life" guided our decisions the rest of her days.

61

Laughter in the Midst of Cancer

The "normal life" that Darlene wanted meant that both of us kept working at our day jobs, she as a developmental pediatrician at Riley Hospital and I as headmaster at Sycamore School. Our future would be punctuated by times of sorrow, but there would be days of joy as well.

My birthday was coming up on Sunday, October 19. The students and faculty at Sycamore had made a practice of surprising me on my birthday every year since 1993, and I was surprised for the first four years until I caught on that their surprises were an *annual* event. This time I decided I would surprise the kids and teachers, and I would ask Darlene to help me prepare for the fun. It was Monday, and the "surprise" was to take place on Friday.

I would be turning sixty-four that year, so I picked up a recording of the Beatles' hit song "When I'm Sixty-Four." I practiced lip-syncing in the car on the way to school and back, and I began developing my moves for the act at home. On Thursday evening, when I had something to show, Darlene and Anna sat together on the couch in our family room for a preview. I went through the act two or three times, and they suggested new moves at certain points in my performance. We must have made six passes through the song before it was ready for the show the next day at school. The evening was well spent, and we were weary from laughter at bedtime.

The next day at school, I gyrated through my moves in a massive wig and something like a Beatles outfit. The kids howled and applauded wildly, mainly because their headmaster looked so ludicrous. The teachers, many of whom had lived through Beatlemania, were in hysterics. They laughed at me, they laughed at the kids' laughter, and they laughed at memories of themselves thirty years earlier. I laughed, too, and it felt good to be laughing during the unfolding medical crisis at home.

62

Hair Loss and More

Like the cells in the mouth, the cells that produce hair grow especially fast and are early targets of chemotherapy drugs. Typically, within two to four weeks, hair loss begins not only on the scalp but all over the body. For most cancer patients, hair loss is distressing, even though it is expected. Darlene responded to this new challenge in her own matter-of-fact, problem-solving way. She knew it would happen and took note of the first hairs on her pillow as though she were tracking the symptoms of someone else. If she felt emotional about it, she didn't show it.

Her hair loss began on Wednesday, October 29, just sixteen days after the first chemo. She first noticed the hair on her pillow, and when she brushed her hair, there was much more on the brush than usual. More came out on Thursday and Friday, but she still had enough to go to work without a wig. She worked all day Friday and returned home at 10:00 p.m. Late nights at the hospital were not unusual, even while she was in cancer treatment.

Darlene turned fifty-eight years old on November 3, 2003. That day also was her second day of chemo. The tumor had shrunk so much that Dr. Storniolo had to search carefully to find it when she examined the breast. We both were encouraged, and the second chemo went as smoothly as the first. She had lost the rest of her hair the previous day, but she took that in stride.

I had started a beard unintentionally during our camping trip in July. It came in so gray and dignified that I just let it keep growing when we returned home. Darlene was okay with the beard until the onset of cancer, but her skin became more sensitive after the first chemo. I shaved my mustache immediately so I wouldn't tickle her when I kissed her, but I kept a halo of beard around my chin and jaw, in an Amish or Abraham Lincoln style. She liked the beard that way, and I kept it until I had masqueraded as Abraham Lincoln in a black suit and a black top hat on Halloween at Sycamore School. The younger students were mildly amused, but I think the older ones thought it was an overly academic stunt. I shaved the beard completely the day after Darlene's birthday.

I went with her for the chemo treatment, watched as her port was accessed, and sat next to her as the chemo fluids slowly dripped into her body. We both read during the infusion and talked a little. We both napped sometimes during the long procedure. When she was thirsty, I brought her water and soft drinks from a hospitality station just outside the room. She couldn't leave because she was tethered to the chemo bag.

The third chemo treatment was on Monday, November 24. By then the tumor had disappeared, and the third chemo went as smoothly as the first two. During and after all three chemo treatments, Darlene had not been sick and had remained active, in good spirits, and working as usual in the Children's Hospital.

Our three kids came for Thanksgiving later that week. Every bed in the house was taken, and it was a joyful celebration. The shock and fear of early October had stabilized. Darlene's energy and serenity calmed us all. We were thankful to have her with us and looking so healthy in spite of the cancer. We feasted and sang together around the piano, living out Darlene's ideal of a normal life.

The fourth chemo was on Monday, December 15. The chemo itself went smoothly, but a new alarming note was sounded. A radiation oncologist said Darlene might need radiation of the axilla, or armpit, next to the affected left breast. The MRI in October had revealed swelling in the lymph nodes, and the oncologist was alerting her that the cancer may have spread there. It was a grim possibility.

On the same day, Darlene met with her surgeon, Dr. Goulet, to discuss her surgical options. A lumpectomy, removal of a lump, seemed out of the question for her kind of cancer. A mastectomy clearly was needed, and she would have to decide whether she wanted to follow it with reconstructive surgery to cosmetically replace the lost breast. We had talked about that decision more than once at home, and she decided not to have reconstructive surgery. She was aware of the potential trauma of that added surgery, and she knew of some women for whom it hadn't gone well. She wanted to preserve her time and energy for other things, for normal life.

Darlene's first Christmas with cancer was a quiet time. We celebrated it early with our children on December 19 because Jenny and Anna had travel plans on Christmas Day. On December 25, Matt went with us to the south side of Indianapolis to be with Darlene's sisters and their children and grandchildren. We told stories about Darlene's parents and our Christmas celebrations years before. Cancer was far from us that day and every cancer Christmas that followed, even the one in 2009. Cancer couldn't stand up to the bright light of Christmas.

63

Mastectomy and More Bad News

On January 9, 2004, the day of Darlene's mastectomy, we were up at 4 a.m. and at the hospital at 6 a.m. A number of tests and interviews had to be done before she was taken for surgery. It was an ominous day, more portentous than we knew in those morning hours. We sat for some time in a dungeon-like examining room in the basement and made small talk. There was little we could say about her imminent surgery: It was serious, necessary, and a milestone we couldn't comprehend. We simply prattled with "normal" talk to keep ominous feelings at bay.

When the time came for her to go in, we held hands and prayed. As she was being rolled out on a gurney, I bent over her and kissed her.

"I love you," I said.

"See you later!" she replied.

I was sent to the surgery waiting room, then the recovery room, and much later to a regular hospital room where she would spend the night. When I finally saw her, she was still coming out of sedation and could only manage a weak smile to acknowledge me.

I had planned to spend the night sitting beside her bed, but I didn't know how I could manage it. I felt exhausted, and I must have been feeling some emotional trauma besides the effects of sitting in the hospital all day. I had sat a few minutes in the hospital room when an "angel" popped in. It was Pam Lemons, a nurse Darlene worked with at Riley Hospital.

"I'll take over now," Pam announced. "I'll stay with her."

I hesitated a moment, and she reassured me. "Get your things and let me take your chair. We will be okay here."

I was too numb with exhaustion to resist Pam's authoritative tone. I mumbled my thanks and a goodnight to Darlene and made my way to the car.

Pam Lemons was a far better helper than I could have been. She knew just what to do during that dark night. That was a hard night for Darlene. She was in pain, and she threw up several times. By morning, though, she was recovering and was able to go home with me before noon.

Since Darlene worked as a medical doctor in the same hospital system as the Cancer Center, she could access her own pathology report on our home computer. On Tuesday evening, January 13, she called me to our computer room. She had just found her pathology report.

"I thought you might want to be in on the ground floor of this thing," she said as she continued reading. "They took thirteen lymph nodes. All of them were positive. They broke out of the lymph sac," she said. "This is really bad."

"Oh, no!" I gasped.

"The cancer cells are now circulating everywhere. They can show up anywhere," she continued.

I had heard enough about other cancer cases to know that one positive lymph node was a bad sign. It meant the cancer had invaded the lymphatic system that moderates many bodily processes. One positive lymph node would have been a bad sign; thirteen was a terrible sign. The fact that the lymph sac had broken probably meant there were other active cancers elsewhere already. Some might even be advanced. We both stared at the computer screen for several minutes before we sat down in another room to think and talk.

We were quiet for a minute or two before she said, "I don't want anyone else to know about this. I don't want to spend the next year just as a dying cancer victim. I want as much normal life as I can have."

We talked then about what this report might mean for her survival. Only the two of us and her doctors knew about the lymph nodes. The medical people were sworn to secrecy by their professional codes. The two of us silently agreed to secrecy too. She especially didn't want to upset our children if this terrible report turned out to be a false alarm.

After talking at length about a "cover story," one that would be true and reveal enough facts to silence further questions, we agreed on a plan. We would tell people about her condition in a general way that we hoped would minimize the news and deflect further curiosity. Above all, we wanted to conceal how bad the news that day really had been.

Finally, we talked about the most serious outcome: She might die within the year. We even talked about where we might want to be buried. Our first thought was Maplewood Cemetery in Anderson, next to Anderson University, where we had both studied and where we had met. We hadn't felt this close to death until now or considered what should become of our bodies afterward, so we thought of burial sites that might in some way sum up our lives. We later dismissed Maplewood but continued to talk privately about cemeteries.

When Darlene and I met Dr. Storniolo and Dr. Goulet on January 15 to discuss the pathology report, I began the discussion by saying, "It seems to be as bad as it could have been."

"Yes," said Dr. Storniolo, "but it is very treatable."

During that appointment, we learned there could be yet another unpleasant surprise after the next scans. If the scans revealed active cancer in other areas, that would most likely be fatal. But with the professionalism Darlene and I had come to rely on, Dr. Storniolo laid out the treatment plan: a second round of chemo, then six weeks of radiation, and then hormone treatment unless the scans led to some other plan. Darlene simply accepted this news as though it were a medical lecture dealing with no one in particular.

After the scans were done at the Cancer Center that morning, Darlene and I went to the basement where the scans were processed. She told the technicians she was a doctor at Riley Hospital and she wanted to go over the scans with them. Setting aside their misgivings, they showed her the scans and interpreted them for her. They said the bone and abdomen scans were clear, but there were four spots in her lungs that might indicate tumor growth.

That news was worrisome, and we had to assume the worst: The spots might indicate more malignant masses.

Darlene was very concerned, but she was still calm and matter-of-fact. I considered this news encouraging, because I thought the scans could have been much worse. A few days later, Dr. Storniolo told Darlene she wasn't worried about the lung spots. Instead, she said she was concerned about the number of small lesions showing on her spine, something the technicians in the scanning lab hadn't mentioned and perhaps hadn't noticed. Dr. Storniolo wanted to get a direct sample of one of those lesions to see if they were malignant. That would indicate the kind of treatment Darlene would need.

Darlene still had one drainage tube in at the mastectomy site, and it was an annoyance to her. She had hoped to be rid of it by that time, and she was unsettled by the continuing bad news. My journal entry on January 19 included the following:

> Monday, January 19, 2004, at 8:45 a.m.: *Things have gone very badly lately. Darlene had her left breast removed on Friday, January 9. That went well, and I had her home by 11:30 the next morning. She is recovering quickly from the main incision. One of the two drain tubes was removed last Thursday.*
>
> *The really bad news is that the lymph nodes removed from her armpit were all cancerous. Even worse, the tumor cells had broken out of the lymph capsule, so there is great danger that they have started tumors elsewhere in her body. She is going to have scans of her chest, abdomen, and bones on Wednesday, the day after tomorrow. We are praying for a miracle—that the scans will be negative—and we are trying to be positive and secretive about her condition.*
>
> *Darlene is amazingly serene about all of this. She is logical and analytical, facing squarely all the issues that come up. She sometimes says she wishes this hadn't happened or that the treatments are going to be aggravating, but she has shown no self-pity. She is a very courageous woman, and she is drawing on great spiritual strength.*

She told a friend that one of her favorite Scripture verses was Joshua 1:9, "Have I not commanded you? Be strong and courageous. Do not be terrified; do not be discouraged, for the LORD your God will be with you wherever you go."

Tuesday, January 20, was a snow day for Sycamore School and nearly all schools in the city, one of the most enjoyable snow days ever. Due to a blizzard, I had closed the school for staff and students. Darlene and I spent the day together at home, and we simply "lived." Sometimes when she wanted to retreat from the world, Darlene would remind me of Varykino, the remote Siberian country house in the movie *Dr. Zhivago*. Many scenes at Varykino show it covered with ice and groaning with the extreme cold. We would sometimes imagine we were there, minus the Siberian snow. Tuesday was that kind of day, a Varykino day, far from the fears and struggles of the world.

The next day, January 21, was a day of more scans, and my journal entry included the following:

> *I'm praying for a miracle. Darlene's research on the internet last night indicated that she might have only eighteen to twenty-four months to live. She couldn't be sure, since each diagnosis is individual, but it wasn't good news.*
>
> *Her tube is still draining too much to be removed—about sixty milliliters per day when it should be less than thirty for the drainage tube to be removed. I'm hoping the drainage is taking tumor cells out of her body so they won't spread, but I realize that's not a medical opinion.*
>
> *I awoke several times in the night and prayed that the fluid discharge would end. By morning she was feeling calm and stronger, and the flow had decreased. That same day, our lives went on normally and quietly. We talked with both of our daughters. Friends brought us food, and our trash truck came—a welcome sign of normal life.*

For a few days, I made no journal entries. Darlene remained at home recovering from the mastectomy, and I was dealing with the ongoing business of school life at Sycamore. We were eating my cooking at home and having long talks. Our kids called often, and Darlene received emails and get-well cards, but I didn't keep a record of all those good, quiet parts of our lives in those dark days.

One night in late January 2004, while we were huddled away from the world, Darlene said to me, "This just goes from one nightmare to another." She was referring to the PET scan she would have on Monday, February 2. The spots on her lungs had been dismissed as normal, but this scan would determine if the spots on her spine were malignant. The bone lesions were too small to be biopsied directly, but a PET scan is especially sensitive and could reveal malignancy. Darlene thought the spots were very likely to be malignant. If so, her prognosis would be very poor.

A note in her Bible I found later showed that she read Psalm 34:18-20 on January 27, 2004, the day she made the remark about "one nightmare to another." The passage reads, "The LORD is close to the brokenhearted and saves those who are crushed in spirit. A righteous man may have many troubles, but the LORD delivers him from them all; he protects all his bones, not one of them will be broken."

At the end of January 2004, several weeks after her mastectomy, Darlene's other drainage tube was removed. The flow of amber fluid from the surgery site had dropped from sixty milliliters per day to thirty on a Tuesday, and by Wednesday morning, the drainage was down to ten milliliters. She called Dr. Goulet's office and was told to come in at noon. She went alone and had a long wait for the ten-minute procedure. During the wait, she cheerfully read a book as though she were waiting for a haircut. She was happy to have the tube out and called me at 3:30 to report. She was asleep when I got home at 6:30 that evening. We had a good dinner of enchilada pie from a Sycamore teacher.

Darlene remained at home for the next several days, still recovering but feeling more comfortable now that the drainage tubes were out and she could heal completely. Many evenings we had dinners that friends from church and our workplaces had brought to us. Those friends knew what we needed better than we knew ourselves.

During those days, we talked at length about whether it was time to tell our kids about the upcoming PET scan and about the seriousness of the situation. We had decided that we would tell them, but on Sunday morning, we decided not to tell them unless it came up in conversation and couldn't be avoided. We didn't know what the PET scan would show, and we weren't sure how we would handle the news, especially if it were bad. I prayed that the places seen in the CT scan would be either benign or remnants of tumors the chemo had already stopped.

On February 6, 2004, I wrote the following in my journal:

> *A miracle! Darlene's PET scan was negative! She called me while I was in a Headmasters' meeting at St. Richard's School at 11:30 yesterday morning. I jumped up and went outside for her call. She cried, and I cried as she told me. Praise God for protecting Darlene! Thank you, God, for preserving her bones!*

The scan had lifted the terror of bone cancer. Life could go on. The spots on her bones were just "bone islands," places with greater density than the rest of the bone. We were still praising God and thanking Jesus for protecting Darlene's bones when she started the next round of chemo with Taxol a week later. I would spend the day with her, as I always did when she had chemo.

Darlene returned to work on Monday, February 9, exactly a month after her mastectomy. Going to work and seeing her pediatric patients and their parents was part of the "normal life" she craved. Her work steadied her and gave her purpose.

At that point, we entered a time of relative peace. Other tests in the next weeks and months were negative. Darlene had been given a reprieve that turned out to be a long one. We didn't tell our children about the PET scan, and we especially didn't tell them or anyone else about the thirteen positive lymph nodes. We also didn't tell them we had gone prowling through the Maplewood Cemetery next to Anderson University in early 2004 while Matt was a student just across the street. Those were secrets we kept for five years.

64

More Passages

During the extended period of normal life following Darlene's mastectomy, our lives were filled with family, work, and church life, just as we hoped. Our desires were simple: lives of worthwhile work, time for each other, shared worship, and occasional travel. Happy life was returning. But life's dramas continued, moving us through more passages.

Six weeks after my father's 90th birthday, he had a devastating stroke that left him partially paralyzed. His treatment and physical rehabilitation in the following two and a half years would be the hardest work of his long, hard-working life. Fortunately, he and my mother were able to continue living in their apartment in Elmore, Ohio.

On Valentine's Day 2004, less than two months after he and my mother celebrated their sixty-ninth anniversary, my father had a second stroke from which he would not recover. The second stroke happened while they were together alone at the dinner table. My father had just told my mother to kiss him. He suddenly went silent and motionless. The Elmore EMT rushed him to a hospital in Toledo, and he died on February 23 without regaining consciousness.

On the evening of my father's memorial service, my siblings and I gathered with our spouses and children along with my mother at my sister's house near Elmore. My mother had just turned ninety and was in frail health, but she seemed at peace and happy to be with the family that night. I marveled at her peaceful, joyful bearing. I wondered if it was unusual for a person who had lost a spouse to be so calm and joyful. I wondered if I would be like that if the time came.

At the end of February, Darlene and I had a happy, noisy party at our house with all our kids, plus nearly all of Darlene's local relatives. The party celebrated several birthdays. There was good eating, lots of talk, and lots of laughter. It was a simple celebration of real life, normal life, as we called it.

A month later, on March 29, Darlene and I accepted an invitation for breakfast with Chad Rasmussen, Jenny's special friend since summer 2003. As we expected, he politely asked our permission to ask Jenny to marry him. We were happy and thankful that another of our children had been given a wonderful spouse. Chad and Jenny were obviously madly in love and had been talking openly of marriage in our family gatherings, so I didn't even try to fake mock astonishment. After that happy breakfast with Chad, Darlene and I went to Anderson and looked at gravesites and headstones in Maplewood Cemetery again, thinking we both might like to be buried there someday.

On March 29, 2004, I wrote the following in my journal:

> Last weekend was a "weekend of love" for our kids. They were all here for Jenny's birthday. Matt brought Kathryn Arrasmith, his first real girlfriend. He met her family for the first time at Valparaiso on Saturday. Jenny and Chad came Saturday evening. They were bubbling and in love. Anna and Greg, the happy married couple, were here on Sunday.

65

Radiation and "Normal Life"

I have repeatedly returned to the idea of "normal life" because it was so important to Darlene. But a normal day is a concept, not a concrete reality. Normal days are ones that fit an ideal we hold in our minds. They are precious, but they don't come reliably when we want them. Darlene used to say, "*Normal* is a setting on the clothes dryer."

Spring 2004 swirled along with only a few scares about Darlene's health. She completed Taxol chemotherapy on March 25. When we met with the radiation oncologist on April 5, I began to understand how serious her condition was. I'm sure Darlene had known much earlier. On April 12, radiation treatments would begin on her left breast area, where the breast had been, and all the lymph nodes in her armpit and shoulder.

The need for radiation and the procedure itself worried me; but as usual, Darlene was able to take it in stride, trying her best to maintain a sense of normal life. On the first day of radiation, she said, "I think I'll take my lunch to radiation to see if they will heat it up on their machine."

That spring we were both immersed in the stresses of our work, both of us working long hours and sometimes having oatmeal for dinner at 9 p.m. Radiation therapy was almost a non-event, even though it lasted six weeks. Darlene would leave home at 7:30 a.m., see patients and their parents at Riley

Children's Hospital, walk over to the Cancer Center at 3 p.m. to "get zapped," return to her work, and get home about 7 p.m. on an easy day. On other, more demanding days, she would not arrive home until much later. Even that scenario was normal for a physician. My days could be long, but I usually got home early enough to have dinner ready soon after she arrived.

Darlene hardly remarked on her thirty radiation treatments, only noting simply that there was something like sunburn at the radiated site. I didn't even make a journal entry when it ended on May 21. She had breezed so easily through the radiation treatments that we made plans for one of our more spectacular camping trips.

66

The Seven-Hour Hike

Darlene and I had been good tent campers throughout our marriage, but we were only moderate hikers. We didn't go on any all-day "death marches" like a few of our camping friends, and we never got into backpacking. Instead we were "car campers": we would pitch our relatively large tent close to our car, set up our stove and cookware, and enjoy the fresh air. Because of our timid approach to camping and hiking, our seven-hour hike in July 2004 became legendary to us. It also was a milestone in Darlene's record of recovery from breast cancer.

Spring was giving way to summer when our thirty-third wedding anniversary arrived on June 12, 2004. It was a Saturday, and we had a quiet day at home. We were already planning a summer camping trip to Glacier National Park in Montana on the Canadian border. We had considered other favorite camping areas like Yosemite and Joshua Tree, but we wanted to see something new. It was a good choice. The mountains, valleys, and waterfalls of Glacier proved to be as inspiring as any we had ever seen, rivaling and sometimes exceeding the sights in our beloved Yosemite.

Darlene's hair had begun to grow again after chemo, and she had it trimmed just before the trip. There was just enough hair to make the trim worthwhile, and she was pleased that she wouldn't need a wig for the trip. Another step in the right direction.

We hadn't heard of Kalispell, Montana, until I began searching online for flights to Glacier National Park. The park's website suggested flying to Kalispell, so I looked it up on a map. It was super convenient and only a short drive from there into the park. I found a flight that would take us to Kalispell after a stop in Minneapolis.

One minor problem happened on that trip. At the Indianapolis airport, I heard my name being called on the PA system. I quickly reported to the ticket agent and learned that the hyperactive security people had confiscated the gas tank from our thirty-four-year-old camp stove, one of our most prized possessions. I had emptied the tank several days before the trip and left it open to dry out, but the security people could detect that it had once contained white gas and therefore decided it might blow up the plane. At least they didn't confiscate the rest of the stove.

The Kalispell airport was blessedly small. We quickly signed for the rental car, collected our luggage, and stepped outside. Our red Ford Explorer was about fifteen steps from the door, and it was a short drive to the Red Lion Inn for the night.

First thing the next morning, we went to Snappy's Sport Senter [*sic*], or SSS, for a camp stove tank. It was almost worth the entire trip just to visit Snappy's and learn of its ancient roots. Inside we encountered a riot of camping and sporting goods filling the shelves and walls, crowding the aisles, and hanging from the ceiling. We found a Coleman single-burner propane stove that screwed into the top of a propane bottle. Voila! The problem of the confiscated gas tank was solved.

Once inside Glacier National Park, we traveled on Going to the Sun Road and other park roads for four days, staying overnight in two of the park's historic lodges. Spectacular scenery spread out before us at every bend in the roads. Snowmelt fell on us in three places where the road hugged a cliff beneath a melting glacier. The mountains had the same rejuvenating effect on us as always, maybe more so in this setting.

We then entered Canada's Waterton Lakes National Park on the north side of Glacier and stayed two nights at the Prince of Wales Hotel. At that dramatic old hotel, we took minimal luggage up to our room because we had to climb a narrow, winding stair high into one of the hotel's steep-peaked roofs to reach our room. Two twin beds faced each other foot-to-foot under the steeply sloping ceiling. Howling winds came up the lake and whistled around our windows all night. We loved the cozy feel of snuggling under comforters for our bedtime reading.

We continued farther north into Canada to Lake Louise in Banff National Park. The Lake Louise campground entrance had all the charm of a Nazi concentration camp: A high, electrified, barbed wire fence was strung between concrete posts that looked like upended railroad ties. There was a good reason for this bristling aura of defense: Grizzly bears were in the area. The high-voltage electrical grid on the road was intended to discourage bears from walking through the entrance for a dinner with campers or a dinner *of* the campers themselves. Grizzlies are dangerous carnivores.

Our campsite was as tidy and manicured as any we had ever used. The tent spot was elevated above the surrounding gravel by a border of 4×4 beams that enclosed a pad of smooth clay. Dinner that night was one of our simple camping concoctions of canned beef stew heated on our one-burner stove, bread, and fresh fruit. Surrounded by tall trees dripping with dew, we felt we were in a kind of fairy world populated by elves, not bears.

Lake Louise is a glacial lake at the base of mountains that frame it on three sides. In front of the lake stands the Chateau Lake Louise hotel. The main attraction in the area is the lake and the hiking trail to the Plain of Six Glaciers. People from all over the world come to see the lake's beauty, and the brave ones take the hiking trail to the famous Tea House at the very top of the trail.

On the day after our arrival, we filled our backpack with a picnic lunch and water bottles and started up the trail in clear, warm weather. We didn't know how far we would feel like hiking, but Darlene wished we could go all the way to the Tea House. "Tea House" was more than a name. We were told that there would be actual tea and other food there. It was delivered by pack mules and helicopters, since there is no real road to the place. Darlene was eager and enthusiastic, and I was cautiously optimistic—or maybe pessimistically cautious.

I was okay as we hiked along the shore of the strangely pale blue lake. The trail was level there. When we were a little beyond the lake and ascending the mountain, I began pleading with Darlene for a rest stop. She relented and allowed me to sit on a stump for a few minutes, but then she wanted to push on. I put the backpack on again and began videotaping Darlene hiking on ahead of me.

I was getting tired and a little hungry, so I began whining and asking Darlene if we could *please* stop and have lunch. I thought we had hiked far enough. She was kind and allowed me to have a sandwich, and she ate something too. When we finished that little lunch, I was ready to go back to the car. She pointed to a turn in the trail not too far ahead.

"Let's just go to that turn and see what's on the other side," she said in a voice that made it sound reasonable and not life-threatening.

We hiked on to that turn in the trail and saw an innocent, fairly level stretch of trail ahead before the trail turned again. Down below was a jumble of boulders that had been pushed down when the glaciers had been active. A small lake shimmered below, and mountains rimmed the Plain of Six Glaciers above.

"Let's go on just a little farther," Darlene suggested, pointing to the next turn at another shoulder of mountain.

By then I was catching some of her enthusiasm, but I kept up some whining, all of which was going into the video recording. I quit whining as we gained altitude and the majestic views expanded.

We continued in this pattern for the rest of the morning: First one of us and then the other would urge that we go just a little farther. We met other hikers who had already made it to the Tea House and were on the downward trail, and they all claimed we didn't have far to go. We believed them and continued. We saw mile markers that reported greater distances than the hikers had said, but still we continued. Near the top, we were exhilarated by the realization that we were going to make it. We rounded another turn in the trail, and the two-story log Tea House came into view like a glimpse of the Promised Land. We had made it!

At last we climbed the stairs to the upper level of the Tea House and were seated at a table on an outside porch. We couldn't stop congratulating ourselves on our long hike and were throbbing with a feeling of good health. When the waitress came, we had tea, since this was a tea house, and we ate a little more of our picnic lunch. To cap it off, we each had a tall square of dark chocolate cake with dark chocolate frosting. It was an ecstatic pleasure.

After a brief rest, we descended from the Tea House restaurant porch and prepared for the hike down to the parking lot. Before we began our descent, a fellow hiker used our camera to capture a pose of us that would become one of our best photos ever. We both looked unabashedly triumphant and joyful with the Canadian Rockies towering behind us. Darlene was grinning and holding my arm. Life was good.

The return trip was all downhill, something for which we were immensely grateful, but it was still a long hike. We fairly whizzed along compared to our slower upward trip. The turns seemed to come rapidly, and I was not whining. I was bragging on us as though it had been *my* idea to take such a recklessly long hike.

At the bottom of the trail, we looked at our rental car at the far end of the parking lot. The parking lot seemed much larger than it had been that morning. We looked at each other, sighed, and shrugged.

"Do you think we should just crawl back to the car?" Darlene asked.

"We may have to," I said, "but let's walk as far as we can."

We walked all the way to the car, flung our gear in the back, and climbed in.

"We did it!" Darlene exclaimed.

"We sure did," I said, hugging her and shaking my head in wonder.

That hike was the highlight of a trip that included many other wonders. Whenever we talked later about our trip to Glacier, we mainly talked about our seven-hour hike at Lake Louise. It had been an 8.7-mile hike with an elevation gain of 1,280 feet, which for us was a huge accomplishment. We had left at ten in the morning and reached our car at five in the evening. We were amazed that we walked that long and that far. Sometimes we admitted that younger, stronger hikers probably made the same hike in three or four hours or even less, rather than our seven hours.

Soon after we returned from the trip, Darlene had an oncology appointment with Dr. Storniolo. We were eager to tell her about our seven-hour hike. On July 11, 2004, I made the following journal entry:

> *Yesterday Darlene began assembling questions for our meetings this week with Drs. Storniolo and Goulet. She talked calmly and frankly about what it will mean if the spots in her back bones*

> turn out to have been malignancies. She is considering not having the next PET scan until after Jenny's wedding on September 18 unless there would be clear treatment advantages in finding out earlier about metastases. She thinks that treatment could only be for comfort, not for cure, if the cancer had spread. We noted again that the trip to Glacier might be our last camping trip, but we also keep talking about possible future camping trips, even one to Yosemite this fall.

"So how was your trip?" Dr. Storniolo asked when the appointment time arrived. "You went somewhere out West, didn't you?"

Darlene was excited to tell the story. She began with the spectacular mountain scenes in Glacier and the little waterfalls that had splashed on our car as we drove under them. Then she announced, "We also made one of our biggest hikes."

She glanced at me, and I waited for her to continue.

"We hadn't been able to take a long hike early in the trip due to all the places we wanted to see, so we decided to take a long one near the end of the trip. At Lake Louise, near Banff, we found a trail to a mountain bowl called The Plain of the Six Glaciers. Well, we hiked all the way up to the Tea House at the top and back down again. It took us seven hours!"

Dr. Storniolo's jaw dropped. She plopped down in a chair, her mouth still open. "You *did*? I can't tell this to any of my other patients! You were just six weeks out of radiation, and you made this hike? I have patients who have been out of radiation since February, and they still can't do their *housework!*"

Darlene smiled proudly. I laughed triumphantly. With that hike, we had purchased a story that became one of our favorites, the story of the seven-hour hike, our longest hike ever. Maybe Darlene was somehow nuclear powered after being "nuked" all those times in radiation therapy. Maybe she was just a very strong woman, determined to make the most of her life when it had seemed it might be nearing its end.

At that meeting, Dr. Storniolo told Darlene that her chance of survival wouldn't be harmed by waiting until after Jenny's wedding for the next PET and CT scans. Darlene decided she was willing to take a risk to avoid the possibility of upsetting Jenny's wedding. She waited.

67

A Wedding and a Gift

After our July meeting with Dr. Storniolo, I told Darlene that I was amazed at how calmly she could talk about things that were so serious for her. She said she "owed that to Daddy." Her dad, Grada Sayers, always took things straight-on and refused to worry about things he couldn't control. Her attitude set the tone for both of us, and I followed her lead as best I could. Jenny's upcoming wedding kept our minds from dwelling on Darlene's health issues.

In September, as Jenny's wedding day approached, Darlene and I felt both joy and apprehension. Darlene was doing well, looked good, and no longer needed a wig. She was living life fully, defying the odds. Still, we both knew that she would have another PET scan and CT scan after the wedding to see if she was still clear of cancer. There could be bad news.

On the morning of the wedding, I awoke feeling sad. My feeling, I felt certain, came from the sense of loss in seeing Jenny marry and move away from us. No doubt it came also from the knowledge that Darlene might be coming to the end of a period of health, happiness, and energy if her tests on September 22 and 27 revealed that the cancer had spread.

It had been a gift from God already that we'd had those months after the PET scan in February when the test result was negative. It would be another great gift if her PET and CAT scans were again negative.

Jenny and Chad's wedding went beautifully. My feelings of sadness and worry were chased away by the joy of the day. Darlene looked beautiful, and we were both thankful that God had given Jenny such a good husband, just as he had provided Greg as a husband for our daughter Anna a year earlier.

Among the many guests for the event were Cliff and Elsie Rasmussen, Chad's grandparents from Nebraska. Both were in their late eighties, but they were wonderful dancers. Everyone loved their lively, expert dancing at the reception, and we all felt younger.

Four days after the wedding, Darlene had a full-body PET scan to determine whether tumors were growing anywhere. She was calm, active, and optimistic as she awaited the results, even though many lymph glands had been affected by the breast tumors.

The results were a gift from God! Her PET scan was clear. It was the best news we'd had on her health in a year, and more good news came soon after. On October 11, I wrote the following in my journal:

> *Darlene's CAT scan was also clear, and we had a good meeting with Dr. Storniolo on Tuesday, October 5. We won't see her again until January 2005! Thank you, Jesus, for your healing, protecting touch!*

With that news, Darlene's cancer treatments and concerns receded from my journal for a time. "Normal life" overtook us, and we enjoyed the autumn time of our lives with new awareness of how precious it was. In November, Anna and Greg told us they were expecting a baby in April 2005, our first grandchild.

68

The Road Clears

*N*early seventeen months after her first cancer diagnosis, Darlene had another PET scan on March 17, 2005, to follow up on the clean scan five months earlier. This scan was to determine whether the spots on her bones were tumors or only what doctors called "bone islands." On March 18, she simply sent me an email to tell me her PET scan the previous day was clear. I called her and cried on the phone as we talked. I had been praying to Jesus that her bones would be protected and her life preserved. And so it was. The road ahead was clear, and our spirits were soaring.

Back in July 2003, while we were camping in southwest Colorado, we had hatched up a plan for a camping trip in 2005 with our whole family. When cancer struck in September 2003, we stopped thinking of the 2005 all-family camping trip. For a time, neither Darlene nor I expected her to be living in 2005.

But God had intervened: The cancer cells that had been released from the affected lymph nodes had not congregated to form tumors. Darlene had bounced back from the mastectomy. We had made our seven-hour hike only six weeks after she finished radiation. And she had worked every day during radiation and continued to work a full schedule.

The 2005 camping trip was back on the agenda, but with modifications. Jenny and Chad were married, and he probably would make the trip with us. Anna and Greg were expecting their first child in April, and they might be able to come with Anna and the baby. Matt would come, but Kathryn was unlikely to make the trip with us.

In January 2005, Darlene and I went to a travel show at the Indiana State Fairgrounds and roamed among dozens of camping trailers and motor homes. The smell of fresh plastic and rubber was intoxicating. We were excited about those little houses on wheels. She decided it was time for us to have a trailer rather than continue to sleep on the ground in our tent, as we had been doing since 1971. After all, I was sixty-five years old, and she would soon be sixty. So we bought a travel trailer that matched our style perfectly and would accommodate our growing family of in-law kids and a grandchild.

It was a hybrid trailer with all the decadent pleasures of a full-scale travel trailer: gas cook stoves inside and outside; gas and microwave ovens; air conditioning; furnace; hot water heater; tiny bathroom with stool, shower, and sink; and even an FM radio and CD player. The main beds were on platforms that tipped outside the trailer to conserve interior floor space and were covered by tents like those on pop-up trailers. There was a queen-sized bed at each end of the trailer, a full-sized bed on one side, and a couch bed inside. We were ready for the 2005 family trip that had so recently seemed impossible.

Darlene and I made our very first trip with the trailer to Bloomington, Indiana, to see Anna and Greg while they awaited their first baby. We arrived after dark on our way farther south for camping. They admired our landed "ship," resplendent with red and yellow running lights at all corners. We gave them a complete tour of the trailer and then set off into the night to find a campsite.

Although Darlene and I were experienced campers, or maybe because of it, we didn't think enough about the possible trouble we could have setting up the trailer for the first time. The fact that we would have to set it up in complete darkness didn't worry us. We also didn't reckon with the problem of finding a campsite late at night.

At one point in our search, I took us down a gravel lane that ended in a farm pasture. I attempted to make a large circular turn in the pasture but couldn't complete the turn without backing up. I backed up in the dark, and the trailer ran over a stump or something—I never knew what. After we got out of that dead-end situation, we found a campground that happened to be on a llama ranch. Yes, llamas, the furry critters from the Andes Mountains.

Once inside the campground, we moved slowly through the dark until we found a pull-through campsite that seemed right for us. With headlamps and flashlights, we managed to stabilize the trailer and hook up the water and electricity. That night we slept in the trailer for the first time. It was a wonderful refuge from the pressures of our professional lives and the recent medical crises. The chilly night air felt like dozens of our camping nights out West.

The next morning, when we peeked out the windows, we seemed to be in rural South America. Llamas grazed placidly, a few goats scampered among them, and free-range chickens pecked at bugs and seeds in the gravel barnyard. And there we were, cooking breakfast in our little playhouse on wheels. We felt healthy and wealthy that day. The maiden voyage with our land-based cruise ship was a success. The way was clear for us to head for the West again and fulfill our dream of one more all-family camping trip.

69

The First Grandchild

Darlene and I were surprised when Anna told us in November 2004 that she was expecting a baby. She was only twenty-four; Darlene had been twenty-five when we were married, and our first baby was born when she was thirty-one. We were surprised and happy. From then on, we lived with happy awareness that we would soon be grandparents.

In early April, Anna began to have false contractions, but by April 7 they were becoming intense. She went to the hospital on April 8, and her doctor induced labor. She called us, and we jumped into action. This was the real thing! Darlene and I put on appropriate "first-time grandparent clothes," which means whatever we could lay our hands on in a hurry, and we headed south from Indianapolis to Bloomington. We were in a race with a baby wanting to see the light of day.

Sometime in the afternoon, Greg emerged from the delivery room. "Anna is having a rough time," he reported. "She's still in labor, but the baby isn't coming out. Also, the baby isn't pointing the right direction. He's facing forward instead of backward. They might have to do a C-section."

The growing tribe of expectant relatives watched as the sun began to dip lower in the afternoon sky. Greg came out again for just a minute. "They're going to do a C-section in a few minutes. Stay tuned."

Darlene and I could only imagine what it might be like to see our first grandchild. Excited conversation was swirling within the welcoming party when Greg came out of the delivery room once more.

"Well, we have a boy!" he announced. "And Anna is doing okay, but it was harder than we expected. Give us a little time and you can come to see the baby."

There were hugs all around and happy, nervous talk while we waited to see the new baby boy. When Greg summoned us, we all trooped in: the four grandparents and Matt and Kathryn. We formed a semicircle around the foot of Anna's bed. She was smiling proudly. We in the audience looked on adoringly and awaited the baby's name.

"I know you all want to know his name," Greg began, and we all took a deep breath. Looking at Anna, he continued, "I think Anna should have the honor of announcing his name."

Anna looked down at the baby in her arms. "We have decided to name him Jacob Sayers Herman."

A collective gasp came from the audience and then, "Wow! Jacob! Can we call him Jake? Sayers is such a good middle name!" and so on.

When Dr. Grandma Darlene was given a chance to hold baby Jacob, she gazed at him lovingly for a minute or two, but then her professional training took over. She stepped to the changing table at the foot of the bed, laid the baby down, and began to unwrap his blankets. Soon he was down to his tiny diaper. She moved his arms and legs and probed gently at his abdomen. We all laughed to see her unbridled curiosity about the developmental condition of her first grandchild.

"What do you think, Doctor?" I asked. "Does he meet your approval?"

"Oh, yes!" Dr. Grandma Darlene exclaimed. Setting aside all the technicalities of more rigorous medical measures of newborns, she announced, "He's perfect!"

70

The Big 2005 Trip

The big 2005 trip began on July 20. Our plan was to spend three days in Alva, in northwestern Oklahoma, for a reunion of my mother's family, the Bruners. My grandpa Bruner, a pioneer, had staked a claim in Woods County as a homesteader on a farm about fifteen miles south of Alva. The descendants of that first Bruner family had been meeting every two years in various places for over twenty years. Cousins gathered from coast to coast and from Alaska to Mexico, and we had an economic impact on any city where we met.

The logistics of the trip were complex. Darlene, Matt, and I drove the Suburban and pulled the trailer from Indianapolis to Alva. Jenny, Chad, Anna, and Greg flew from Detroit to Oklahoma City with three-month-old Jacob. The five of them then drove to Alva in a rental car.

The daytime temperatures in Alva that summer were averaging 112 degrees. Darlene, Matt, and I arrived in shimmering heat and set up the trailer in the steamy, graveled truck parking area at the Western Motel, where our family had stayed during several Bruner reunions since 1982. We strung our extra-long, heavy-duty extension cord from a power pole to the trailer so the trailer's air conditioner could keep five of us comfortable. Anna, Greg, and baby Jacob stayed in the motel.

The reunion with the Bruner family was from Friday to Sunday. Church volunteers and local family members set up a reception center in the Church of God, and we ate some of our meals there. A program of singing and story-telling was augmented by genealogical information from Aunt Irma, my mother's sister. As we had at every reunion we sang "O Kansas Land," a whimsical song that had become the family's national anthem.

After the reunion, Anna and Greg were scheduled to fly back to Detroit with the baby so Greg could get back to his work at the Ford Motor Company while the rest of us continued our trip. As planned, they left Alva after lunch on Sunday, but I soon had a call from Anna. They had stopped at a large filling station and convenience store outside Medford, Oklahoma, fifty miles straight east of Alva. Greg had to go on to Oklahoma City for his flight, but she wondered if we could work it out so she and Jacob could go with us to Colorado. She had felt sad about missing the rest of the family trip. With the help of my brother Owen and his rental car, I was able to retrieve Anna and Jake from the gas station where they had taken refuge. Within an hour, the Colorado travelers were assembled for our drive west.

Our Chevy Suburban had a beefy V-8 engine, a towing package, and seating for seven. When we were ready to set out for Colorado late Sunday afternoon in the sweltering heat, every seat in the seven-passenger vehicle was taken. Matt and I were in the front. Jenny and Chad were behind us. Jake was in the far back seat, wedged in between Anna and Grandma Darlene. Still new at pulling a trailer, I mistakenly dragged it through a shallow ditch while making a U-turn through a parking lot in Alva. From then on, I had several people supervising my driving, advising me to "pull wide" for every turn.

By 11 p.m. we had reached the cooler altitude of La Junta, Colorado, and set up the trailer in a broad, sandy campsite. The next day we stopped at the Colorado Springs Airport so Jenny and Chad could rent a car to relieve crowding in the Suburban for the remainder of the trip. We then stocked up on supplies before entering the mountains.

We arrived at the Blue Mountain Campground near Lake George in early afternoon. Campsite 13 did not have enough level space for the trailer, so we chose a place on the other side of the campground. We were far from the outhouse that had attracted us to Campsite 13 in 1978, but we had brought our own restroom with us in the trailer. Like the Eagle Scout he was, Matt decided to sleep the first night in our small tent next to our picnic table rather than in the trailer with the rest of us.

Near bedtime on the second night, we heard a tremendous crash from the direction of Campsite 13. We surmised, correctly, that a bear was raiding the trash bin next to Campsite 13's outhouse. The next morning, we saw the overturned trash bin and more: There were bear tracks in a mud puddle beside the tented bed where Anna and baby Jacob had slept that night. Our collapsible five-gallon water jug on the picnic table next to Matt's tent had been pierced by bear teeth. Matt gathered up his clothes and sleeping bag and slept in the trailer with the rest of us after that.

Despite the bear scare, we had an idyllic day of fishing for trout on the South Platte River in Eleven Mile Canyon, adjacent to our campground. Darlene and Anna took turns with baby Jake high on the shore while the rest of us floated our baited hooks into deep, emerald-colored pools between small rapids. Time and again, an unseen force deep in the water grabbed the bait and dived under a boulder. Up came a glistening, beautiful trout.

When nearly everyone had caught a fish, we took our catch to the campground for dinner. Because of the bear episode in the night, I cleaned the trout in an unoccupied campsite about 75 yards from the trailer and carried the trout remains to the distant trash bin. We didn't want to do anything to encourage that curious bear. We had a feast of rainbow trout, and no sounds or thoughts of bears disturbed our sleep that night.

The next day, a gentle rain began in the afternoon and continued all night. Jenny and Chad took their rental car to see friends in Colorado Springs while the rest of us huddled snugly in the trailer. I baked a gooseberry pie, and we told stories, sang songs, and enjoyed the soft whisper of the mountain rain.

When it was time to leave, the long trip home stretched out dauntingly before us. We pondered the logistics of getting Anna and Jacob home to Detroit. We had intended to take them back with us in the Suburban, but they would have ended up in Indianapolis with no way to get on to Detroit unless we drove them. The long, hot trip did not seem good for the baby or his mother. Greg said he could meet Anna and Jake at the Detroit airport if we could find a way to fly them there.

I remembered that I had built up frequent flier miles on my credit card. I had never tried to use those miles, and I wasn't sure about the rules, but it seemed worth a try. There was no cell phone service there, so I left everyone at the campsite and went to a bar in Lake George to use the phone. The owner directed me to the pay phone in a hot, dusty hallway. I called the number on the back of my credit card and learned that I could get a free ticket for Anna and baby Jake just by showing up with them at the Colorado Springs airport.

The next day, we put Anna and Jake on a plane to Detroit. It was a relief for everyone to know they would be at home that night rather than bouncing along with us overland for two or three days. The rest of us pointed our "covered wagon" toward the lush, green hills in the Land of the Hoosier.

Our dream of one final family camping trip to Colorado had been fulfilled.

71

Peaceful Years 2005 to 2008

*I*n January 2004, Darlene's prognosis was so poor we thought she might die that year. But all the tests later that year were clear, and we slipped into a smoother stream of life as 2005 began. It is said that good news does not make big news, but these four years were eventful and rich. A few highlights may be enough to convey the flavor of our lives.

In November 2004, while she was still under the shadow of cancer tests, Darlene ran a conference at our church on Down syndrome for parents and medical practitioners. Researchers and practitioners spoke in sessions all day. It was a victorious moment for Darlene. She enlisted our immediate family, and church volunteers joined Riley Hospital staff members to arrange the rooms and offer directions to visitors.

In January 2005, I informed the Sycamore Board of my intention to retire on June 30, 2006. I released a letter to the parents explaining that by 2006 I would have been at Sycamore for thirteen years, and I would be sixty-six years old. The early announcement was good private school practice, and it gave the Board time to plan their search for my replacement.

I had been invited to a Liberty Fund conference at a resort in Tucson, Arizona, in February 2005. Darlene went with me and lived as a vacationer while I was in conference meetings. It was like a taste of what we thought retirement might be. We took afternoon hikes in the desert, waded in a shallow stream in our new hiking boots, and were like newlyweds again. One evening I found her eating alone at one end of the resort's dining room where I had come to have dinner with the other conferees. Her dinner had arrived, and she had a book propped open on the table. She was at peace and beautiful, enjoying the moment. I stopped and we talked. It was like flirting with my own wife.

That summer we took the all-family trailer trip to Colorado that I have reported elsewhere, and we entered a period that resembled normal life. Darlene and I were immersed in our work, and any spare time was for home, family, and church activities. All of our kids were away from home now. Jenny and Anna were married, and Matt was away at college in 2005.

Like most married couples, our lives were mainly filled with the small, repetitive things of life. We had our morning coffee and prayer time together, then started the race to work. Darlene often took a breakfast of yogurt topped with Grape Nuts cereal and fruit in a plastic box. At the hospital, she could eat in her office while she checked her overnight email and finished dictating charts. I was usually the first one home in the evening, so I cooked the majority of our meals. If we couldn't eat together, we talked while she had a reheated dinner later. When we both worked late, we often had a dinner of oatmeal. Fortunately, we both thought oatmeal made a fine late dinner, and we often gave thanks that we both liked leftovers: free, fast, and the food often tasted better the second or third time around.

We often had pancakes and bacon on Saturday mornings, just as we had in Wisconsin when the children were at home. We ran errands on Saturdays and sometimes went to a movie or a party in the evening. Sundays were church days, often with an early start for her choir practice. I started teaching a class in 2004, so I had a reason to go early, too. We often came home for a late breakfast, afternoon naps, and sometimes a Netflix movie together in the evening. We were inveterate homebodies.

A fact of married life, at least our married life, is that it tends to be dominated by work and other responsibilities. Being married did not mean being preoccupied with an endless string of entertainments, hobbies, or complex social life. It did not mean being continually absorbed in marital romance, either. It was a good life, but it was never simple.

When I retired from Sycamore School in 2006, the school gave me a travel voucher as a parting gift. We decided to spend the voucher on a trip to Europe that would include a conference of Darlene's and some places we had both wanted to visit. We charted out an overly ambitious itinerary that started in Paris, included time in Poland, and ended in Vienna.

A few weeks before the trip, Darlene asked if we should take Matt with us. He was between college and med school and hadn't lined up a summer job. He would soon be engaged to Kathryn, and they would marry in May 2007. We thought he would enjoy the trip before the rigors of medical school, and he could help us with our luggage and logistics. He agreed to go, and we later wondered how we would have survived the trip without him. It was a beastly hot summer in Europe, and we were on and off trains, planes, and automobiles all summer. Matt was a strong young man and could wrestle our luggage on and off trains with ease. He was better at map reading than either of us, or we might have turned up missing that summer.

Our trip began with Darlene's conference in an industrial area on the north side of Paris. While she attended sessions of the World Conference on Infant Mental Health, Matt and I took the Metro to tourist sites: the Eiffel Tower, the Louvre, and the Monet museum. One night we lay in the grass in front of the Eiffel Tower while he took long exposure photos.

When Darlene's conference ended, we flew to Gdansk, Poland. On the cab ride from the airport, we saw only Soviet-era concrete apartment blocks of indescribable ugliness. I wondered if going there had been a mistake. But our hotel was on the edge of the old medieval city of Danzig, and the more humane ways of earlier times were alive, well, and happy. Our primary object in going to Poland was to visit Slupsk, the city that had been the home of Kardatzke ancestors before the family immigrated to America. Slupsk had been the Prussian city of Stolp for nearly a thousand years before World War II, but it became the Polish city of Slupsk when Soviet Russia expelled all Germans and installed Poles. From Poland, we went to Prague, and it lived up to the rave reviews we had heard from friends. A concert in a beautiful church near the Charles Bridge was like being inside a Christmas ornament. A four-hour train ride took us to Vienna, the place Darlene most wanted to see. She took us to the Sigmund Freud Museum at the psychiatrist's former office. We visited the Heeresgeschichtliches Museum and saw the car in which Archduke

Franz Ferdinand and his wife Sophie were assassinated in 1914, the opening shots of the First World War.

Back in Indiana, Darlene went back to work, and I soon began work as a Senior Fellow at Liberty Fund, an educational foundation I had valued since my days as an economics graduate student. I had used Liberty Fund materials when I taught at Marquette University and at Brookfield Academy, so for me this was a celebrity appointment. The work took me back to my economics roots for a final brief career.

In my new job at Liberty Fund, my main role was managing seminars for academics and professional people in hotels and resorts around the U.S. and in other countries. The seminars explored the nature of freedom and responsibility through readings in literature, philosophy, theology, political science, and economics. It was like returning to graduate school but in many disciplines, not just economics.

Darlene went with me to some of those weekend conferences; I had to pay her expenses but all of mine were covered. We shared my hotel rooms, and we paid for everything else for her. Her first trip with me was to Tucson, and the next was to Savannah with her two sisters while I handled conferences in both places in fall 2006. The most amazing trip we had for Liberty Fund was to a conference in July 2007 at a retreat center on Lake Como in northern Italy. It was one of the most beautiful places either of us had ever seen. When I had free time, we took short excursions along the lake. When I was busy, Darlene went shopping at Bellagio, a renowned resort that was a short boat ride across the lake from the conference hotel. She only *looked* at the pricey items in the shops there. After the conference, we stayed three more days in the town of Como and took a short train trip to Milan. The Milan Cathedral was one of the highlights of the trip and included a stroll around the roof of that great church. We wondered if such a building could be built now, or even be imagined.

Jenny was pregnant in 2007, and Darlene was thrilled that a second grandson was on the way. We bought plane tickets for a trip to Houston just prior to the baby's due date. Jenny's doctor induced labor, and we were in the hallway outside the delivery room door when little Samuel Wayne Rasmussen announced his arrival with healthy cries. Darlene and I jumped up and hugged and shouted. A male nurse at the nearby nurses' station seemed startled and puzzled. We thought he should have been accustomed to such goings on in his line of work.

In 2007 and 2008, our lives were rich and full. Darlene continued her very full-time work in the hospital, and I had many more Liberty Fund conferences, mostly in the United States. Darlene went with me on a few more trips, and I made several alone when she couldn't spare the time away from the hospital. She went with me to a conference in San Diego, and she was thrilled when I rented a convertible for her to drive while I was busy in meetings. For a moment she was embarrassed at the extravagance, but pictures show her beaming when she drove it with the top down, her hair streaming behind her head.

On March 1, 2008, we flew to Los Angeles for a Liberty Fund conference that would start five days later. This was our chance to go back to our romantic roots at Joshua Tree National Park, where we had learned to camp on the weekend we were engaged. Our rental car was just big enough for our camping gear and luggage, and we were soon on our way east on Interstate 10. At the top of a rise, our field of view was suddenly filled with the sight of gigantic wind turbines that seemed like Quixotic monsters, slashing the air above the otherwise peaceful mountainsides. We began to dislike those unaesthetic machines. Joshua Tree itself was as we remembered, except this was still technically winter, and we were in the high desert where winter temperatures can go below zero. We pitched our tent in an open area and nearly froze that night. Even our reliable mountain bags were not warm. We didn't have a thermometer, but it was surely the coldest place we ever camped. The next day we went into the town of Joshua Tree and bought warmer clothes in an all-purpose drug store. The next night was better, but still very cold. We were willing to give up camping and return to the warmth of Santa Monica on the Pacific coast. We had renewed our friendship with the desert where camping life had propelled us into marriage in 1971.

In July 2008, Darlene and I pulled the trailer to Wichita for a Kardatzke family reunion. We camped in a commercial campground on the west side of the city for the weekend reunion at the home of one of my three Kardatzke cousins who had grown up in Wichita. We then headed for the mountains to begin planning an all-family trip to Estes Park in 2009. We scouted out places to stay on that trip, including a collection of large rental homes in Estes Park.

Darlene had always loved Rocky Mountain National Park, and we took three drives into the park that summer. There were two poignant moments. We went to the Forest Canyon Overlook where a viewing point stands at the rim of a deep canyon, and the river below is barely visible. Across the canyon is a mountainside with curious rims and valleys of its own. Off to the east, clouds hung over a range of mountains in the middle distance. Darlene looked into the canyon in all directions while I took pictures of her in her camping hat and sweater. The beauty of the place clearly spoke to her in poetic or even spiritual terms, and I know that her mind had been on her precarious future.

Two days later, we roamed in our car at a lower altitude. We had packed a lunch, and we found an inviting picnic site called Upper Beaver Meadows. She unpacked our lunch while I brought out our lawn chairs. After lunch, I set up the lawn chairs facing the meadows that sprawled across a valley just beyond a rock outcropping. When I saw Darlene sitting peacefully gazing at the rock formation and the meadow, I took pictures of her in that reflective mood. Retirement had been on her mind for months, and it was now less than a year from her projected retirement date. I labeled one of the pictures "Darlene Retired." I made prints of that photo three years later when its full meaning became clear to the family.

When I was a teenager, I plowed wheat fields in Oklahoma after the wheat harvest in three summers starting in 1956. I was working for my uncle Silbert Lanman, husband of my mother's sister Ella. Uncle Silbert was a public school principal during the school year and a wheat farmer at planting and harvest times. Known to me as "Uncle Sib," he was a joker and a teaser who loved kids and kept us guessing about what he might do next. He was a favorite uncle. While on a visit with two of his daughters in Alaska, Uncle Sib had died of a heart attack on December 31, 1987. His body was flown to Oklahoma, and he was buried during a furious blizzard in January 1988.

My Aunt Ella was in Alaska visiting their children when she, too, died there in November 2008. Ella was to have a funeral in Hutchinson, Kansas, where she had lived in her later years, and a second funeral in Alva, Oklahoma, where she and Uncle Sib had lived in retirement not far from their birthplaces on farms. Because of my close relationship with Sib and Ella's family, Darlene and I went to Hutchinson for the first of Aunt Ella's two funerals on Thanksgiving Day. Alva, Oklahoma, is 125 miles southwest of Hutchinson, and we decided to start the trip on Thanksgiving evening. The route took us southwest to Pratt, Kansas, and then directly south to Alva. We planned to spend the night in Pratt.

As we drove into Pratt looking for a motel at 6:00 p.m., all the businesses were closing. Even Pizza Hut was closing. We hadn't thought of the fact that it was Thanksgiving night. We drove all the way through town looking for a place to eat, and it was looking grim. We turned around at the end of town, and we could see that nearly all restaurants were closed. We thought we might have to buy sandwiches at a gas station. Darlene then remembered that we had passed the Pratt County Regional Medical Center. "They probably have a cafeteria," she said. "They have to feed the patients and visitors. Maybe we can eat there." We pulled in at the hospital and found a side door unlocked. A maintenance man saw us looking for directions and asked, "Are you looking for somebody?"

"We're looking for the cafeteria," Darlene said confidently like the doctor she was.

"It's right down that hallway," the man told us, "but you better go right away. They'll be cleaning it up pretty soon."

The cafeteria was open, but we were the only prospective customers. A complete Thanksgiving dinner was laid out in the warmers in a glass case: turkey, dressing, mashed potatoes, gravy, sweet potatoes, cranberry sauce, overcooked vegetables, bread, and pie and cake, plus drinks.

We went through the line and asked the serving lady to fill our plates with everything they had. We took our trays to a table, and Darlene went back to pay. She came back to the table and told me in a secretive voice, "It was only $3.00 each! I told the lady, 'That's a real bargain,' and she said, 'Well, we do it for our visitors. You *are* visitors, aren't you?' I told her, 'Yes, we're visitors.'" She laughed softly and told me to start eating. We were, in truth, visitors to Pratt, but we weren't visiting anyone at the hospital that night. We quickly ate our bargain dinner and cleared out before anyone came to ask questions.

During Aunt Ella's funeral in Alva, fine scriptures were read, and we sang familiar hymns. My cousin, Kim Lanman, is a pastor, and he led the service. He asked if anyone present would like to share some memories of Ella Lanman. There was a respectful silence that went on a little too long, so I volunteered to speak. I went up front and began to tell my story.

"I have been fortunate to be almost a part of Sib and Ella's family," I began. "Uncle Sib invited me to come out and plow wheat land for him when I was in high school so he could follow the harvest north. I plowed the farms near Dacoma and Capron.

"Aunt Ella was so kind to me. She took me in like one of her own kids. One day while Uncle Sib was up north in the harvest, I ran out of water out in the field and came in so thirsty I couldn't eat. She fixed two quarts of Kool-Aid for me, and I drank all of it. I was too hot and tired to eat. I told Aunt Ella I wanted to go straight to bed. She looked me over and must have shuddered. I was covered with sweat-caked red dust.

'Can you take a bath before you go to bed?' she asked.

"I was so tired that I didn't want to take a bath, but her pleading tone of voice told me I should. The bath water that night probably could have supported a small crop of wheat."

My speech went on. "As you all know, Aunt Ella was a real saint. Not only did she put up with me as an unwashed farm hand, she put up with a lot of distress in life in her soft-spoken, kind way. But I heard Aunt Ella curse a number of times."

Startled people took deep breaths and braced themselves.

"Yes, I heard Aunt Ella curse. More than once I heard her say, 'Well, I never!' She also said, 'My lands!' And sometimes for emphasis she said, 'Boy, howdy.' Even a saint like Aunt Ella had her curse words."

I suspect some people silently thanked God when my talk was over. Darlene surely did.

72

Late Autumn: March 2009

Thanksgiving and Christmas 2008 were happy times. Our children and their spouses came, and the two grandsons entertained all the adults. Darlene's sisters and their families came and added their food to ours, and we repeated the beloved foods, games, songs, and traditions of both holidays. Darlene played the piano, and we sang "Let all Things Now Living" for Thanksgiving and many carols at Christmas. Life was wonderful, but Darlene had no illusions.

"I'm not a survivor," she said one day when she had passed the five-year mark since her mastectomy. "Not with that pathology report," she added, meaning the thirteen positive lymph nodes in 2004.

She said no more and went on with what she was doing.

In January 2009, I had cataract surgery on my left eye. This is an easy surgery that can clear your vision after years of seeing things through a haze. Because of the anesthesia involved, someone has to take you to and from the doctor's office, and Darlene was my driver on the way home. As Darlene drove me home, we heard forecasts of a blizzard that night, and it was already beginning to snow. We wondered how she would get me back to the doctor's office for the required next-day checkup.

The next morning, the snow was nine inches deep, and the Suburban, with its big engine, four-wheel drive, large tires, and hefty weight would be able to overrun the snow, but it was sitting outside in the driveway. It could make it through the snow, but could we get to the Suburban? I was not supposed to do any lifting or other physical work for a couple of days, so Darlene put on her warm black coat, gloves, and a hat and began to dig out the Suburban. I took pictures as she dug a path to the car for herself and one for me. We were among the very few cars on the snow-packed streets, and there was plenty of room in the parking lot at the eye clinic. The eye surgeon was surprised that we had made it there and had even arrived on time. The pictures of Darlene shoveling snow that day soon became poignant sights, freighted with meaning.

Darlene was saving vacation days for another Liberty Fund trip with me to Destin, Florida, in early March. The weather there might be spring-like, and she was ready for a few days away from the hospital. We were both looking forward to a spring trip to Florida.

PART FIVE

Wintertime: 2009 and 2010

73

Cancer Returns

The weather in Destin, Florida, was too cool for swimming, but the salt spray was refreshing and we weren't there for swimming. It was March 2009, and Darlene and her sister Beverly had accompanied me on a Liberty Fund trip. I was managing a conference on an esoteric comparison of Adam Smith and Jean-Jacques Rousseau. Cancer was far from our minds, or so I thought.

Darlene hadn't spent time with the older of her two sisters in several months, and this trip would give them time together to visit, shop, and eat out, all far away from Darlene's hectic schedule at the hospital. I would be working most of the time, but I would see Darlene during breaks between sessions and in the evenings.

The trip was also a time for Darlene to do what she rarely had time to do—go shopping with me. During one afternoon break, she and I went to an Eddie Bauer outlet store. She bought a couple of things for herself and insisted on buying three pairs of slacks and a shirt for me. That shopping trip would become an important memory for me.

"We should be very thankful that we can still walk this well at our ages," I said as we started on an afternoon walk to the beach. We were enjoying the sunshine and the brisk breeze, but Beverly was resting at the hotel.

"Yes," Darlene replied as we stepped over a curb and started down a concrete walk dusted with sand. "It's good to be able to walk."

Her next words were a shock. "I have made an appointment with Dr. Storniolo next week," she said. "I have had this annoying cough for a couple of weeks. Last week I coughed hard, and I have had a pain in my rib cage since then. I want to make sure it's nothing too serious." We completed the trip, but I was no longer at peace about her health.

After examining her, Dr. Storniolo, said "This may be just an ordinary cold. Let's do an X-ray just to be sure."

The X-ray revealed a cracked rib, evidently a result of her coughing episode. It also showed a spot on a lung. The spot warranted further investigation, so Dr. Storniolo ordered a CT scan, which would include a larger area. The CT scan showed a large abdominal mass just below her ribs. Her kidneys were enlarged too. Dr. Storniolo and Darlene were both alarmed. A second CT scan was scheduled for Friday morning, March 20. This scan would include all of Darlene's lower abdomen to explore the abdominal mass and her enlarged kidneys. Darlene calmly told me on Thursday evening of the new scan. She was apprehensive but calm, as always.

On Friday, the day of Darlene's scan, I had to be at Liberty Fund offices near our home to manage a seminar on the United States Constitution. The seminar would start at lunchtime on Friday, and the last session that day would end at 9:00 p.m. Meetings would continue all day Saturday. On that Friday morning, I wrote the following in my journal:

> *March 20, 2009. Darlene has a CT scan of her lower abdomen and pelvic area this morning. She had a chest CT scan on Tuesday, March 17, to follow up on the X-ray that revealed a spot on a lung. That CT scan showed a blockage from the kidneys. The blockage could damage the kidneys, so there is urgency about the diagnosis and treatment.*
>
> *Darlene has mentioned these things that are of concern: the kidneys and lungs, liver, pain in her hip, and the general concern for reproductive organs that are sometimes sites of cancer. We are praying that all these concerns will be dismissed or minimized by the CT scan today, but we are both very concerned.*

When the Friday evening session of my conference ended, I left immediately for home. Darlene was in the family room when I walked in. She seemed calm but serious. I took a seat next to her on the couch.

"I heard from Dr. Storniolo about the CT scan," she began. Everything she had feared was indeed present in the scan. "The cancer has spread. It's in my liver and bones and maybe my lungs. There's a large tumor in my abdomen. That's probably why the kidneys are enlarged."

She took a breath. "It's devastating."

I could only blink and listen. I leaned over and hugged her.

This news was serious, maybe fatal, but she remained calm and explained to me the probable course of further testing and treatment. The patient was a doctor, and she was tutoring me, her caregiver. The abdominal tumor was probably constricting the flow of urine from the kidneys through the ureters. If true, her kidneys were being compromised. The evidence of cancer in her pelvis indicated a widespread metastasis: Cancer could be in many other places.

She shared more details as I listened and asked questions, trying to be as calm and analytical as she was. There were major concerns about kidney blockage and the damage that may have been done already. There were also several lesions in her liver. She said she believed she was full of cancer and might have only a few months to live, but she was serene and factual in telling me.

That night we talked until nearly midnight about the next steps, telling the kids, our jobs, and the need for prayer. We prayed together and were thankful for the many good experiences we had enjoyed since the disastrous pathology report in January 2004 when the thirteen lymph nodes were taken.

We were both in shock, I think, when we headed for bed. She was coughing, and I needed to be up early on Saturday morning for my conference. We talked as we prepared for bed, and I kissed her and tucked her into our bed. I went to our guest bedroom so I could leave in the morning without disturbing her. As I slid into bed, I prayed for Darlene and for both of us in the days ahead. I wanted to protect her and prevent what was happening, but I knew I had to give her to God for his care.

Darlene was still sleeping in the morning when I left for the conference. I was in a daze all day. I did my best to listen to the complex conversation among academics around the table. I took notes mechanically, wishing time would speed up and take me back to her. My mind was far from the United States Constitution.

At home on Saturday night, we made a pact of secrecy. We would go to church together the next day, but we wouldn't say anything about her dire diagnosis. As when her cancer had first appeared nearly six years earlier, she wanted to control the information and share it carefully only when the facts were definitively known. She didn't want to send out false alarms, and she didn't want our children to receive the news indirectly from others. There was still time to pray for a miracle.

On Monday we both packed lunches before her morning appointment at Indiana University Hospital. We had been told the doctors would take a tissue sample for a biopsy to determine the kind of cancer and plan treatment. Taking a biopsy sample usually was a simple outpatient procedure, so we were prepared to go on to work.

As she was registering at the hospital, the nurse asked who had driven her in that day and would that person remain to drive her home. That question was a bad sign. The doctors clearly had something bigger in mind, something that would involve anesthesia. The nurse went on to say specifically that Darlene would not be able to drive home after her procedure.

We didn't dare exchange knowing glances. We knew she was not going to have the simple procedure we had thought. The cancer had returned with a vengeance. The season of our lives had changed again.

74

Gruesome Procedures

*T*he news of the cancer's return had hit us both hard, but we had been hardened to this possibility by the seriousness of her pathology report in 2004. God had sustained us through many earlier crises, and our relationship with each other was strong. We couldn't have anticipated the gruesome events ahead, so we merely prepared to take the next steps.

Due to the severity of the situation, the doctors moved as quickly as possible. My diary entries detailing the procedures started with the following on Wednesday, March 25, five days after the recurrence was found.

> *Today Darlene is to have stents installed in her ureters, the tubes that lead from the kidneys to the bladder. The CT scan on Friday showed some damage to one of the kidneys, so this is an urgent procedure.*
>
> *On Monday they did a needle biopsy of a suspicious spot on the top right-hand edge of Darlene's pelvis. They would have biopsied the liver, but the spots there were too small for them to hit with a biopsy needle. We thought the bone biopsy would be a short procedure, but we were there all day. The unexpected*

difficulties with the biopsy that day convinced us that we needed to tell the children.

The stents, small cylindrical devices that are designed to expand after insertion, were the least invasive procedure for maintaining the necessary flow of urine.

On Monday evening, we called each of our children. They were calm and curious as we shared the news with them, but I knew they would have their private emotional moments when they got off the phone. We assured them that we had come this far by faith, and we would continue. Because of our shared belief in God's goodness, they understood the need for them to pray and depend on God to guide us. We all felt sure that none of us would be shattered and hopeless, no matter what happened. As events unfolded, our adult children were continual encouragers.

Monday's procedure was the first of multiple biopsy attempts, a nightmarish sequence of pain and long-term damage. The hip bone biopsy was painful, but that pain was minor compared to what followed.

At home on Saturday afternoon, Darlene felt pressure on her side and then pain. The ureter stents were failing, and urine was backing up in her kidneys. By early afternoon, she was nauseous and vomiting. She had not been able to pass urine for several hours. Chills shook her. Something had to be done to relieve the pain.

We reached the emergency room at 3:30 p.m., and we sat for a few minutes in a tiny waiting room. Darlene was still shaking and nauseous when a nurse guided her to an examining room and helped her change into a surgical gown. An IV needle was inserted into an arm. I told her I loved her and returned to the little waiting room.

I was alone in the waiting room only a few minutes when my cousins Greg and Monika quietly slipped in and sat next to me. I had forgotten that I had texted them before we left home, and I was comforted to see them. They smiled greetings and asked how Darlene was doing.

"She has been better," I began. I told them about the sudden onset of illness that day and her pain and nausea. "I don't know how they are going to fix this, but they seem to know what they are doing."

We prayed, talked more, and waited. Greg and Monika stayed with me until a nurse came and said the procedure was over. Darlene was being taken to a room upstairs, and I could meet her there. I thanked Greg and Monika for coming, and I went alone to Darlene's room.

As we had feared when the stents were put into the ureters, the stents had failed. The pressure from the abdominal tumor had squeezed them shut, and the flow of urine had been dangerously blocked. Now tubes had been surgically installed directly through Darlene's back and into her kidneys. These were called nephrostomy tubes, and they made it possible for urine to drain from her kidneys into plastic bags outside her body. The bags hung from the sides of her bed and could be strapped to her legs when she was out of bed. There were markings for measuring the rate of flow, and they were transparent so the condition of each kidney could be monitored by the color of the output. I stayed with Darlene at the hospital Saturday night, and the nurses taught me how to empty and clean the urine collection bags. Darlene was moved to a hospital room, and we spent the night together there.

Sunday morning had an unearthly feel. Darlene was in pain, and I was in a fog from the night's crisis and lack of sleep. Sun streaming through the windows of that old part of the hospital gave the room the feel of a prison. Dr. Storniolo had called two of her colleagues for additional opinions, and oncologist Dr. George Sledge came early that morning to review Darlene's case.

Dr. Sledge told us about several kinds of cancer cells and their treatment. It was still unclear where Darlene's new tumors had come from, since the cancerous breast had been removed five years earlier. Dr. Sledge said he would consult with Dr. Frederick Stehman, the prominent gynecologist and oncologist Dr. Sorniolo also had contacted. Darlene would have to remain in the hospital at least another night for that evaluation.

Dr. Stehman came Monday morning to review Darlene's records and evaluate the likely source of the cancer. Were the tumors a recurrence from her breast cancer in 2003, or were these metastases arising from a new ovarian cancer that had spread? If these tumors were from an ovarian cancer, few treatment options were available. Thankfully, Dr. Stehman concluded that her new tumors did not come from ovarian cancer, and he referred Darlene's case back to the oncology and urology departments.

Since the hip biopsy attempt had failed, another one was needed to harvest enough cells to stain and analyze to determine the type of cancer and the appropriate treatment. Even though Darlene would have to endure yet another painful biopsy, the fact that ovarian cancer had been excluded was a glimmer of good news.

We were still in the hospital on Tuesday, March 31, when that bit of good news was shattered. We learned that that first hip biopsy sample taken so painfully on Monday had not collected enough material for analysis. Darlene was to be taken to surgery for a second biopsy attempt that would actually incorporate three procedures.

First, a biopsy sample would be taken from the sacrum, a triangular bone made of fused vertebrae between the two hipbones of the pelvis. An active tumor was present in her sacrum and had already dissolved some of the bone mass, so it was logical to try to get a sample of it. Second, liquid nitrogen would be injected into the sacrum to freeze the tumor and stop further growth. In the third procedure, plastic cement would be injected into the hollowed sacrum to stabilize what remained of the partly dissolved bone.

The biopsy attempt on the sacrum was unsuccessful. The sample taken was again too small for analysis. Far worse, freezing the tumor and injecting the cement into the sacrum had damaged the nerves to her right leg. Her leg was completely numb immediately after the procedure.

I brought Darlene home the next day, April 1, with her kidney drainage bags and a walker. Within a few days, the numbness in her leg subsided and the walker became unnecessary. Even though walking was painful, she insisted on walking as much as she could tolerate.

We previously had liked to walk nearly a mile to an intersection at the bottom of a hill in our neighborhood and then back. After her leg nerve injury, we walked only a half mile down to a stone bench beside a small creek, rested, and then walked back up the hill. Darlene had lost her only real form of exercise, and she quietly mourned the loss. Although she accepted the situation stoically, a few times she showed a tinge of anger about the doctor who had performed that bungled procedure.

The kidney drain tubes and bags presented special challenges. In daytime, Darlene wore ankle-length skirts to conceal the urine bags strapped to her calves. At night, the bags had to hang down on each side of the bed. Our king size bed was actually two twin beds lashed together by the frame, so I took it apart and gave us each a twin bed. The nephrostomy bags were then suspended from the bottom sheets on both sides of her bed.

I placed my twin bed close to hers so I could monitor her during the night. She sometimes got up by herself at night to record the level in the bags and empty them, but I usually checked them at least once in the night and emptied them. We both slept surprisingly well despite the tubes and bags.

We weren't emotional about all she was going through. She was stoic and matter-of-fact, and she depended on me to be the same. We were both guided by the simple logic of doing the next necessary thing, taking the next step. We had managed to adapt our lives to gruesome procedures, and we were determined to find a new sense of normal life again. We knew we were engaged in a grim battle, and we were determined to see it through to a good end.

75

Darlene's Retirement

For at least ten years, Darlene had a love-hate relationship with her medical career. She loved the work and the science behind it, and she loved caring for her young pediatric patients. She valued her colleagues. She hated the pressure, her feeling of inadequacy, and the enormous time demands. She was often exhausted by her hours. Especially after her first bout with cancer, she longed to have time for reading, singing, and the watercolor painting hobby she shared with her friend Jeanne Smucker. She wanted more time with our growing family of grandchildren. She knew that if she lived long enough to retire, her time might be short. She wanted to have as much of it as possible.

Sometime in 2007, she calculated the date when she could retire based on how long she had worked. She wanted to be sure she would retain health insurance coverage for both of us under the Indiana University plan. The calculations were based on a formula that included her age and her years of employment at the university. The magic numbers showed that she could retire on May 31, 2009. She began eagerly counting the days.

When cancer came back in March 2009, Darlene realized that she could not return to work. The nephrostomy tubes and urine bags would present a sanitation issue at the hospital. In addition, the nerve damage to her leg limited her mobility. She would have to retire immediately, two months earlier than she had planned.

It would not be the healthy, happy retirement for which she had hoped. We would not be like the silver-haired retirees shown frolicking in financial planning ads on TV. Hers was a retirement of grim necessity. Cancer had snatched her retirement plan away at the last moment.

Easter Sunday was on April 12 in 2009, and our three children and their spouses and children came home for a visit. We all went to church as though everything was normal, and we had a traditional family dinner at noon. After the meal, we assembled in the backyard for a family photo.

Darlene smiled broadly and triumphantly in the middle, surrounded by family. Her long skirt concealed the urine bags tied to her legs, and she looked ready for an afternoon walk. Grandson Sam was small enough to sit on his father's shoulders for the picture. Jake stood in front of Anna, her tummy bulging with the next baby. Jenny's tummy, baby aboard, pressed against Darlene's arm. The new babies were due in May and July. After the photo, the little boys kept the adults entertained hunting plastic Easter eggs their parents had hidden around the yard. For a day, medical problems seemed far away.

On Monday, April 20, Darlene had her third and final biopsy. My journal didn't report the site from which tissue was taken, but it must have been taken from the abdominal mass that was blocking her ureters. That would have been an easy target, but this required a major surgical procedure.

She was in great pain immediately afterward and had to be given additional pain medication in the surgery recovery room in the hospital basement. That medication made her so loopy that she slid helplessly out of her wheelchair nearly to the floor. Two nurses and I managed to lift her back into the wheelchair for the trip upstairs to a hospital room, where she was rolled onto a bed. The nurses there made her comfortable and brought blankets for me to sleep in a recliner at the foot of her bed.

After that ghastly, painful evening, she awoke the next morning surprisingly alert and pain-free. We left the hospital at mid-morning, feeling encouraged. The bright sun and crisp spring weather made it seem like a second Easter.

The third biopsy attempt was successful: enough tissue was gathered to clear up the questions about the origin and type of her cancer. This allowed Dr. Storniolo to choose the appropriate chemo for this specific cancer.

As it turned out, Darlene's final day of work was March 19, 2009, the day before the recurrence was found. Her retirement became official on March 31, while she was on medical leave. There were no traditional retirement parties. This retirement was not one to celebrate.

76

Chemotherapy Again

Darlene had received chemotherapy treatments from October to December 2003. Chemo was stopped then so she could regain strength for the mastectomy in January 2004, which was followed by another round of chemo in March and then radiation. The port used to deliver the chemo had been removed in 2004, but the cancer recurrence in March 2009 meant that a new port had to be installed for new rounds of chemotherapy.

Early one morning in April 2009, we went to a hospital on the west side of Indianapolis for the procedure. The port installation this time seemed almost a normal part of our abnormal life. Darlene changed into a surgery gown and was wheeled to an operating room. Unseen by me, she was sedated, the incision was made, the port was installed, and the covering skin was secured to heal. We chatted in the recovery room as though this procedure had been nothing out of the ordinary. By noon we were headed home during a brisk spring shower that had created shallow pools in the streets that reflected the sky when the clouds parted.

We had learned that all the receptors on Darlene's cancer cells were negative, which meant that some of the newer, less toxic treatments wouldn't work. She would need chemo again. On the day of the port installation, I wrote the following in my journal:

> *This is all so awful that I'm sure it isn't fully registering with either of us. Darlene has already had four painful procedures before treatment starts. She doesn't expect to live long. Yesterday she talked of starting a "bucket list" of things to do before she dies. The main things on her list are organizing memorabilia for our kids and selecting pictures for her funeral. I wonder if things are really much worse than we know. I wonder if the cancer is in more places than we know. I wonder what the mass is that has blocked her ureters.*

The day before the port was installed, Darlene's friend Susie McCracken died of cancer at the age of forty-nine. Susie was a mother of four teenage girls. She and Darlene sang in the Church at the Crossing choir together, and her girls and our children were friends. Susie had been treated successfully for melanoma a few years earlier, but it had returned. Darlene baked meatloaf for the family at least twice during Susie's treatment time. She and I had visited with Susie and her husband, Scott, in the hospital and at their home.

We were having our morning coffee in our front sitting room when I told Darlene that Susie had died. She thought about the news for a few moments and said, "That's sad, but it's a relief. If I were Susie, I would have wanted to be released from all of that."

We never discussed it, but she must have seen Susie's cancer recurrence and death as preceding hers on her own path to the end of life.

The new chemo routine started two days after the port was installed and continued for three Thursdays in a row, followed by a one-week break before three more Thursday chemo treatments. A week after chemo started, Darlene and I talked about my job at Liberty Fund. I was disturbed about the time I was spending away from her. She urged me to keep my job. She wanted us to have something normal in our lives, and my work at Liberty Fund provided that degree of normality.

My supervisor was very understanding and flexible about my need to be with Darlene at her medical appointments and chemo treatments. I kept going to the office, planning conferences, and writing reports on the conferences

I managed, but I usually could come home for lunch with her. I went to the office each morning at eight, and she had her quiet time. If the weather was good, she took her Bible and coffee outside for what she called her "deck devotions." For a few months, this pattern was our new normal.

77

CaringBridge

We soon found that the rush of events was too great for our usual modes of communication with family members and friends who were eager to know Darlene's condition and offer their help and prayers. During Darlene's first cancer episode in 2003–2004, she and I had communicated by letters, phone calls, and emails. There was a risk of overlooking someone who cared deeply for Darlene, and it was sometimes hard to keep up with events.

When Darlene's cancer returned in March 2009, Dr. Jeanne Smucker, one of Darlene's hospital colleagues, told us about CaringBridge, a website on which one can post information about a seriously ill family member or friend at no charge. We began to post reports on Darlene's condition on CaringBridge so people could consult it at will at any time of day. Friends could sign up for email notifications when we posted something. It was a great asset during a difficult, busy time.

We began our posts on April 30, 2009. Our posts continued through her death on October 25, 2010, and soon after I included an obituary. (All the information and pictures posted for Darlene on CaringBridge is still available online. The link to Darlene's section is https://www.caringbridge.org/visit/dkardatzke).

78

Alumna of the Year

Darlene had accepted her retirement and the new round of chemo treatments as calmly as she took everything else. But her years of service as a medical doctor had not gone unnoticed. In May 2009, she was honored as Alumna of the Year at Southport High School, where she had graduated in 1963.

"Guess what," she told me when she opened a letter from the Southport Alumni Association, "they want to make me Alumna of the Year. I guess my high school diploma is finally paying off!"

We both chuckled. It was like her to minimize this honor, but I'm sure she was pleased. She was suddenly being elevated within her large graduating class.

The class of 1963 was large, and Darlene could count only a few members as friends. She maintained contact with those few, and we had gone to one of the class reunions a few years earlier. As a quiet, conservative girl, she had not been one of the more famous members of the class but became one of the few who held graduate degrees. What's more, her degree was from the local medical school, Indiana University. Her most recent medical practice had been in a demanding subspecialty at Riley Hospital for Children, one of the finest pediatrics hospitals in the country. One of her colleagues at Riley, Sue McIlvried, was also from Southport and had told Darlene's story to the alumni association.

When Darlene learned of the honor, her thoughts must have turned to the long path that had taken her from the Southport Elementary School where she and her friend Connie had broken the playground swing. She had gone on from there through high school, college, medical school, and years of work in California, Wisconsin, Kansas, and Indiana. Her award would be presented at the alumni association's annual program at which scholarships for members of the graduating class were announced.

As we drove to the high school, Darlene mused over her life's journey and the speech she would give that night. She had worked on the speech for three days, and she was unusually calm, given her aversion to public speaking.

"I hope I'll say the right things," she said.

"I'm sure you will. You sounded good when you rehearsed the speech for me. And you have a lifetime of experience to share. You'll be great," I said.

At the awards ceremony, Darlene and I sat on the raised dais with the school principal, the alumni president, and other dignitaries. Darlene's sisters and their husbands were seated with our children and their spouses directly in front of us, where we could enjoy their reactions to all the proceedings. Beyond them was a sea of upturned faces of high school students and their parents and teachers. As scholarship recipients were announced, each honored student came to the dais to receive a letter confirming the award.

In announcing Darlene's award as Alumna of the Year, the president of the alumni association cited Darlene's family roots in Southport and her progression into the medical profession. Darlene smiled calmly, listening to the accolades she never would have sought for herself. She then gave a brief talk and thanked the alumni association for honoring her.

Her talk that evening included a story about speeding on the way to school more than once and how the driver's training teacher had called her "lead-foot Sayers." She then told about her journey from high school to college, medical school, pediatrics, and finally to developmental pediatrics. She closed with these words of advice and blessing, which I recorded in my journal:

> *I received a good education at Southport High School, went to Anderson College, and studied what interested me most, the biological sciences. I ended up in medical school intending to*

do research and teaching. During medical school, I fell in love with pediatrics and became a pediatrician.

In the years when my husband and I had three young children, being a mom was my first priority, so I worked part-time in pediatrics. In mid-career, I was fortunate to return to Riley Hospital to do a fellowship in Developmental-Behavioral Pediatrics. I have worked in this challenging and rewarding field for the last thirteen years. I have had the opportunity to work with such fine colleagues as Sue McIlvried, whose three daughters graduated from Southport High School.

I am impressed with the number of students here tonight to receive recognition and awards for their hard work. It is an honor to be here with you. I congratulate you.

When you let us gray hairs get up in front of a group of young people, we can't resist giving some advice. So here is mine. I encourage you to continue to give your best efforts to make the most of every opportunity you encounter. Seek wisdom and guidance from a source higher than yourself. Seek ways to serve and care for those around you. My personal way of doing this is to strive to love God with all my heart, mind, soul, and strength and my neighbor as myself.

When times of adversity come, maybe you will remember this quote I once heard. "Life is not about waiting for the storm to pass. It's about learning to dance in the rain." Life goes by quickly, so work hard, love well, and laugh often. Enjoy!

Thank you again. God bless.

A standing ovation followed, and I was the first to congratulate her. She was not a confident public speaker, so it had taken iron determination for her to write and give that speech. She was always reluctant to be the center of attention, and she was especially reluctant to receive praise. The speech had drawn heavily on her limited reserves of strength, and the walk to the parking lot would have been painful and a great effort because of her damaged leg. She accepted congratulations from school officials and family members while I brought the car around to the entrance for the ride home.

79

New Grandchildren

With the port installed and chemo again in progress, Darlene felt well enough to travel. A new grandchild would arrive soon, and she didn't want to miss the moment. Anna and Greg's second baby would be delivered in a scheduled C-section in Waukesha, Wisconsin, on May 23, 2009. We planned our travel for that date so we could be there on the day of the C-section. We would have to return to Indianapolis promptly to conserve Darlene's strength. She would have chemo again a few days after the baby's birth.

Making the trip to meet her third grandchild, Benjamin Daniel Herman, met Darlene's deep desire for normal life once again. The trip was a triumph of sorts: She didn't want to simply cower at home, even though she had been weakened considerably by the cancer treatments as well as the cancer itself. Pictures showed her looking unnaturally old in her thinning gray hair. A blood vessel stood out on her neck where a tube passed from her port to a main artery, but she was beaming as she held newborn baby Benjamin.

During this short trip, Darlene's nephrostomy tubes remained in her kidneys. She concealed the urine collection bags on her legs beneath a long dress. We took a motel room with two twin beds so the tubes and bags could hang on both sides of her bed as they did at home. Having seen and held the new baby, she was ready for the trip home and our quiet routines.

Soon after that Wisconsin trip, Darlene asked me to cut off her remaining hair. It had become thin, and what remained was an annoying, scratchy stubble that was just long enough to itch. I used our electric barber clippers to buzz off her remaining her hair until she was nearly bald. She had me leave only a little hair around her ears that might show under a wig. I thought she looked younger with her head shaved than she had with the thin, gray hair. She felt better, and she rubbed her remaining stubble vigorously to celebrate.

On Saturday afternoon, June 1, she awakened from a nap with chills and a fever. She was shaking and in pain. We hurried to the Indiana University Hospital downtown and spent five hours in the ER. She was given intravenous antibiotics for a major bladder infection and an antibiotic prescription to fill before we returned home that night.

At 4 o'clock on Sunday morning, I heard a loud thump and moans. She had fallen on the way to the bathroom to empty the urine bags. She was already getting up from the floor by the time I reached her, and she said she was okay. We returned to bed, but this fall was a warning.

The bladder infection and Darlene's fall made me wonder if I should quit my job at Liberty Fund immediately. I would be managing a conference in Los Angeles at the end of the week. After prayer and talking with Darlene, I decided to continue my work a little longer and go to the conference at Hermosa Beach, a few miles south of the Los Angeles airport.

While I was there, she called to tell me that a bone tumor specialist had looked at the recent MRI of her shoulder and had seen something troubling, possibly a new tumor. We both felt this news sounded ominous, but she remained upbeat and unconcerned. I wrote in my journal, "Darlene is a very brave woman."

We learned that the new MRI had revealed a tumor in her left arm, her dominant arm. It would be treated by her ongoing chemotherapy, and we thought no more about it. On June 28, 2009, I wrote the following in my journal:

> Darlene's nephrostomy tubes were capped on the outside on Friday, June 12, and the tubes were removed on June 19 after her CT scans on June 16. Those CT scans were good, and Dr. Storniolo said, "Awesome results!" I was literally thrilled to tears, but that evening Darlene cautioned me that there are tumors in her

> bones, liver, kidney area, and the front of her abdomen. Various doctors have read the June 16 CT scans to see if anything can be done about the neuropathy in her right leg. It appears that there may not be a surgical procedure that will help.
>
> I don't want to become complacent now that Darlene is feeling better and her scans show progress. I don't want to waste the next month or more on office work only to find that these were the last months when she could do things. That thought could cause me to quit work before the end of August.

As it happened, we were easing onto a smoother highway with happier events along the way. Jenny gave birth to Clara Ruth Rasmussen, our fourth grandchild, on July 16, 2009, at the Memorial Herman Medical Center in Houston, Texas. Because of Darlene's chemo appointments, we couldn't be present when Clara was born. Jenny's mother-in-law was there for Clara's birth and to help care for two-year old Samuel. Three weeks later we flew to Houston. At Jenny and Chad's house, we both had long hours of holding Clara when she cried her way through the nights. It took four adults in relays to give Clara the attention she needed. Darlene had been a colicky baby, and she was well-prepared to help care for one.

The trip to Houston to meet yet another new grandchild seemed like a miracle. We had been able to make not just one but two trips to meet two new grandchildren in that short span of three months. We were amazed and thankful to have four grandchildren: Jake was four years old, Sam was two years old, and the babies Ben and Clara were just getting started.

80

Returning to Colorado

During her treatments, Darlene and I managed to resume some of our camping and traveling. Our all-family camping trip in 2005 with one grandchild had been so much fun that we immediately began thinking of another family trip to Colorado. We wondered if such a thing could be possible with our growing family and Darlene's health challenges.

In July 2008, we pulled our trailer to Wichita for a Kardatzke reunion. We had a rowdy weekend with my cousins and went to Central Community Church, where we had been active the year we lived in Kansas. After the reunion, we drove on to Estes Park and set up the trailer in a commercial campground in town. Darlene felt this location was rather sissified for experienced campers like us, but she was seduced by its convenience.

While we were there we scouted out the YMCA of the Rockies and rental homes in Estes Park, but when Anna and Jenny both announced their pregnancies in late 2008, a Colorado family camping trip seemed unlikely. When Darlene's cancer returned in March 2009, we were sure the trip was off and we doubted we would ever take another family trip. But by August 2009, the two new babies were thriving, and Darlene was well enough to travel. We un-canceled the trip.

Colorado had always been a place of emotional and spiritual healing for both of us. It had cast a mystical spell over me as a young boy when I first experienced a cold, pine-scented summer morning there with my parents and siblings in 1949. Darlene had come to love it too during our many camping trips there with our kids.

Returning to Colorado in 2009 as a family that included all three married children and four grandchildren seemed to take on meaning we couldn't clearly discern. We sensed that it would become historic.

On Wednesday, September 23, our son Matt and his wife Kathryn flew to Denver with Darlene, three days ahead of the rest of the family, and drove to Lake George. Kathryn had been hearing about Campsite 13 for as long as she had known Matt, and Darlene wanted her to see the mythical place. The campground was closed to vehicles for the season, so the three of them had to hike in from the entrance gate.

Despite Darlene's painful neuropathy, she hobbled along on the hike, telling stories about earlier times there. The three of them had an untypical camping picnic of Subway sandwiches and soft drinks at the same picnic table where we had first eaten in 1978 with baby Jenny. Knowing she would never be there again, Darlene insisted on trimming her fingernails at the Campsite 13 picnic table "to leave something of me here," she told them. The three of them then headed north to meet the rest of the family.

The other nine members of the family converged on Denver from three different cities on Friday. Anna and Greg flew from Detroit; Jenny and Chad flew from Houston; and I flew from Indianapolis. Four young grandchildren, two of them babies, made the journey as well. It was a logistical triumph. Everyone arrived at about the same time, and we bought $322 worth of groceries to stock the house we had rented in Estes Park.

Family trips would not be complete without at least one unexpected event. One of our excursions included a picnic inside Rocky Mountain National Park. Just after lunch, Anna discovered she was missing her engagement and wedding ring set. She confided the loss to me and whispered she didn't want Greg to know. I quickly went to the rented vans and searched inside. Nothing. I looked under the vans and under the vehicles parked next to them. Nothing.

Suddenly Anna realized what must have happened. As soon as we entered the park, I had stopped the lead van to look at the park map at the pullout just past the entry station. When I stopped, Anna jumped out of the other van and ran up to find out why I had stopped. She remembered taking off her rings to put lotion on her hands as we were waiting to enter the park, laying them temporarily in her lap. When she jumped out to see why we had stopped, the ring set must have fallen out of the car.

When she told me this sequence of events, we decided I should hurry back to search for the ring before someone else found it or ran over it. Back at the picnic table, I surreptitiously but quickly gathered a few passengers and property into one van and left the others, including Greg and Anna, to come in the other when they were ready. Darlene, Matt, Kathryn, and I went to look for the ring.

As we approached the park gate, we saw where I had pulled off earlier and stopped where both vans had stopped that morning. I made a U-turn and stopped only halfway off the pavement at the pullout. I didn't want to risk running over the ring. Leaving Darlene and Kathryn in the van, Matt and I walked along the edge of the pavement, searching for the ring. We hoped it hadn't been run over and crushed by a vehicle, but we saw nothing on the pavement.

"I found it!" someone behind us yelled.

We spun around, and there stood Kathryn, dancing along the side of the road waving the ring overhead. She had silently jumped out to join the search and immediately found the ring. It had fallen into sand at the edge of the pavement, and there was just enough of it showing to be seen, glittering in the sun.

We gasped and cheered. Just then the second van arrived, and Anna nearly risked her life to run across the busy road to us. Greg had been left out of the secret until then. It took him a few minutes to take it in.

Of all the lovely things we did on that all-family weekend at Rocky Mountain National Park in August 2009, the recovery of the lost ring stands out as one of the most vivid memories. A photo of our group at the picnic table shows Anna's left hand without the ring, before she discovered it was missing. That picture has become a lasting memento of the story of the lost ring, something like a parable about "that which was lost was found."

81

My Retirement

I finally retired on Thursday, October 15, 2009, just four days before my seventieth birthday. I was older then than some people's idea of a retirement age, but I had long hoped to work until I was seventy. I nearly made it.

It was difficult to leave my work at Liberty Fund, but there were reasons why it was right for me to retire fully, and there were reasons why that specific day was the right day. Circumstances convinced me that I was doing the right thing at just the right time.

Darlene's health made me more eager to retire. I knew her improving health could worsen at any time. As long as I held onto my job, I had to be in the office from 8:00 a.m. until 5:00 p.m., five days a week. In addition, I had to make frequent four-day trips for conferences. I concluded that it would be a huge, grievous mistake for me to spend the last months of her life in the office while she was at home alone.

On August 1, I informed my colleagues at Liberty Fund that I would retire on Thursday, October 15, 2009. As God would have it, that date was exactly a year before Darlene's rapid, final decline. We had more time together in that final year than at any other time since we had met forty-four years earlier. For us, my retirement became the beginning of our "medical honeymoon."

To complete the terms of my retirement, I had one more Liberty Fund conference to manage. Blissfully, it was at Hermosa Beach, California, at the same small resort where I had been a few months earlier. I was surprised when Darlene said she wanted to go with me. She assured me she felt strong enough and was eager to go along.

On that trip, she acted as though she was restored to complete health. She spent a long afternoon on the beach, and she even enjoyed getting a sunburn, something she had always been careful to avoid. When I joined her on the sand later, we waded into the Pacific Ocean and looked toward faraway China. That evening I took her to a local pizza restaurant I had discovered on my previous trip to Hermosa Beach, and we felt almost like youthful honeymooners on a moonlit evening.

After that trip and with both of us retired, we decided to travel as much as we could. For our first trip after my retirement, we drove to Lindsey, Ohio, the town where I was born in a rented farmhouse. A patch of weeds in a farm field marked the place where the long-demolished house had stood. Darlene took pictures of me there, virtually in the shadow of the town's grain elevator on the abandoned railway right of way.

On her sixty-fourth birthday two weeks later, we went to Lebanon, Indiana, to see the place where she was born. We had driven past this town many times on our trips from Milwaukee to Indianapolis, but we had always been preoccupied with making it to our destination in either direction. We had never pulled off Interstate 65 to see the Witham Hospital where Darlene had been born in 1945.

The town had a sparkling new hospital on the north side of town, and on the site of the old Witham Hospital was a Walgreens Drugstore. The former nurses' home still stood next to the store. I took pictures of Darlene in the Walgreens parking lot and in front of the nurses' quarters. We were making history.

As a retired couple, we continued to make our everyday lives as happy and as normal as possible. Our days were brightened by our little celebrations of daily coffee, meals at home, and short walks.

Darlene gave occasional talks on infant mental health for residents at Riley Hospital. Together we visited elderly church friends in hospitals. One, a woman named Phama Wickheiser, had declined treatment when her cancer returned, and she waited many days before death took her. Another church leader, Ray Harden, seemed likely to die soon of recurring spinal cancer, but he outlived Darlene by more than a year.

Darlene enjoyed basic chores. When her hair grew back, she went on her own for a trim. She mended Matt's sport coat for a medical residency interview. She had me take her and her sewing machine to church so she could help women sew tote bags to be sold by widows at a mission in Kenya. She cooked intermittently that year and kept up her "meatloaf ministry" to people who were sick or grieving. In July, we invited my Sunday school class to our house for a picnic. The weather was hot, so we had the pitch-in picnic inside. Nearly everyone in the class attended, and Darlene was active in preparing and hosting the event.

In the evenings after dinner, we often watched Netflix movies on DVDs. Darlene watched all the *Foyle's War* series, and I joined her for most of it. One night we placed her laptop on a TV table in front of the fireplace so we could watch a movie and the fireplace simultaneously. We knew how to have a good time together.

On November 2, 2009, the day before her last birthday, we signed our new wills. We no longer needed to depend on Lawrence and Rachel Smiley to care for our children if we both were to die before the children reached eighteen. They were grown and married by 2009. Our children would receive equal portions of our not very great wealth, and we specified several charities to receive small portions of the remainder of our estate, if there was any after our deaths. Signing our new wills was such a low-key event that we simply went home afterward for lunch and an afternoon nap.

Cancer receded into chilly shadows when our children and grandchildren spent a noisy Thanksgiving with us in 2009. Like other holidays, ours was a celebration of real life. Thanksgiving had always been a favorite holiday for all of us, especially for Darlene. The repetition of turkey, cranberries, and mincemeat pie affirmed that all was well. We were indeed thankful.

My journal entry on December 20, 2009, was the following:

> *We are busy with the small, hardly defined tasks of retirement: eating, sleeping, laundry, cooking, reading, watching rental movies, and talking on the phone. It's a good life, but a life*

with few boundaries. I wonder if we will tire of it, but medical appointments punctuate our time.

Our activities may have seemed mundane to others, but they were the lifeblood of our normal, retired lives. They gave us positive, real life. Even though my journal entries continued to report concerns about Darlene's low energy, possible new tumors, and the side effects of treatment, we dealt with them all and continued our "new-normal" lives.

82

A Celebration of Life

*I*n November 2009 we held a celebration of life event at the Church at the Crossing. It was initially Darlene's idea, but our children and I then took over much of the planning. This event was a celebration of Darlene's relatively good health despite continued heavy cancer treatment and of our long-lasting marriage and our family. It was also, without it being said, a "living funeral," a time to gather family and friends at a time other than an actual funeral. Our celebration contradicted the lament heard so often at funerals: "I wish we would get together like this sometime other than funerals."

On that chilly Sunday afternoon, friends and family members came from Ohio and Kentucky as well as Indiana. All our children and their spouses were there with the four grandchildren. My siblings came, and many cousins did as well. It seemed that nearly the entire choir was there, as well as dozens more from the church. An ensemble of choir members sang a medley of songs selected especially for us.

Friends were there from earlier chapters of our lives. Dean Norman Beard, my employer at Anderson College at the time Darlene and I met, gave a raucous speech that cast doubt on my competence and virtue but praised Darlene to high heaven. Colleagues from Riley Hospital and Sycamore School gave speeches to wish us well, and a choir of sixteen friends from the church serenaded us. It was a happy day with none of the foreboding there could have been.

Darlene knew better than we that her remaining days might be few, and she had wanted a special time with her family members, church friends, and neighbors. The event fulfilled one of her important last wishes. Between us, we thought of the day as "a funeral for the living."

Two days later, she learned the results of her most recent CT scans. She was concerned but she said little. After learning the results, she went forward for prayer at church the next Sunday. The scans had shown new lesions in her liver.

83

Deep Conversations

*I*n her last year of life, Darlene showed her view of life in short comments more often than in long, sustained conversations. Her short quips sometimes sounded like proverbs and conveyed deep thoughts. Some were funny. Some revealed the philosophical and spiritual way she looked at her illness and coming death.

She was a woman of prayer, but sometimes the rush of crises and treatments didn't give her time for long, quiet, meditative prayers.

"Sometimes I just have to fire off bullet prayers," she told me one day. "Sometimes all I can say is, 'Lord! Help me!' and he does."

As we talked about the changing chemo strategies one day, I said to Darlene, "It's as though there is an evil monster inside you, and it keeps bobbing and weaving to avoid everything we throw at it. It says, 'I'm over here now! Try to hit me here! No! Now I'm over here!'"

She thought a moment. "Yes, that's pretty much the way it is. Cancer is like that. It can keep changing."

The enormity of her health condition sometimes struck one or both of us suddenly. Just walking through the kitchen one day, she suddenly blurted, "My God! I'm going to die!" She said no more about it, just that sudden realization. It was a fact she suddenly saw differently than before, and she then set it aside.

In summer 2010, she mused over one of her medical reports. It was written factually but in language she thought was overly diplomatic, an attempt to encourage her. She laid the report on our kitchen table and declared, "I just want the truth!" She had always been unblinking in facing the truth about each diagnosis, each procedure, each treatment. She wanted no gloss, however well-meaning, to dim her view of what was happening.

"I know I'll be healed," she said that same summer. "I just don't know which way." Her words expressed her confidence that she was in God's care despite what she was going through then. She talked other times of death as "the great healer." She knew she would be healed that way even if all chemo treatments failed.

The reality of the cancer was horrific, yet we both remained so matter-of-fact about it. I said to her one day, "Darlene, I wonder if we really understand what's happening. Should I be more hysterical about your condition?"

She snapped at me. "Don't you go getting hysterical on me! Just keep doing what you are doing!"

She wanted me to take her lead, dealing with each event factually as a problem to be solved, not as an excuse for an emotional outburst. Clearly, emotional outbursts from me would make it more difficult for her. The grief that her illness and death would bring our family was enough. She wouldn't be helped by displays of emotion. We just needed to do what we could each day. If Darlene ever wept over her cancer, I didn't see it. I cried a few times when reality hit me, but I more often teared up over good news. She watched my reactions, but she didn't cry.

"The wake closes quickly," Darlene said after cancer forced her into retirement. She knew that Riley Hospital and her colleagues and patients would all adapt quickly to her departure. Later, thinking of her death, she again used the same aphorism. She didn't say it bitterly or sentimentally, only factually. Life would go on without her.

Closer to her death, she said, "I only regret that my grandchildren won't know me." Sensing that there might eventually be more than four, she longed to know all of them.

More than once in 2009 and 2010, she said, "He numbers our days. There will be just enough days to complete our lives." Those words echoed words from Psalm 139:16, "Your eyes saw my unformed body. All the days ordained for me were written in your book before one of them came to be." The same thought was expressed in Job 14:5: "Man's days are determined; you have decreed the number of his months and have set limits he cannot exceed." She was comforted to know that she would have just enough days; her life would be just long enough. "I'll have just the right number of days," she said calmly.

Darlene sometimes said when we hugged, "I'm just the right size." At first I chuckled, but over the years I came to realize that she *was* just the right size: just tall enough, just rounded enough, just warm enough, and just huggable enough.

After her leg was damaged in the 2009 procedure, Darlene sometimes took one of the electric shopping carts when she went for groceries. She could drive around the store, pick up a few things, and be on her way. She liked to tell about a day when she had shopped and was in the checkout line in her motorized cart. She had to stand to reach into the basket to retrieve her items to place them on the conveyor. Behind her was a young boy with his mother. The little boy was astonished. "Look!" he said to his mother, "she *can* walk!" The embarrassed mother apologized, and Darlene laughed. She then owned that story and told it often.

84

Milestones of 2010

*I*n 2010, we experienced several joyful milestones. As the seasons of our life together changed, we became more acutely aware of the gifts God was giving us.

The first milestone in 2010 was the removal of Darlene's ureter stents on January 5, never to return. The stents had kept the tubes from her kidneys to her bladder open, but they pinched painfully when she moved certain ways. Without them, she could move more freely and without that particular discomfort. The procedure gave her new freedom and new optimism. Removal of the nephrostomy tubes from her back in June 2009 had been a big step; this was another.

One day soon after, talking about the nephrostomy tubes and the ureter stents, Darlene said, "I don't think I would be willing to go through that again. I wouldn't agree to it again."

I accepted that decision as I had her others about her health. She had been through so much already, and she questioned her strength for more challenges.

The next milestone was our son Matt's baptism on Sunday morning January 31 at the Church at the Crossing. Like Jenny and Anna, Matt had been a Christian since childhood. The girls had both been baptized as young adults a few years earlier, and he wanted his mother to see this important expression of his faith. He could have waited until the next date for baptisms in May, but he felt urgent about doing it in January. He wanted to make sure his mother was there.

March 2010 brought two more milestones. Matt learned on Match Day that he had matched with Riley Hospital in Indianapolis for his pediatrics residency. And Darlene's colleagues held a reception at Riley Hospital and surprised her by announcing a lectureship on infant mental health in her honor. She was embarrassed but deeply pleased. She must have felt she had reached a moment of completion for the medical part of her life.

Our years in Indiana had been punctuated by our children's progression in their education. Jenny had graduated from Anderson University in 1999 and had completed a PhD in school psychology from Ball State University in May 2009, during the dark days of Darlene's recurrence. Anna had graduated from the Indiana University-Purdue University campus in Indianapolis in May 2004 soon after Darlene completed radiation treatment. Matt's graduation from medical school on May 8, 2010, after four years at the IU School of Medicine, was a major life milestone, and it led directly to his residency in pediatrics at the same medical center beginning June 24. As we had when Jenny and Anna had graduated, we all gathered for his graduation ceremony, and we held a reception for him at the house that afternoon. After the reception, when only our immediate family remained, Darlene shared how the day had been a moment of completion for her as well.

"When my cancer came back last year, I prayed that I would live to see Matt graduate from med school," she said that day. "I know another woman who had breast cancer, and she died before her son graduated from med school." She told us she had hoped that scenario would not happen to her, adding boldly, "And here I am!"

After purchasing the trailer camper in 2005, we had thought our days of tent camping were over. Not so. Darlene was so much stronger and more mobile that in January 2010 we began making plans for a springtime tent camping trip to Yosemite National Park in California, a place that had enchanted us since our first visit there in 1971. I checked typical California weather for May, the time we knew the waterfalls in Yosemite Valley would be most spectacular. We decided on late May, after Matt's graduation.

In early May, I printed the list of our camping supplies that we kept on the computer. Reliving our years of packing for camping trips was exciting, and the packing list was almost like the outline of an adventure story. The thought that we would be retracing some of the paths from our earliest years together energized us. As she had done throughout our camping years, Darlene began sorting and arranging our camping supplies three weeks before the trip. She spread them around the family room and checked each item against the list we kept on our computer. Her list included big things like our tent, ground pads, sleeping bags, and stoves. It included small things like matches, insect repellent, salt shakers, and small containers of cooking oil and dish soap. She loved to perseverate (a word she taught me) over the camping gear, no doubt remembering many of her favorite scenes from "way out West." I doubt I could survive a camping trip now without her preparations.

Scans in early May showed that the liver lesions were growing, but on May 25 we boarded a plane for our camping trip. We hadn't gone to Yosemite for over thirty-five years, so this would be a sentimental journey. We would see Yosemite together again, and this time would be our last.

85

Final Camping Trip

*B*efore boarding the plane, we had loaded vast supplies into our checked luggage, including our small tent, camp kitchen, sleeping bags and pads, warm coats, and camp tools. At the San Francisco Airport, we took pictures of each other in front of the mound of luggage that overtopped our luggage cart. That trip to Yosemite would be our final camping trip, and we intended to make the most of it.

At the car rental counter in San Francisco, the agent asked if we would like a small SUV instead of the Chevy Impala I had ordered. It would be a Nissan Rogue, a car I hadn't heard of. I glanced at Darlene. "Would you rather have the SUV?"

She thought half a second and nodded eagerly. She liked the idea of a sportier car, and it was a good decision. The Nissan Rogue had a flat rear deck that would make it easy to get our luggage and camping gear in and out. We felt like a frisky young couple as we left the airport.

Our route took us several miles south before it turned us east across farm country and into the forests and mountains near Yosemite. Campsites in Yosemite were not yet open for the season, so we had reserved a room at Yosemite View Lodge just outside the park for two nights. Our back patio was only three feet from the rushing water of the Merced River, and we had coffee on the patio each morning, hardly able to talk over the stream's roar.

We were giddy with excitement when we made our first drive into Yosemite. At the entry gate, I flashed my Golden Age Passport that allowed us to enter free. It felt good to be so old! We collected all the free information offered and decided to visit sites that had enthralled us in the 1970s. We again found the improved spring beside the main park road that poured clear, cold water from a cliff. The water was free for the taking, and we had some again this time. The "nose" of El Capitan still attracted daring climbers and seemed to silently boast of defeating many climbers, some of whom had died there. Half Dome still stood at the other end of the valley, majestically gazing over the valley as though it had eyes under its famous "visor."

In 1974 we had climbed to the top of Yosemite Falls. This time we were content to take the short trail to the thundering base of the falls. Even that short hike was too much for Darlene. She waited a hundred yards back and sat on her cane/chair combination while I went on to a bridge that faced the roaring waterfall. Behind the flowing water was a solid granite wall, but a strong wind seemed to be blowing sprays of mist out from the falls. It seemed strange that a strong wind could be coming from that granite wall. It took me a few minutes to realize that the plummeting water was carrying air with it, and that air was blowing out from the falls with the mist. Darlene smiled serenely when I rejoined her and told her of the wind blowing from the solid rock wall.

At the Mariposa Grove of giant sequoia trees, we fortified ourselves with a small picnic lunch from the back of our car and then walked slowly up a paved trail among the trees. Again Darlene used her cane chair, and I took a picture of her beaming as though her rest stop was a prank she was playing on me.

We had arrived on Wednesday, and Memorial Day weekend loomed. Throngs of tourists would soon clog the roads and trails. We congratulated ourselves on our good timing as we drove away on Friday morning ahead of the crowds.

Winding mountain roads took us next to the south shore of Lake Tahoe, where we would camp in our small tent for two days. We found a dry tent site in the Meeks Bay Campground, though much of the ground was soggy from snowmelt and rain and large puddles stood in the roads. Lake Tahoe's deep, clear waters and bright blue surface invited us to walk along its shore as far as Darlene's strength would allow. We took pictures of each other at every stop.

On our second evening in Tahoe, we heard a loud commotion at a travel trailer about fifty yards from our tent. People were yelling and banging pans. The noise soon subsided, so we thought little more of it. Much later, at 3:00 a.m., Darlene awakened me for our usual nightly bathroom trip. I took a flashlight and my trusty headlamp for the short walk to the lighted restrooms. I waited outside the women's side for Darlene.

The lighted restroom windows cast a half-light into the grove of trees where I stood. In the dimly lit trees, an especially dark shadow caught my attention. As I watched, the dark shadow began to move. Suspecting I was seeing something other than a shadow, I turned on my headlamp. There stood a pudgy black bear about thirty feet away. I waved my hand to urge her away, and she lumbered back and then went around behind the building.

Unwisely, I circled around the building in the other direction to get a better look. She had made a wide loop and was by then a comfortable distance away, shambling across a meadow toward another patch of woods. I shone my light at her, and she looked over her shoulder at me. Her brilliant green eyes reflected my flashlight beam, but she ambled away at a leisurely pace, seemingly disdainful of me. I was thrilled. I had finally seen a wild bear after forty years of camping.

When Darlene emerged from the restroom, I told her excitedly about my encounter with the bear. Far from being disappointed, she shuddered and said she was glad she had missed the bear. We learned later that the commotion at the trailer the previous evening arose when a bear tore open the trailer door. Before the owners could chase it off, the bear had torn open their refrigerator and food cabinets and enjoyed a fine meal of almost everything inside. That bear may well have been "my" bear.

Our last campsite was at Donner Pass, where thirty-nine members of the Donner Party had died during blizzards in 1847 on their way to California. A monument near our campsite marked the place where many of the travelers froze to death. Markings on the side of the monument showed the twelve-foot snow depth that had covered the doomed travelers. Five feet of snow had fallen on them in a single night.

We drove a mile or two into the town of Truckee, at the crest of Donner Pass. A sign on the street attracted us to the Dragonfly Restaurant that claimed to be a gourmet eatery. The restaurant was having a half-price sale, so we boarded a rickety elevator to the second-floor entrance. We were led to a cozy table for two at a window overlooking the tracks. We beamed at each other, held hands, and waited for the first train to pass. We hoped to see one of the trains that rumbled through the pass several times each day.

Our hope was fulfilled and our vigilance was rewarded by four long trains being dragged through the mountains by strings of rumbling diesel engines as we ate our meal. Our dinners, as the sign had said, were "gourmet." The regular prices were daunting, so we were thankful as well to have been there during their half-price sale.

Unlike those pioneers, we had comfortable weather on June 1, our final night of camping at Donner Pass. The campsite provided a welded steel box for food storage as defense against bears, but thankfully no bears came that night.

San Francisco was the end point of our trip. We crept across the Bay Bridge the next day in heavy traffic, barely able to glance north or south at the bay. Darlene asked if we could go across the peninsula immediately to see the Pacific Ocean again. She had gazed silently into the ocean's infinite distance at San Diego and Santa Monica on our other trips, and and we had often visited the ocean when we lived in Los Angeles in our early years of marriage. She wanted one more look.

I watched as she walked close to the gentle surf until the toes of her hiking boots were in the brine. She gazed out over the cold, gray water just as she had on other ocean visits. I took pictures of her, and we held hands a few minutes and then searched for lodging.

We found a motel near the airport, and the next day we took a harbor cruise under the Golden Gate Bridge, around Alcatraz Island, and back to Fisherman's Wharf. I took pictures of Darlene in front of Ghirardelli's "Original Chocolate Shop," a mecca of sorts to her. That night my nephew David Kardatzke and his wife, Sarah, took us to dinner on a floating island in San Francisco Bay. We were completing our last tourist trip, but not the last trip of Darlene's life. She still had some living to do.

86

The Last Summertime

Darlene and I enjoyed a pattern of living from June until October 20 of 2010 that resembled the lives of many retirees, except we had a larger number of medical and financial appointments than average. It seemed we might live together like this for several more years, maybe many more years. It would be the last summertime of our lives.

One afternoon, I reflected on the early years of our professional training and my subsequent work on my doctoral dissertation while teaching at Marquette. I realized that I might have abandoned that work had it not been for Darlene.

"I was thinking just now," I said to her, "that if it hadn't been for your example of hard work and self-discipline, I might never have finished my dissertation. That would have left an important part of my life incomplete."

She looked at me thoughtfully for half a minute. I could see that it meant something to her.

"Thank you for saying that," she said.

We both felt better.

In mid-June, Matt and Kathryn came to a chemo session at the Cancer Center with us. My pictures of that day show Darlene looking healthy and happy, as though she were leading a party game. All of us were laughing as though chemo was a party trick. She opened her shirt just enough to allow the technician to access her port and start the chemo.

On July 8, Darlene initiated a conversation with me about "end-of-life matters," as she called them. We talked about what each of us might do after the death of the other, depending on who died first. Even at that time, we acknowledged that I could possibly die first even though she was in the middle of heavy cancer treatment.

She sat at the kitchen table as we talked, and I prepared our dinner. At one point I washed a pan and laid the dishcloth in a wad on the edge of the sink. I noticed that *she* noticed, and I quickly spread the cloth out to dry. We both laughed at the thought that her life would improve if I were to die first: The dishes would be cleaner and there would be no more wadded dishcloths.

Darlene said she did not intend to donate her body to the Indiana University Medical Center even though she'd had a lengthy career there as a student and later as a clinical professor. Matt was a pediatrics resident there, and although he would never encounter his mother's body in a dissecting room, the mere knowledge that it was there could have been disturbing to him.

In that same conversation, we talked of burial and cremation. She had already decided she wanted her body cremated, and she had told me she wanted some of her ashes scattered at the Forest Canyon Overlook in Rocky Mountain National Park, an especially breathtaking place we had visited several times. We agreed that some of her ashes and some of mine would be buried in a cemetery in Oklahoma where my mother's parents are buried. The purpose would be to maintain a connection to my mother's family.

The Bruner family had been pioneers, and their westward trail had ended in the open prairie of northwest Oklahoma in 1894. A burial site with my Bruner relatives would give our children and grandchildren a reason to know something about my mother's pioneering family. The burial sites of her parents and mine were well-known, and they were not likely to be soon forgotten.

Looking toward the end of her life, which she knew could come soon, Darlene bought two children's books that summer to comfort the grandchildren. Both books were compassionately written and illustrated in color. One book was *What Happened When Grandma Died?* The other was *Someone I Love Died*. She was caring for her grandchildren, even in her physical absence.

More than once at dinnertime, I looked at her left arm, since it was nearest me as we sat at the table. I thought about the other healthy parts of her body and her intelligence and her strong spirit, and I thought about the nearness of death, and I thought, *What a waste.* Then I thought, *God is in charge, and we all die, but I still think her death would be a waste, from my viewpoint.* I did not share this thought with her.

That summer we continued to enjoy ordinary things: meals at home, Netflix movies, gardening, long conversations, and as much walking as Darlene could tolerate with her damaged leg. She even did some gardening. In early July, she bought green knee pads so she could get right down among the weeds she was attacking. I took a picture of her looking like a Teenage Mutant Ninja Turtle. She didn't thank me for that.

We flew to Houston in July to see Jenny's family. We again arranged for a wheelchair to meet us plane-side. The pain in Darlene's hip and neuropathy in her leg had made walking difficult, and we weren't too shy to ask for help. I wheeled her from the airplane's walkway through a labyrinth of hallways to the exit. Though we needed a wheelchair at the airport, pictures later that day showed her sitting cross-legged on the carpet at grandson Sam's exercise class. She was an active grandma at Clara's first birthday party a few days later.

Our last road trip was to Wisconsin in August to see Anna and her family. On the way north, Darlene sat in a middle seat in the Suburban and studied a road atlas, imagining past and future trips. At Anna's house, both of us sprawled on the floor to play with fifteen-month-old Benjamin and his big brother Jacob. We visited our beloved neighbors Bud, Edna, and Joanne. We gazed again at our house on Summit Drive, the place where we had lived during the years Darlene had called "the summertime of our lives."

Back in Indianapolis, Darlene's sisters and cousins and my nieces and nephews came for visits. Perhaps these visits were not intended to be portents of an approaching end, but our visitors may have sensed they were. We laughed and talked of food and family and old memories, not of the days ahead.

Darlene always looked good to me, but I reminded myself of two other women who had looked beautiful only two weeks before they died. Mary Jane Staples, wife of one the Elmbrook Church pastors, had looked beautiful until very shortly before she died.

Darlene had been startled when Mary Jane called one day near her death.

"You weren't expecting to hear from me, were you?" Mary Jane said.

I also remembered a young mom at Sycamore School whose breast cancer returned after treatment, but she remained active in her children's school life. The last time I saw her, she was helping manage a special event in the school gym. She died a month later.

Darlene's good looks do not mean she isn't near death, I cautioned myself.

On August 18, Dr. Charles Zeanah gave the first lecture in the series that Darlene's colleagues had established in her honor. He spoke to the residents and house staff at Riley Hospital for Children for their early morning "Grand Rounds" lecture. Darlene chatted comfortably with the famous specialist in infant mental health with our son, Dr. Matt, by her side.

After Dr. Zeanah's presentation, there was a luncheon in his honor at a restaurant that was best reached by the monorail train that connects two of the big downtown hospitals. Darlene and I took the train to a stop between the hospitals and then the elevator from the train platform down to the street. She held my arm for support and limped as we walked toward the restaurant.

"I think they are just doing this lecture and luncheon now because they think I won't live much longer," she said quietly.

"Oh, no, Darlene!" I objected. "They are doing this because they love you and admire the kind of doctor you are!"

Her comment was typical of her clear-eyed view of her health condition, and it was also characteristic of her self-deprecating attitude. She was never comfortable with the reality that she was a highly competent doctor with an exceptionally humane manner of dealing with her young patients and their parents.

Darlene continued to have worrisome symptoms, but in spite of them, we planned an early fall road trip to Colorado with our travel trailer. She even suggested we might drive to Yosemite in California. We spent some August and September afternoons cleaning the trailer and patching a crease on the roof that had leaked. We hoped to start our road trip on October 1.

The Suburban had a serious electrical problem in late summer and had to be towed to our mechanic. While it was there, I told my mechanic we were planning a road trip to Colorado. He said I could have waited for new tires, but with a long road trip coming up, it would be best to have fresh tires. I bought the tires.

It was exciting to be planning a trailer camping trip to the West again, but I questioned my own strength for it. I knew Darlene couldn't do much to help me set up the trailer each night as we traveled, but if that's what she wanted to do, I was determined to make it happen.

87

The Trip Not Taken

On Tuesday, August 31, we both saw the CT scan of Darlene's liver on Dr. Storniolo's computer screen. The main tumor seemed to be about an inch across and was clearly visible, and it had continued to grow since the last test. The tumor shone brightly and looked like a cluster galaxy of stars in outer space. The main tumor was surrounded by an ominous cloud of tiny white stars where other tumors were forming.

Dr. Storniolo ordered that Taxol and Avastin treatments be stopped and Gemzar started on September 1. *"This is a serious development,"* I wrote in my journal that day. Darlene wrote a factual email to our children about the scan results and the change of treatment, but she minimized the potentially dangerous implications. She was running out of treatment options.

Darlene struggled with pains in her legs, troubled sleep, occasional diarrhea, and lack of energy. She became weaker, but we still assumed we would drive to Colorado in early October with our trailer. We didn't realize how serious some of her symptoms were, or at least I didn't. On Wednesday, September 15, she was coughing at 6:00 a.m. and asked me to go to CVS for an albuterol inhaler. She'd had to skip chemo the previous day because the blood test showed her platelets were too low, and now she was coughing. She took one puff on the inhaler and went back to sleep.

On Sunday, September 26, I wrote in my journal that her energy level had increased but every exertion still tired her. While I was writing, she was taking an afternoon nap to recover from attending church and Sunday school and singing in the choir. I added these words at the end of my entry.

> *We have been discussing over and over our plans for a trip in early October. We now plan to go back to her first idea: drive to Estes Park with the trailer, but no farther. Right now I feel too tired, but if Darlene wants to go, I'll do it. But I'm feeling tired now myself.*

The next morning, I wrote the following:

> *Last night Darlene sat down in our bedroom, exhausted from climbing the stairs. She told me she had to rest at the landing before coming to the top. She said she questioned whether we should take any trip, let alone pull the trailer to Colorado.*
>
> *In the very early morning hours, I heard her coughing in the bathroom and asked if she was throwing up. She said she was only coughing. When I could finally awaken, she was in her study in the big green recliner, covered with a blanket. She said she was better there and had spent the rest of the night there.*

That day Darlene asked me to sit with her on the couch in our music room, the room named for the piano, violins, and guitars that lived there. She put her arm on the back of the couch and asked me to put my arm over hers there too. She took a beige shawl that a friend had crocheted for her and covered both of our arms in a little ceremony.

"I think we have to decide not to drive to Colorado," she said and looked for my reaction.

I looked at her and sighed. "I'm sure you're right. It would have been fun, but I don't think we are up to it."

We were both relieved that we had made that decision. For a few hours, we felt we could focus again on simple living. Our decision had given us a little new strength for that day.

Darlene had chemo and a chest X-ray at the Cancer Center the next day, September 28. The X-ray showed nothing new, but her coughing continued. After dinner at home, she asked me to go to CVS for a "spacer" for her inhaler. She thought her breathing problems might be due to asthma. When I returned from CVS, she was in a chair in the family room, bundled up in a blanket and doubled over in pain. She could barely turn to look at me.

"I need to go to a hospital," she whispered. "Take me to the ER."

We immediately started for the hospital (now Indiana Health North) on North Meridian Street. The hospital was affiliated with the Indiana University Medical Center, where our daughter-in-law Kathryn was on staff as a nurse. I called Kathryn and asked her to call ahead and alert the ER that we were coming. I asked her to pull rank if she could. Darlene needed immediate attention.

At the hospital, I pulled in the ambulance entrance, right up to the ER door. I helped Darlene to the door and put her in a wheelchair. The staff was expecting her, and they took her directly to an exam room. The young doctors may have been a little nervous when they realized their patient was a more senior physician than themselves, but they went to work to help her breathe.

Tests that night showed a lot of fluid on her lungs. She was diagnosed with congestive heart failure and admitted to the hospital, where she would remain until Friday.

During that hospital stay, Dr. Darlene joked about her congestive heart failure. One of the chemotherapy drugs she had received in 2003, Adriamycin, was known in some cases to lead to an often fatal kind of congestive heart failure many years after the treatment. Dr. Darlene knew this, of course. She laughed as she told people, "Adriamycin kept me alive long enough to get congestive heart failure!" It was as though she had earned a Girl Scout badge.

Darlene also requested a visit from a hospice care representative. The hospice lady spent more than an hour with us and explained the nature of hospice care and how it would be done at home. We talked about equipping our music room as a hospice bedroom. We felt assured by the competence of the hospice lady, and we felt we could make the hospice decisions if it became necessary. The consultation seemed like a wise, long-range precaution, not an urgent matter.

I stayed with Darlene at the hospital each night, and when she was released on Friday, we resumed normal life. She was weaker and tired more easily, but she was breathing better and was able to work at emptying the file cabinets in her study.

We ate at home most of the time, and we read or watched Netflix movies for entertainment. She finished the *Foyle's War* series and started *Reilly, Ace of Spies*. She also read novels by Sue Grafton, whom I called "The Alphabet Lady" because she was working her way through the alphabet with titles starting with each letter of the alphabet, such as *"N" is for Noose*. Darlene had read many books by C.S. Lewis and reread some of them that year. One piece of information about her love for Lewis books didn't stand out to me until later. Lewis died seven days before his sixty-fifth birthday, and Darlene would die eight days before her sixty-fifth birthday.

88

Nearing the End

Darlene had another PET scan on Tuesday, October 12, in preparation for another chemo session on October 19. We waited expectantly at home for the results of the scan, hoping to receive them before the weekend. We had reason to believe the news would not be good, but bad news would be better than a weekend of anxious waiting.

The phone finally rang late Friday afternoon. Dr. Storniolo told Darlene the liver tumor had continued to grow despite treatment with Gemzar. She said she would call on Monday with a treatment plan.

When the call ended, Darlene turned to me with the news. She told me calmly and frankly, and I remembered the large, bright tumor I had seen and the cloud of tiny menacing little tumors that shone like stars.

"This is not good," she said.

"No, it's not," I said.

We sat for a moment just looking at each other, absorbing the news.

That gloomy moment passed when Matt and Kathryn stopped in for an impromptu dinner with us. They knew nothing of this news, though they knew the recent reports had not been good. Darlene told them calmly about the scan results and pointed their attention hopefully to her chemo the next week. We had a good evening of conversation, and they asked if they could spend the night in our guest bedroom rather than going back to their house. It was the best possible way to finish the evening. It was fun to have a sleepover.

On Saturday morning, the four of us carried on our family tradition of pancakes and bacon, our favorite Saturday morning breakfast since our Wisconsin days. The day then rolled along with activities too pleasant to have made it into my journal. We put together a makeshift lunch of sandwiches.

That Saturday night, while talking with us in the family room, Darlene had severe abdominal pain. Until then she'd had only mild pain or sometimes just an awkward discomfort, but this time the pain was severe. She shifted her position often to find a less painful posture. At bedtime she told me that the pain probably meant her liver was in serious trouble.

On Sunday, October 17, Matt and I went to church together and left Darlene and Kathryn at the house. We went forward at the end of the service to be anointed for prayer on Darlene's behalf. I was choking up and in tears as I told Pastor Rennick about Darlene's bad news on Friday. He anointed Matt and me, and we knelt at the altar to pray.

My journal entry on Monday, October 18, recorded the following:

> *Darlene had increased pain on Sunday. I have started asking her what her pain level is, and it was as high as 7–8 yesterday. While watching TV, she would shift her position often to try to control the pain. She took two Tylenol pills during the evening and said she would take a Norco at bedtime, but when she awoke at 5:45 a.m., she said she hadn't taken Norco because she had found a position in which she was comfortable, or at least the pain was minimal.*

That day Darlene's sister Beverly and her husband, Wilbur, called to ask if they could come for an evening visit. I wouldn't have encouraged a visit that night because Darlene had been weak and in pain for several days, but she said she wanted to see her sister, undoubtedly sensing that her condition was very serious.

During their visit, Darlene needed to be in bed, so we gathered upstairs beside her bed. We formed a small semicircle around her and talked about family members, Darlene's condition and recent treatments, and our children's plan to see us that week. We told them that Darlene would have an oncology appointment the next day to discuss a new treatment plan.

89

The Baby Gate Crisis

During Darlene's increasingly serious medical events in October 2010, a minor crisis arose that would become a comical part of our family's folklore. This episode is remembered affectionately within our family as "the baby gate crisis."

Darlene's sixty-fifth birthday on November 3 was approaching, and I was uncharacteristically planning ahead. She was pleased when I told her on October 8 that I was going to buy a flat-screen, high-definition TV for her birthday. We expected the new TV to enhance our evenings of movie watching. As it turned out, I didn't buy her a flat-screen TV. Something more urgent was on her mind.

Our daughters were planning to visit on October 20, and Darlene became obsessed with concern that the two toddlers, Ben and Clara, might fall down the stairs that led to our second floor. With Darlene's prodding and over a period of three weeks, I bought several adjustable gates, one after the other, to block access to the stairs at the top and also the bottom. The stairs could not be blocked at the top by any of the commercial safety gates I kept buying, testing, and returning, rather than shopping for and buying that flat-screen TV.

I knew Darlene would not rest until the children were protected from our stairs. I promised her I would solve the problem somehow, but nothing I said calmed her worries. I was at the brink of drilling holes in the hallway wall at the top of the stairs to install some sort of crude, heavy-duty gate of my own design. It would have been about the quality of a farm gate or an industrial barrier, but it was all I could think of to do.

Matt and Kathryn were the ones who finally resolved the baby gate crisis. During their visit on the weekend of October 15, I told them of the various baby gates I had bought. I told them about my plan to drill holes in the wall and install some sort of gate at the top of the stairs. They listened earnestly, possibly suppressing feelings of alarm at our frenzy. They may even have suppressed laughter about my plan for a homemade baby gate.

Thankfully they pointed out the obvious. Our first two grandkids, Jake and Sam, had never toppled down the stairs. Ben and Clara, both a year old, would be in direct parental care at all times and would not have access to the stairs. They also said that we could even use a couple of baby gates to confine kids in upstairs bedrooms if necessary (and it never was necessary).

Darlene was persuaded by Matt and Kathryn's calm reasoning, and the baby gate crisis was over. Apparently she trusted the advice of pediatric specialists over that of an aging, retired economist.

By the time the baby gate crisis ended, it was too late to get that flat-screen TV for Darlene's sixty-fifth birthday. Events suddenly moved too swiftly.

90

Looking Toward the End

Tuesday, October 19, was my seventy-first birthday and the date of Darlene's chemo appointment. Birthdays had always been more important to her than to me, and she apologized that she hadn't been able to plan anything special. In fact, she had ordered three shirts for me from Land's End on Friday, the day when we found out the results of the PET scan and Matt and Kathryn had come. I told her it was okay about my birthday as we struggled to get her dressed and ready to leave for her appointment.

She was feeling so sick that I suggested we cancel the appointment, but she was determined to go. She became annoyed with me when I called from the car to let the Cancer Center staff know we were running a little late. They said not to worry.

In the examining room, Darlene was in great pain. At times she doubled over and held her stomach. Dr. Storniolo's face and manner seemed to express a repressed concern. She went over the aspects of Darlene's treatment that were going well, including no increase in tumors other than in the liver. She then showed Darlene the CT scans of her liver from the previous week.

They agreed that the liver was now heavily involved in tumors as I sat and listened. The large tumor we had seen the month before had grown even more, and the little menacing tumors that had formed a star cloud were larger and more numerous. For some reason, I didn't step over to see the monitor but kept taking notes. Maybe this time the tumors seemed too serious and personal for me to see.

The three of us then talked about several chemo options, and the only one that seemed even plausible was something called Carboplatin. The very name seemed foreboding, like a coal mine or a steel mill. The other treatments were out of the question. One would have had her in chemo treatments four days each week. There wouldn't be much time for conversation or anything else for as long as she received those treatments. *What kind of life was that?* I wondered.

I asked how long Darlene might live with the best chemo that seemed plausible. Dr. Storniolo thought it might work for a year. I was hoping she would say more than a year.

Dr. Storniolo took a deep breath and paused. We were not prepared for her next words.

"This is likely to be your last Christmas," she said.

At least we will have this Christmas, I thought. *It might be a sad time with the end of her life looming, but at least we would have another Christmas with the kids and grandkids.*

Since the treatment options were so time-consuming, energy-draining, and uncertain, I asked how long Darlene could live with no further treatment.

"Three or four months," Dr. Storniolo said.

I envisioned the coming months. If she stopped treatment, she might die in February or March of 2011. *What would the coming months be like?* I wondered.

Dr. Storniolo recommended that Darlene not start a new chemo that day but take the rest of the week to decide on further treatment. I thanked God silently for her wisdom. Darlene was eager to leave. She was tired and felt very sick. She must have been in pain but didn't say so. We made an appointment for her to return for chemo on Tuesday, October 26, and then made our way slowly down to the lobby. I had a wheelchair for her that day, as I had done a couple of times before, and we waited for the valet parking men to bring our car.

On our drive home, we had one of the more significant conversations of our lives. We probably talked about small matters and medical decisions part of the way, but I started the heavier conversation by sharing a thought that had come to me that week.

"If you think about just the span of human history, let alone all the time in eternity, it won't be long before I will follow you," I said.

She was listening closely.

"I'll be looking for you," she replied.

As we were getting off Interstate 465 at the Shadeland Avenue exit, she then said, "Don't get involved with women for the first year."

She had earlier warned me about making major decisions in the year after her death.

"Humph," I said. "Who is going to want a withered seventy-one-year-old man?"

"Don't kid yourself," she said. "There will be lots of widows after you. You're good looking, intelligent, and a good conversationalist."

I disregarded those compliments and we changed the subject, but it was clear that she was looking toward the end of her life. The day was sunny, but in my memory, it was covered by a dark cloud and fog.

At home, Darlene went directly to bed. I went to CVS for oxycodone, OxyContin, and Zyprexa—two powerful pain medicines and a treatment for anxiety. She took at least one of the pain pills and was up for a brief time in the evening. It was a relief to turn off our lights at 11 p.m.

91

Last Day at Home

*T*wo months earlier, our daughters had begun making plans to come to see us on October 20. We later looked on this "coincidence" as a miracle: All of us had focused on this exact day, and we would all be together. We knew there could be serious issues at hand by October, but Darlene and I looked forward to their visit in our favorite season of the year, thinking of it as another happy family weekend. Jenny and Chad would fly from Houston with Sam and Clara on October 20. Anna and Greg would drive from Milwaukee with Jake and Ben that afternoon. Matt and Kathryn lived only three miles from us. All of them would be converging on our house on Wednesday, October 20. As it turned out, that was Darlene's last day at our home.

I was up early that morning to clean the kitchen, vacuum, and do whatever I could to get ready for our family gathering. Darlene's sister Evelyn and her daughter Lisa were coming a little later to help me. Events moved so swiftly that I couldn't keep up with my journal writing. The following is what I wrote three months later:

> *On October 20, I was up early completing cleaning and laundry that was needed before Jenny and Anna and their families would arrive that night. I don't remember now if Darlene was*

> awake before Evelyn and Lisa came at maybe 9:30 to help with the cleaning. I took them upstairs to see Darlene, and I took her some coffee then, if not before. She could only sit on the bed and sip a little of the coffee. Darlene began to visit with Evelyn and Lisa, and I went downstairs to continue my work.
>
> They came down later, and we all worked at vacuuming and dusting and tidying up. We ate some lunch in the kitchen and went upstairs to do some work there. They had left Darlene in her room, going back to sleep in late morning. The half-full cup of coffee was still on the desk next to the bed when I returned from the hospital on October 25 after her death.

Lisa and I took a break in mid-afternoon to get Kathryn from their house. She was feeling sick and was too weak to drive, but she wanted to be at the house when Jenny and Anna arrived. Kathryn went upstairs to see Darlene, and Darlene recognized her and smiled. Kathryn lay down on the other side of the bed next to Darlene. Evelyn, Lisa, and I continued to clean the house.

I was in the "Upper Room" (what we called our guest bedroom) when my cell phone rang a little later. It was Dr. Storniolo's nurse, Vivian Murphy. She said Darlene had called a couple of hours earlier saying something about being confused about her medications. Vivian asked if Darlene was okay. I was astounded.

"You mean Darlene *called* you *today?*" I exclaimed.

"Yes, she called because she was concerned about her medications."

"We thought she was sleeping!" I nearly yelled and thanked her.

Evelyn, Lisa, and I hurried to the master bedroom. Darlene was lying on the bed awake. Her speech was incoherent when she tried to talk to us. I could barely understand her.

"I made a mistake with one of my medications," she managed to say at last.

We finally understood her concern. She had taken her Zyprexa too soon, at 11:00 a.m., when she shouldn't have taken it until 11:00 p.m. She must have called Dr. Storniolo's office when she realized her mistake.

When she said she needed to urinate, I tried to walk her to the bathroom. She nearly collapsed, and it took all three of us to help her into the bathroom and get her seated. She couldn't urinate, and I thought it might be because there were people in the room. We tried to give her some privacy, but she was so unsteady she couldn't sit on the toilet by herself and still couldn't urinate.

With great effort, we got her back to the bed, but she wouldn't lie down. She sat on the edge of the bed and slumped over the desk next to the bed in an odd posture, wedged between the bed and the desk. We tried to move her, but she was too heavy for us to lift. Charlie Eldridge, Evelyn's husband, arrived about then and helped us. Somehow the four of us managed to get her to lie down again.

The nurse had told me the excess medicine would wear off, but it would take longer because her liver couldn't metabolize the Zyprexa very fast. We were seeing no sign of improvement.

Meanwhile, Jenny and Chad were preparing to fly from Houston with Sam and Clara. Anna and Greg were on their way by car from Milwaukee with Jake and Ben. They both called with periodic updates on their progress. I gave them reports on Darlene.

It was about 7:30 p.m. when I finally called Dr. Storniolo at her home and told her the situation. At first she thought the Zyprexa would wear off soon enough, but after talking it over for a few minutes with me, she said I should call 911 and send her to a hospital. The hospital would be able to stabilize her and could put in a urinary catheter, if needed.

I called 911, and we all awaited the ambulance. By this time, Lisa's husband, Manny, had come, and so there were five of us there helping Darlene.

Five minutes after my call, we heard the siren and an ambulance backed into our driveway. Two fire trucks also arrived and sat in the street with their lights flashing. The whole neighborhood was lit up with flashing lights.

Several emergency men and women hurried into the house. They brought a stretcher to the front door, but when they saw the turn in the staircase leading upstairs, they left it outside. I led them to the bedroom, and they immediately started taking Darlene's vital signs. They tried to talk to her, but her speech was still sluggish. I heard her say that she'd had an accident with her medication.

The person in charge said they would need a chair to take her out of the house. A couple of people went for it, but the bedroom and hallway were still crowded with people.

Darlene asked me what they were doing, and I said, "They're going to take you to the hospital."

"The hospital! No, not the hospital!"

"You really need to go to the hospital," I told her. "Do you want to go to Clarion North again?"

"No, go to University Hospital," she said firmly, and that turned about to be the obvious and excellent choice.

The emergency crew bundled Darlene up and carried her out of the house strapped to a narrow metal chair. Charlie was standing next to the front door when they carried Darlene out. He was sobbing.

Matt was on call at Riley Hospital next to University Hospital, so Kathryn called and told him to meet the ambulance at the hospital. She said she would go with Darlene in the ambulance. Little did I know that Kathryn was so weak that she needed to be rushed to the hospital herself.

I stayed at the house just long enough to gather things to take to Darlene at the hospital. Evelyn said she and Charlie would stay at the house until Anna arrived, since she and her family were now fairly near.

That morning, before her Zyprexa accident, I had prayed that Darlene would have one more lucid day with all our kids. It seemed that she might die at any moment, so I prayed again.

"Lord, please just let her live until the girls arrive!"

I quickly gathered up my shave kit, pajamas, a change of clothes, and a few other things for myself. I got Darlene's makeup kit, having learned from our last hospital excursion how important her cosmetics were to her. I also grabbed undergarments for her. As it turned out, she wasn't able to use any of what I brought for her.

The ambulance was long gone by the time I got out of the house and started for the hospital. I parked in the garage next to the emergency room and found Darlene there with Matt and several doctors and nurses. Matt had run over to University Hospital when Kathryn called. A doctor was working on Darlene, and she was more coherent than before. She recognized me, but she was still giving her history to the doctors.

Anna called my cell phone to report that she was on I-465, nearing our house. Jenny texted to tell me their plane was delayed in Houston and they might not arrive until after 10:00 p.m.

Meanwhile, Kathryn was lying on a gurney in the emergency room hallway just outside Darlene's room. Kathryn was weak from dehydration. She had been vomiting frequently for more than a week, and the loss of fluids had caught up with her. Matt asked the ER nurses to start Kathryn on IV fluids, and she took three full units. The doctors continued to work on Darlene throughout the evening.

When Anna reached our house, she dropped her husband and kids off there and hurried to the hospital. Jenny's plane had taken off from Houston, and we learned that it was due to arrive at Indianapolis after midnight. Anna and I discussed who should go to the airport to get Jenny and her family. Matt was needed in the ER with both Kathryn and Darlene. We decided that Anna should be with Darlene. I would be the airport shuttle man.

Jenny, Chad, Sam, and Clara were waiting in an exit vestibule at the airport when I arrived there. The young kids had traveled well and were happy, even so late at night. Sam was active, running in circles, and Clara was just quietly looking cute. On the way to the hospital, I told Jenny and Chad the latest on Darlene's condition and the events of the day. As soon as we arrived at the hospital, Chad took the kids to our house in my car. Jenny and I went to see Darlene.

By this time, Darlene was in a regular hospital room. She was awake just long enough to greet Jenny and have a short visit. After checking on Darlene, I fell asleep in a recliner across the room. After talking with the girls a few minutes, she lapsed into a deep sleep, not disturbed even by the nurses' frequent visits. We realized we might never speak with her again.

92

Second to Last Conscious Day

When I awoke for a moment sometime during the night, Jenny was in a straight-backed chair next to Darlene's bed, gazing at her silently. Anna had gone home to rest and check on her kids. Medical people must have come in often during the night, but I didn't notice. When I awakened again in early morning, Jenny was dozing upright in her chair. I got up and traded chairs with her so she could sleep in the recliner. We would all need rest for the day that was ahead.

A team of nurses and physicians arrived at 7:30 in the morning, and by then Darlene was awake enough to talk with them. They checked her vital signs and medication schedule. She answered questions and seemed to understand what was going on. She was heavily medicated, but she was comfortable and seemed cognizant of everything.

When I first stepped out of the room that morning, David Casterline, our church's choir director, was waiting just outside the door. He looked tired and concerned. He apologized for just showing up without calling.

"That's just fine," I said. "Thanks for coming. Would you like to see Darlene now?"

"Sure, if I can," he said. "I won't stay long."

I led him in, and Darlene recognized him and smiled. They talked for only a couple of minutes. He assured her that choir members were praying for her, and he prayed briefly with her before he left. He was the first of many visitors that day.

Darlene sensed that this day, maybe only this morning, might be her last chance to speak with any of us in this lifetime. She asked me to call her two sisters. They came quickly with their husbands. Our children and their families arrived in two groups. Our three children came first. Greg and Chad brought the grandchildren just before lunch. When everyone was there, our children presented Darlene and me with a small, professionally-produced booklet of family photos. Pictures taken that day at the hospital show her smiling as she leafed through the book.

Other pictures that day show her turning partly on her side and smiling at our children and grandchildren at her bedside. She wanted to hug each grandchild, but they sometimes squirmed away so she had to be content with touching them, as in a blessing.

When Matt had a few minutes alone with Darlene in the hospital room, he reminded her that Kathryn had been sick for several days and had needed IV fluids in the emergency room the night before. He told her why. They were expecting a baby. She smiled radiantly when hearing of her newest grandchild.

In the early afternoon, Darlene was transported for a procedure in the hospital's basement. Matt and I went with her. After the procedure, we waited in a basement hallway for a transport aid to take her to her room. Darlene was quite alert. Matt stood beside her bed and cleared his throat. Since he hadn't told me the news, he reenacted his announcement.

"Mom and Dad, I have something to tell you," he said.

Darlene turned her head to see him fully.

"Kathryn and I want you to know we are expecting a baby. We just found out. It will come in early June, we think."

Though her strength was fading, she was clear-minded in this moment, and a beautiful smile spread across her face. The smile remained as she was wheeled back to her room. For the time being, the news was a secret for Darlene and me and the new baby's parents only. Baby Ezra was on his way.

Darlene's face was swollen, and an oxygen tube was in her nose. She was not allowed to drink fluids, but our children and I were allowed to wet her lips and tongue with small sponges on wands. I took pictures of our daughters and their families in little groups with Darlene. Her face was pale but peaceful. She seemed to be fully present mentally.

We learned that her kidneys were beginning to fail due to the liver's decreasing function. By midday we had heard widely differing estimates of how long she might live. We showed the hospital staff a copy of her advance medical directive. That document instructed them to avoid extraordinary means to keep her alive if her condition was irreversible. By the end of the day that Thursday, we believed that we'd had our last conversations with Darlene. Everyone went home, and I went to sleep in the recliner in her room.

I thought this day had been the answer to my prayer for our children to have one more day with her. When that prayer was answered, I asked for three more days with her, and it was as though God said, ever so quietly, "No."

93

Resurrection Day

At 3:30 a.m. on Friday, October 22, Darlene awakened. I went to her side and used one of the sponge swabs to moisten her lips and mouth. She was alert, more than she had been on Thursday. The overnight change was completely unexpected.

"I want to drink something," she said.

"Are you sure you should? I don't want you to choke," I said, thinking that her swallow reflex might be poor.

"I think I can. I'll drink just a little."

She was able to hold the glass and she took a few sips of water. She then asked for the box of juice from a shelf across the room. I inserted the straw, and she drank some. The day before, she had choked when she tried to drink and couldn't hold a glass of water in her hands. Somehow she had gained strength during the night and could hold the drink and swallow.

"That's enough," she said after drinking about half of the juice. She laid her head back on the pillow, but she couldn't hold down even that small amount of liquid and threw it up. I watched her for a few minutes, and she went back to sleep.

At 4:00 a.m. she was awake again and wanted me to take notes in our ever-present notebook I'd been keeping on her medical condition and procedures.

She wanted me to make sure she was enrolled in Medicare D before her birthday on November 3, and she wanted to make sure that our children would remember some safety precautions for the grandchildren at our home.

We talked about her night and about the people she wanted to see that day. We had thought we might never talk to her again after her murky day on Thursday, but here she was. Far from dying in the night, she was perfectly clear-headed on Friday. I later would say that Friday was her "resurrection day," because she had returned to us seemingly from the dead.

I fell asleep again at 4:15 a.m. What followed next was a series of short and important last conversations.

"How long will I live?"

At 7:50 a.m. Darlene saw me begin to wake up and she told me to sit up, get out our medical notebook, and start taking notes again. From 4:30 until 7:50 a.m. she may have been awake in bed, thinking and praying about the day that might be her last.

I went over to her, and she told me she loved me and began her to report on her night.

"The oncology resident was here at 4:30 a.m.," she said. "I asked him how long this will go on."

"What do you mean? How long will *what* go on?" I asked.

"How long will I live?" She said it calmly, as though she were talking of someone else. "He said I might live one or two days."

Like other times when difficult news came, we registered it mentally as another grim fact to deal with. We sat quietly for a moment. Neither of us said more about it.

"Now hurry and take your shower, before they come on rounds," she urged me.

"Don't Take Extreme Measures."

At least five medical people came on rounds that morning. One would have been the hospital doctor in charge. The others may have included nurses, residents, and a medical student. One seemed to be a hospital official whose job was to verify Darlene's advance medical directives, since it was clear that she wouldn't live long. The usual vital signs were checked, and the hospital official made notes on her clipboard after asking us a few questions. She reminded Darlene of the measures that could be taken to extend her life, if only for a short time: a feeding tube, breathing machine, and kidney dialysis.

Darlene thought for only a few seconds about each item. When the list of options had been read, she said, "Oh, no, I don't want any of that."

The hospital official made a note and then left.

The doctors' visit was somber, but Darlene was undaunted. She was a physician and knew the sequence in which her vital organs were failing but said nothing about the process of dying that had already started. When the medical people left, Darlene had a list of more things for me to do. She had been making a list in her head, perhaps ever since 4:15 that morning.

"Make sure they are safe."

Darlene had been thinking about the four grandkids running or toddling around our two-story house without her there to oversee their safety. She admonished me to make sure they were safe.

"Tell Jenny and Anna to put the covers on the doorknobs to the basement and the kitchen bathroom," she directed. Those plastic covers fit over the doorknobs, and they slid unless an adult gripped them tightly, so little kids couldn't open the doors.

"Make sure they don't fall down the other stairs," she added. She didn't mention the baby gates that day, but the kids' safety was still on her mind.

"Heavenly Birthday Party"

One of the first dictations Darlene gave me after 7:50 a.m. was a way to explain her death to the grandchildren when they were old enough to understand. Since her birthday was approaching on November 3, she wanted me to explain that she had been invited to what she called her Heavenly Birthday Party. She had received her invitation, she said, and she would be going soon. She knew it would be a great party. She wanted the grandchildren to know that all of us would eventually get an invitation to a Heavenly Birthday Party as well, but we wouldn't know when that day would be until the time arrived.

"Have you forgotten me already?"

While we were talking, my cell phone rang. I could see it was Matt calling, so I handed the phone to Darlene.

"It's Matt," I told her. "You answer."

"Hello?" she said clearly but quietly. There must have been a pause at the other end. Matt apparently was confused because he thought he might be speaking to one of Darlene's sisters. He didn't know she had survived the night and was so alert.

"Who is this?" he asked at last.

Without missing a beat, Darlene said with mock indignation, "It's your *mother!* Have you forgotten me already?"

That quip, "Have you forgotten me already?" became one of the watchwords for her last conscious day.

No, we hadn't forgotten.

Darlene handed me the phone, and I told Matt about the doorknob covers. We both chuckled. The knob covers were already on. People were awake at home and would soon come to the hospital. Darlene was awake and asking for them.

Wisconsin Calls

Shortly after 9:00 a.m., I was back beside Darlene's bed and my cell phone rang again. It was Darlene's dear friend, Roselyn Staples, a pastor at Elmbrook Church in Wisconsin. I passed the phone to Darlene, and Roselyn asked if she should drive down from Wisconsin.

"No," I heard Darlene say. "Don't try to come. We're going to do this right now, right here."

She held the phone to her ear and smiled as though Roselyn were there with her, just as when they had talked during our visits to Wisconsin after 1992. I took a picture of Darlene as they talked. Except for the pillow under her head, she looked so happy that she might have been having coffee with Roselyn in Wisconsin. They may have talked five or ten minutes, and Darlene smiled lovingly as she said, "Good-bye."

"Jaunty angle"

About 10:00 a.m. our children and their spouses arrived with the four grandchildren. Pictures showed all of us smiling and laughing as though we were at a party, which we were. We were celebrating her life and the fact that we had her this one additional, unexpected day.

In one picture she held the little sponge-ended wand she was using to wet her lips. She held up the wand as though it were a magic wand or maybe a royal scepter.

One by one the grandchildren were brought to her to touch and hold, if they would hold still long enough for a hug. The scene was like that of a biblical patriarch, in this case a matriarch, blessing each family member before departing.

We took pictures of her with each of the three married couples and all the grandchildren and all the other visitors. It was a day of celebration, even though we all knew she was leaving.

I bent over her and took several close-up pictures of her face. She smiled joyfully and peacefully. A little later, she had a fever. The kids and I took turns placing cool, damp hand cloths on her forehead. She was beaming when I bent over her again for a picture of her wearing one of the cool cloths. The cloth slipped to one side.

"Jaunty angle!" she said, and we both laughed. "Jaunty angle" was a special little joke just between us.

"You are a *soul* that has a *body*."

During the day, she said several other memorable things worth recording. She quoted her beloved author, C.S. Lewis, several times.

"You don't just *have* a soul," she said more than once. When people looked startled, she would continue.

"You don't *have* a soul. You *are* a soul. You *have* a body. You aren't a *body* that has a soul. You are *a soul* that has a *body*."

"Resting in Jesus"

When Pastor Steve Rennick visited, he commented to her on how peaceful and comfortable she looked. She just smiled and replied seriously, but I think also whimsically.

"I'm resting in Jesus!"

"Don't wear yourself out asking why."

Darlene reminded people that day of a line from Proverbs: "Don't wear yourself out to get rich." (Proverbs 23:4). She also advised her visitors, "Don't wear yourself out asking why."

Throughout her cancer episodes, she had never asked why. She never said, "Why me?" and she never claimed that her cancer was "unfair." She seemed to shun that thought.

"That will be enough."

Darlene and I had written out a plan for her memorial service, and the girls had brought it to the hospital for us to review together. She was fully alert as we talked through the order of service and made a few changes. We included her favorite hymn, "Great Is Thy Faithfulness," and the rousing spiritual, "When We All Get to Heaven." For the concluding benediction, she affirmed that the great benediction at the end of the Book of Jude should be read.

When I had a moment alone with Darlene, I asked her, "Do you want to have your body embalmed for showing at your service?"

She had sometimes commented earlier about the value of seeing the body for the sake of closure in the living. She thought a few moments.

"No. Just cremation. Everyone who needed to see me has been here. That will be enough."

A Child Will Be Born.

Matt knew that Kathryn's pregnancy would soon be obvious, so he decided he wanted to tell his sisters and their husbands as well. He wasn't sure Darlene remembered his telling her on Thursday, so while we were all together on Friday, he said, "Well, Kathryn and I have something to tell you. We told Mom yesterday that we are expecting a baby next summer."

The room filled with gasps and cheers. Jenny and Anna ran to Kathryn, then to Matt, and then to Darlene. Darlene was smiling happily. *This* she remembered! The expectation of a new baby filled the room with joy, even as the baby's grandmother was slipping away.

With the help of one of the children, she chose a blanket for the new baby and ordered it online from her hospital bed. It arrived on the day of her memorial service.

"Be kind to yourselves."

"Do you have any advice for us?" Anna asked Darlene on that last conscious day. "When you are gone, and I miss you, what can I do?" Anna asked.

We all knew that Darlene was leaving us, and she knew it too. We couldn't foresee all the emotional shocks that might lie ahead. Anna asked Darlene for guidance.

Darlene thought a few moments.

"Be kind to yourselves," she said.

That has been a watchword for us. When we missed her, when we wondered what else we might have done, when we felt the anguish of loss, we remembered her advice. It was a way she could love us, even though she would be absent. She made it easier for us to be without her.

"We have much to be thankful for."

Darlene and I had our last private conversation in early afternoon on Friday, October 22, 2010. We knew we would have only a brief time together, and it might be our last time alone.

I said, "When we decided to get married, I knew that you were the one God intended for me. It was God's will for me to marry you." She smiled, and I continued, "I knew there could be no life for me apart from you."

We held hands, and she listened as I continued. I mentioned our children and their spouses and the four grandchildren. I talked about some of the good times we'd had, the ways we had been blessed, and the difficult times we had come through together.

Thinking of our children and grandchildren and our lives together, I said, "We have had a good, productive marriage."

"We have much to be thankful for," she replied.

"Yes," I said.

We didn't know it then, but we had in those simple terms spoken our benediction on our thirty-nine years of marriage.

"I was thinking it."

Then I remembered a conversation we had *not* had. I had consciously avoided that conversation, and she had never brought it up. I had something to tell her, and it seemed urgent for me to say it then.

"Darlene," I began, "I want you to know that I noticed that you never complained about having cancer the first time or the second time. You never said, 'Why me?' and you never complained or blamed God. I knew that it was a terrible disappointment that the cancer came back when you were only two months from retirement. I didn't compliment you or say anything about how you were handling this because I thought it would only make it harder for you if I brought it up. You never talked about those disappointments."

"No," she said, "but I was thinking it."

"I'm *going* on a trip!"

Late Friday afternoon, Darlene looked beautiful and strong so I said to her, "Darlene, you look so good that I think I should just take you home so we can pack for a trip."

She turned her head toward me and gave me an almost impish smile.

"I'm *going* on a trip!"

That statement became another of the watchwords for Darlene's "resurrection day." She was going on a trip.

It was in that spirit that she spent her last wakeful day, as she had spent most of the nineteen months since the cancer returned. She had faced everything frankly and confidently, and on that day she faced a future she was confident would be beautiful and joyful. A few days earlier, in an email to many relatives and friends, I had said, "She is confident of her future."

Racing from Milwaukee

Darlene's nephew Doug Guffy called and asked if he could drive down from Milwaukee to see Darlene. "You can come if you want, Doug," I said, "but there's no way to tell if she will be with us when you get here."

"I'm coming," Doug said.

My sister Annette in northern Indiana offered to come too, but I discouraged her from coming. It seemed unlikely that Darlene would survive until she arrived. I later regretted my advice to her that day.

At about 4:00 p.m., the nurse in charge announced that Darlene was to be moved to a room in the Cancer Center. Up to that point, she had been in a room in the Indiana University Hospital that was barely adequate for the stream of visitors. The two hospitals are connected, so her bed would be rolled through a labyrinth of halls and elevators to the new room.

I carried Darlene's belongings and mine to the new room. On the way, my cell phone rang. It was my cousin Greg Hale.

"Monika and I wonder if we could bring you dinner," Greg said. "We are at the Capri and would like to bring dinner."

I said that would be great. Those of us in the room were beginning to feel weak after the long day.

"How many are there?" he asked.

I counted around the room and then said there were just four of us: our three kids and me. Darlene was awake but couldn't eat. Greg and Monika brought a lovely Italian dinner within an hour, along with cloth napkins and stainless steel utensils that the restaurant had insisted they borrow. Darlene was awake, and Greg and Monika visited with her briefly. Darlene was comfortable and content.

The new room was spacious compared to the other. It had three or four places for visitors to sit and there was a couch that could be made into a twin bed. The bathroom was larger, and there was ample space on both sides of Darlene's bed for visitors.

It was early evening when Darlene's nephew Doug Guffy arrived from Milwaukee. He had battled heavy traffic around Chicago and was later than he'd expected. Darlene was delighted to see him and was alert enough to talk with him. He was the last visitor to arrive while she could talk.

Our three children and I took turns standing or sitting at her bedside that evening. At 11:00 p.m., Darlene was feeling weak and was in pain. A nurse came and injected pain medication into her IV tube, and she was soon in a deep sleep. We'd had our last conversation.

94

The Kiss Test

Saturday, October 23, was a day of watchful waiting. Our children and their spouses came to the Cancer Center in rotations throughout the day and evening while others watched the grandkids at our house. We all took turns at Darlene's bedside, holding her hands, stroking her head, and talking to her softly. We dampened her mouth with the little sponge wands. She did not respond to these touches or to our voices, but about mid-morning, I leaned over and kissed her firmly on the mouth. Two of our kids were watching. When our lips met, she kissed me back! I was astounded and kissed her again. She kissed me again.

"Darlene, are you there?" I asked.

She moved her jaw slightly but couldn't talk. From then on, every hour or two, I kissed her again. She kept responding all morning, but by afternoon there was only a weak response. The kids and I called it the "kiss test." It was our only measure of her awareness and responsiveness that day.

That same morning, Kathryn called her mother, a hospice nurse who had witnessed many deaths and the various ways death had approached her dying patients. Kathryn asked how those of us at Darlene's bedside would know when she was about to die.

"You really can't tell until it happens," Kathryn's mother said. "Death doesn't follow a smooth, downward path. Sometimes a person will revive for a while when they seemed near death. Other times, death comes suddenly."

After a pause, she added, "People tend to die as they have lived. If a person is a loner, she will wait until everyone has left, and she will die alone. If a person is a social party animal, she will wait until all her family and friends are around, and then she will die."

From this conversation, we decided that Darlene probably was not on a smooth glide path like that of a plane landing or like a wheel gradually ceasing to spin. We wouldn't be able to foresee her death.

But we also saw contradictions in Darlene's nature. She was in many ways a loner, driven by her own thoughts and her sense of duty and of God's calling. She was also sociable and caring. Which one of these natures would appear at the time of her death?

95

The Benediction

*O*ur children and their families went to church on Sunday while I stayed with Darlene. She was sleeping peacefully. There was barely a response to the kiss test in the morning and then none at all by noon.

At about noon, Pastor Jim Cook came for a visit. He talked to Darlene on the chance she could hear him. He pulled out the Bible he carried on his many hospital visits and read a passage to her. After his visit, he and I sat at a table down the hall. I shared with him some of the food that Darlene's colleague Jeanne Smucker had brought for visitors. I filled him in on the events of the previous five days, and he assured me of his prayers and those of the church. His words gave me calm assurance for our continuing vigil.

In mid-afternoon, our good friends Lawrence and Rachel Smiley arrived with their daughter Ericka, who was about Jenny's age and deeply spiritual. She had felt led to come and pray for Darlene's healing and restoration to life. She wanted to pray for a miracle.

We talked a few minutes and then gathered around Darlene and put our hands on her. One by one, each of us prayed. After the prayer, Pastor Steve Rennick arrived, also intending to pray. We gathered around Darlene again and prayed.

Soon I was alone with Darlene as she slept so quietly. I remembered my prayer on October 20 asking God for one more day. When things improved on October 21 and she had been so clear-headed, I had timidly asked God if we could have three more days with her. By Sunday afternoon, I could tell that God definitely had said, "No."

Our three adult children and their spouses arrived in late afternoon again, this time with pizza and salad for all of us. Darlene's niece, Anita, was with the kids at our house. Darlene continued to sleep silently as the rest of us settled in for an evening like we might have had at home a few weeks earlier. On those evenings, we might have been intent on a football game, and Darlene might have watched intermittently while reading or working on a little project.

Here we were having an evening of normal life together, but it was at Darlene's bedside in the hospital. Still, it was comforting to have one last quiet evening with her. It was a Sunday evening like many others, but Darlene was in a deep slumber. She was perhaps listening in on our chatter and the hum of the commentators on TV, or perhaps she was only resting, beyond all sensations of this world.

After dinner, the "in-law kids" left to relieve the babysitter and put the grandchildren to bed. Only Darlene and our children and I remained.

During the game that evening, we took turns crossing the room to see Darlene. Each time we found her unresponsive to our touch or to speech, sleeping deeply. When the game was over, we checked on her again and went to work tidying up the room for the night. We picked up all the remnants of our dinner, and Jenny and Anna made up my bed with sheets and blankets.

When the room was ready for my overnight vigil with Darlene, the four of us gathered around her bed. Jenny, Anna, and Matt were about to go home to their children and spouses. Two of us stood on each side of her. I was on Darlene's right side beside her knees. Anna was to my left beside Darlene's head. Jenny was across from Anna, and Matt was facing me. We all placed our hands on Darlene.

Jenny and Anna sang a beautiful duet and then another. Their singing led all of us to sing three or four of Darlene's favorite hymns. I then recited the words of the great benediction from Jude 24–25. Darlene and I had decided on Friday that these words should conclude her memorial service: *"To him who is able to keep you from falling and to present you before his glorious presence without fault and with great joy—to the only God our Savior be glory, majesty, power, and authority, through Jesus Christ our Lord, before all ages, now, and forevermore. Amen."*

The moment I said "Amen," Jenny exclaimed, "She's stopped breathing!"

We all gasped and listened. Darlene's quiet breathing had stopped. I felt her wrist for a pulse and then her neck. Nothing. Her heart must have stopped before she took her last breath.

The young nurse who had been attending Darlene had just entered the room, and she stepped forward with her stethoscope. Pressing it against Darlene's chest and then her neck, the nurse said, softly, "Yes, that was it."

Jenny screamed, cried, ran to the side of the room, and crumpled to the floor, sobbing. The rest of us stood in stunned silence and Jenny rejoined us. We would all have our times of weeping ahead, but at that moment were in awe of what we had just seen: wife, mother, doctor, and spiritual leader had slipped away into the arms of God the moment the benediction ended. She had waited for permission to leave, and she left with her children and husband by her side.

I looked at the wall clock. It was 12:35 a.m. on Monday, October 25, 2010.

We stood around her vacant body for a short time. Within seconds, it seemed her face was transformed from that of a beautiful lady sleeping peacefully to one who no longer had life. She looked ashen and pale.

"Her soul has left her!" one of the children whispered. "You can see how she has changed."

We all stood, gazing, and we could all see how she had changed.

"Her spirit has left her," someone else said.

It was a sacred moment as we looked at the visible change in her appearance. It was a sign to us that we had to let her go. The woman we loved was no longer with us. She had been healed, completely healed, as she had said she would be but didn't know how. And she had gone to her Heavenly Birthday Party, as she said she would.

I looked around the little circle at our three children. We were all there! This could have been different. Darlene might have died alone later that night. Or one or two of the children might have been at the house when she died. Like our plan two months earlier that we would be together on this particular weekend, it was a great blessing, perhaps a miracle, that we had all been present, exactly as Darlene would have wanted. Perhaps she timed it so.

I went to an empty hospital room and called Darlene's sisters. The news was not unexpected, but death always seems sudden. Her sisters could only murmur their first grief then, in the middle of the night, knowing we would all be together often in the coming week.

A physician came from another part of the Cancer Center to officially document Darlene's death. The kids and I gathered up all of Darlene's belongings and mine. It was disorienting to realize we had to leave the hospital while her body remained there.

I went to her side and lifted her left hand and gazed at her wedding ring. I had placed it on her finger many years earlier, and in that moment, I had to slip it off. We had taken our rings off together only once while I was rock-climbing in California, but this was the only time I ever removed her ring. Only she had ever removed the ring before, and only rarely. Taking her ring was another benediction, one just for me.

96

The Aftermath

The unfamiliar events that follow death were about to unfold. Her body would be taken to a morgue in the hospital's basement. Her death would be further documented there, and her body would be held there until it was received by the mortuary in charge of her cremation. All these events would move along without us. We needed only to leave her body for the professionals, taking with us the knowledge of her life and the story of her amazing, confident, joyful death.

It may have been the next day when one of us remembered Kathryn's mother's explanation of how people die, that they die as they lived in relation to other people. Darlene had been a loner but also a social, caring person who was focused on children and family. That was indeed how she died! She waited until she was surrounded by her family, her children and her husband, and when they had sung to her and spoken the benediction, she left silently.

97

Memorial Service

When someone dies, the survivors have much to do. Cultures vary greatly in the rituals they perform at the time of death, and those rituals help carry the grieving family beyond the point of death and into life without the one they have lost. Beginning early Monday morning, October 25, there were many decisions to make, even though we had written most of Darlene's memorial service with her help at the hospital on Friday. On that Friday she told me she didn't want her body to be embalmed for viewing at her memorial service. "Everyone who needed to see me has been here," she explained.

"Which funeral home should I use?" I asked.

"Flanner and Buchanan," she replied immediately. It must have been the most familiar name and one she trusted.

Even with those plans laid, there was much to do between Monday morning and the memorial service on Saturday. I think you can never be fully prepared for the death of a family member. Death is always sudden, even after a long illness.

My first visitor was a cousin my age, Phyllis Miller. She arrived Tuesday morning unannounced with a sheet cake, and she and I talked in the music room while others cut the cake. Phyllis would follow Darlene in death four years later.

Many other visitors came, and we were overwhelmed with their sympathy and good wishes. Time and again, thinking of Darlene's confidence as she died, I told grieving visitors "Don't grieve like those who have no hope!"

Pastor Rennick came and reviewed plans for Darlene's visitation on Friday and the service on Saturday. We gave him the fairly detailed order of service that Darlene had revised and approved on her last wakeful day. Before the funeral on Saturday, Steve added comments and prayers by two other pastors and he composed a sermon titled "She Taught Us." He offered a brief history of her life and her cancer journey. He said she taught us how to live and how to die as people of faith.

On Wednesday, someone called from Flanner and Buchanan to tell me that Darlene's body had arrived at their funeral home on Shadeland Avenue at I-465 only three miles from my home. I needed to go there to verify Darlene's body before cremation. Jenny and Anna decided to go with me, and they brought the four grandchildren. They initially did not intend to come inside to see Darlene's body and would wait outside with their children. In the actual event, we all saw her body. Jenny and Anna and I took turns watching the kids outside while each of them came in to view her body. The day was chilly but bright, and the trees outside the funeral home were a playground for the little kids. The funeral home had the right body, but Darlene's mind, personality, energy, beauty, and spirit were elsewhere.

I don't understand the modern distinction between a funeral and a memorial service. The only difference I know is that the body is not present at a memorial service. It seems like a petty, unnecessary distinction. Funerals follow death. Does the body have to be *present* for that?

Darlene's service was memorable. There was a large crowd of family members, church friends, former colleagues, college friends, and neighbors. Some friends drove from Kansas and other states. The service included her favorite hymn, "Great is Thy Faithfulness," as well as "When We All Get to Heaven," and "It is Well with My Soul." The church choir sang "The Majesty and Glory of Your Name" at her request.

Our cousins, Greg Hale and Monika Nyby, talked of ways Darlene had served in the church: singing in the choir, serving on the Board of Elders, and guiding parents of children with physical or developmental disabilities. Greg told how Greeks marveled at Christians in 124 AD. "If any righteous man or woman among the Christians passes from this world, they rejoice and offer thanks to God, and they escort this body with songs and thanksgiving as if this person were setting out from one place to another nearby." We were celebrating Darlene's move from one place to another nearby, Greg said. Darlene had told Monika that one of her favorite verses was Joshua 1:9: "Be strong and courageous. Do not be terrified; do not be discouraged, for the Lord your God will be with you wherever you go."

When the time came for family remarks, our three children and I went to the platform. I was afraid I would lose my composure and embarrass everyone by bursting into tears, so I made a very short speech. I thanked everyone for coming and said I would defer to our children. Then the kids took over. Their talks were detailed, funny, and touching.

Jenny talked about Darlene's courage as she went through painful procedures and rounds of chemotherapy. "But," she said, "all of those were nothing compared to her fear of insects. She could walk into a room and spot a spider on the ceiling in a far corner of the room, and it had to be killed before she would enter."

Anna told about a time when she was sick with a fever as a young girl. She had asked Darlene, "Mom, am I going to die?" Darlene, the doctor and theologian replied, "Yes, you're going to die, but probably not of this."

Matt said, "Mom extended her love to each of our spouses as they were added to the family. She found ways to make each of them feel like her own children. One way she did this was with nicknames. While us siblings were Jenn-Pen, Ducky Dolly, and Buddy Squirrel; our spouses became Chaddy, Greggy-Poo, and Kathryn was affectionately called 'Daughter-in-Law.' The bond between them was special, and it was important to me that my wife was accepted so warmly into the family."

Anna spoke for all of us: "There will be difficult days ahead but we are rejoicing that her suffering is over, she is whole and healed and at peace. She is, as she told us on Friday, 'resting in Jesus.' Praise God for all his mercies, his blessings, and his care for us in innumerable ways. Thank you for your prayers that have sustained us to this point."

The service closed, as Darlene herself had requested, with Jude's benediction that had been Darlene's own benediction at her bedside nearly a week earlier.

By the day of her memorial service, Darlene already may have been zooming forward and backward through time. She probably had confronted Paul and some of the disciples and prophets with questions that had puzzled her as she read her Bible. She may have investigated the steps of creation and how God had populated the Earth with people and animals. She may have gone 800 million years into the future to see how the Earth will end, and she may have seen, with God, how all of our lives will be played out. Not only did she teach us, as Pastor Rennick said in her funeral service, but she may be a lifelong learner, even in eternal life.

98

Closing Words

When Darlene was in heavy treatment after her cancer returned in 2009, she and I were both reading *The Four Loves* by C.S. Lewis (1960) from separate copies of the book. On October 13, 2009, I wrote in my book that Darlene wanted a passage read at her funeral. We both forgot her request and we didn't read it at her memorial service. Let these words from C.S. Lewis be her closing words.

> For the dream of finding our end, the thing we were made for, in a Heaven of purely human love could not be true unless our whole Faith were wrong. We were made for God. Only by being in some respect like Him, only by being a manifestation of His beauty, lovingkindness, wisdom, or goodness, has any earthly Beloved excited our love. It is not that we have loved them too much, but that we did not quite understand what we were loving. It is not that we shall be asked to turn from them, so dearly familiar, to a Stranger.
>
> When we see the face of God we shall know that we have always known it. He has been a party to, has made, sustained and moved moment by moment within all our earthly experiences

of innocent love. All that was true love in them was, even on earth, far more His than ours, and ours only because His. In Heaven there will be no anguish and no duty of turning away from our earthly Beloveds. First, because we shall have turned already; from the portraits to the Original, from the rivulets to the Fountain, from the creatures He made lovable to Love Himself. But secondly, because we shall find them all in Him. By loving Him more than them we shall love them more than we now do.

The Girl Who Broke the Swing

Closing Words • 337

On the Trio Tour in 1965

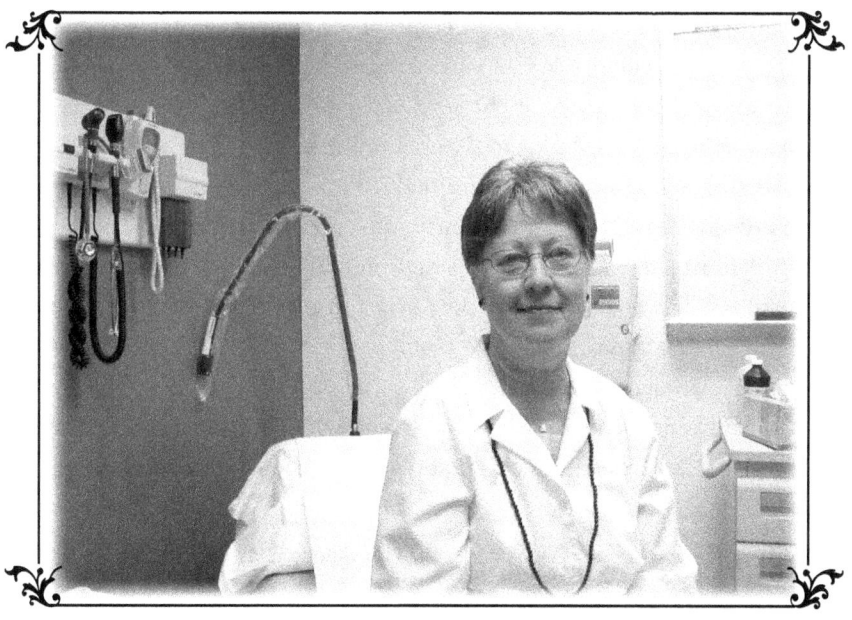

Dr. Darlene as a Cancer Patient

Epilogue

Although the summertime of our lives has ended, Darlene's life continues to enrich those of us who knew her and many who didn't know her. Her legacy as a physician continues as well, impacting the lives of many who will never know her personally. The lecture series created in her honor continues her work on early childhood mental health among physicians in Indiana.

Within the immediate family, the date of Darlene's death is a memorial day each year. Sometimes the adult children and I talk of her "monthiversary" on the twenty-fifth day of other months. Jenny, Anna, and Matt continue to tell their children the stories recorded in this book about their grandmother as they come to mind in the ordinary course of their lives. We remain a tight-knit family, bound together by our common experiences and love.

Six of our ten grandchildren have been born since their grandmother's death. She would have loved to know each of them here. Perhaps she can, as she expected, see them from heaven. As for me, I often ask myself, "What would Darlene do?" when faced with decisions large and small. That question usually brings me to my senses. Truth be told, she may roll her eyes over some of my choices.

In August 2011 the kids and I mounted another whole-family trip to Colorado to deliver half of Darlene's ashes to places she loved. We placed some ashes at Campsite 13 west of Colorado Springs before going to Rocky Mountain National Park.

At Estes Park, we rented a house large enough to contain our whole family of eleven. It was in the same collection of houses where we had stayed in 2009 with Darlene. When we began to sign the guest log for the house, one of us remembered that Darlene had made an entry in the book at the other house in 2009. We hurried to that house and found the book. There was Darlene's entry in her own words, in her own beautiful handwriting. We took pictures of those pages, and the book probably is still in that house.

At the Forest Canyon Overlook, the place Darlene had chosen for her ashes, our three children went with me with ashes in a small plastic bottle. I felt we should be secretive about the fact that we were going to scatter cremation ashes. Crowds filled the official viewing plaza, so we circled around to another place a few yards away where we could have a degree of privacy.

We sat on jagged rocks overlooking the canyon and I took out the bottle of ashes. We each gave a prayer of thanks for Darlene and her life. I opened the bottle and shook out a few ashes. The ashes blew up in our faces, so the others dropped ashes closer to the rocks. I handed the bottle to Jenny and then each of the children shook out some ashes. I shook out what remained when the bottle returned to me.

We were disappointed that we couldn't scatter the bulk of Darlene's ashes at the Forest Canyon Overlook. As a partial remedy, Jenny and Chad took a few ashes to other scenic places in the park. I still had most of the ashes I had brought to Colorado. Then I remembered a place that seemed right. I remembered having a picnic with Darlene beside an alpine meadow on our exploratory trip in 2008. I had taken a picture from behind her as she sat in a lawn chair gazing at the rock outcropping at the near side of the meadow. When I remembered that scene, it was as though Darlene had chosen that place for her ashes rather than the Forest Canyon Overlook.

The girls and their husbands were keeping their kids entertained, so Matt and Kathryn and baby Ezra went with me to find the place I remembered. From the park map, I could tell it must have been at Upper Beaver Meadows. At the end of a narrow gravel road, we found the picnic site just as I had remembered it. The concrete picnic table was there beside the steel campfire pit, just as I remembered. And the place where Darlene had sat was just as I remembered.

Leaving Kathryn and Ezra at the car, Matt and I walked to the rock outcrop and circled behind it. Wildflowers were blossoming behind the rock, and a grove of aspen trees rattled in the breeze nearby. Darlene loved wildflowers and aspen trees. This was the place.

Matt returned to the car so I could scatter Darlene's ashes by myself. It seemed I should do this alone, since Jenny and Anna weren't there. Just when I returned to the car, a gentle mountain shower began, settling Darlene's ashes among the wildflowers, nourishing them until the end of that summertime.

Delivering her ashes was an act of completion, and we are thankful we can visit those special places. I have visited there twice since 2011. I have whimsically called the rock outcrop "the rock of ashes." Darlene might have smiled or maybe she would have frowned.

Darlene and I agreed to have a place in memory of the two of us in the small cemetery in northwestern Oklahoma where my mother's parents and others of her family are buried. The plot is to remind our children and grandchildren of my mother's pioneering family that might otherwise be forgotten as well as the two of us, who pioneered in our own ways. I placed a headstone in that cemetery in 2014 with the benediction from Jude engraved on the reverse side.

Four years after her death, I wrote the first of my previous three books. That first book, *Widow-man: A Widower's Story and Journaling Book,* contains practical suggestions for men who have lost their wives. When I introduced

the book to a group of volunteer Stephen Ministers in January 2015, one of them asked, "Did her death weaken your faith?"

"No," I explained. "My children and I were all strengthened in our faith. She lived confidently and joyfully to the end. The way she lived and the way she died made our faith stronger."

In her last year of life, Darlene said more than once, "The wake closes quickly." She meant that after a person leaves a place of employment or a neighborhood or leaves this world, life goes on. A person's wake in the sea of life closes quickly, and other people continue their own life journeys. She made that remark thoughtfully, without regret or bitterness about her own passing; it may have assured her that those of us who knew her and loved her would live full, busy lives without her.

If Darlene were here to help me end this book, I think she might say something like this to you:

"Well, now you have read our story, or at least my husband's version of it. He could have written more, but this is enough, just enough. I hope you have had fun reading parts of it. Some parts may have been hard to read, but those parts may help prepare you for difficult times you may face. Now that you have read our story, close this book, put it away, and go on living your own life. Trust God to guide you now and always as you go."

Chronology:
Life of Darlene Sayers Kardatzke, MD

1945 Born November 3, 1945, at Witham Hospital, Lebanon, Indiana
1963 Graduated from Southport High School
1963 Entered Anderson College in pre-nursing
1964 Entered nursing school in Indianapolis
1965 Left nursing school and returned to Anderson College
1965 Met Nyle Kardatzke and began dating
1967 Graduated from Anderson College and entered the Indiana University School of Medicine
1971 Graduated from medical school and married Nyle Kardatzke the next day, June 12
1971 Pediatrics residency at the UCLA Medical Center, Los Angeles
1974 Completed UCLA residency in June and moved to Milwaukee in July
1975 Began part-time pediatrics work in Milwaukee area hospitals and clinics
1976 Began attending Elmbrook Church and bought first house
1977 First child born, Jenny Elizabeth
1980 Second child born, Anna Katherine
1983 Third child born, Matthew August
1992 Moved to Wichita for Nyle's job at Wichita Collegiate School
1993 Moved to Indianapolis for Darlene's fellowship in Developmental/Behavioral Pediatrics at the Indiana University School of Medicine

1996 Completed fellowship and became Assistant Clinical Professor of Pediatrics
2003 Diagnosed with breast cancer
2004 Mastectomy and bad prognosis, but cancer went into remission
2009 Cancer recurred and heavy treatment followed
2010 Death on October 25, 2010, at the Simon Cancer Center, Indianapolis, at age 64

Appendix

Grandma's Cooking

Nostalgic stories of our mothers' and grandmothers' cooking are the stuff of memories. Darlene was a good cook, but she didn't especially like to cook. She did have a few specialties that are worth noting. These stories about Darlene's cooking and some of her favorite recipes are included especially for our grandchildren.

Lasagna: Darlene may have cooked more lasagna for company than any other dish. She used lasagna noodles she cooked herself, not the no-cook kind, and she used a half-gallon jar of Prego sauce for her double lasagna recipe. I don't think she added special seasonings except some added oregano. Her lasagna was a staple when our children were still at home, and she cooked it often for church events or for shut-in church friends.

When Anna was still eating pureed Gerber baby food, Darlene gave her a bite of lasagna. Anna's eyes widened, and she looked accusingly at us. "Do you mean you have been eating this wonderful stuff while you have been feeding me that flavorless baby glop?" she seemed to say. If she ever ate flavorless baby glop after that, it was not for long. Darlene's lasagna had introduced her to better things.

Meatloaf: Darlene's meatloaf recipe was basic but delicious. She used dry Lipton Onion Soup and kneaded it into a combination of ground beef and ground pork. She seldom slathered ketchup on top as some cooks do; in fact, I don't remember her doing that.

Besides serving meatloaf for our family, Darlene carried on what she called her "Meatloaf Ministry." When a friend from church was hospitalized or was convalescing at home, she would prepare two meatloaves. If they weren't needed immediately, she'd wrap them in foil and deliver them frozen for later use.

Pie crust: One of her deepest, darkest secrets was her recipe for pie crust. Darlene didn't approve of store-bought mixes or the kind that comes rolled up two to a package. She insisted on making her own pie crust. I wasn't attentive enough to her procedure, so after her passing I tried to re-create her pie crust. I got good recipes from our daughters and our daughter-in-law, and suggestions came from Darlene's sisters and a niece. Then at Thanksgiving 2017 in Houston, Jenny found her own handwritten notes on how to make pie crust from a phone conversation with Darlene in 2009. The following is believed to be the authentic recipe.

Pie Crust

Ingredients
1½ cup sifted flour
½ tsp salt
½ cup shortening (She used Crisco, but lard will do at least as well.)
4–5 Tablespoons ***very cold*** water

Procedure
Sift, then measure the flour.
Mix flour and salt.
Add shortening with pastry cutter in portions.
Mix ice water into dry ingredients.
(*Don't mix too much. When the crust sticks together, roll it out.)
Chill and roll the crust.

Jenny added this note: Users of this recipe are dependent on the words recorded by a daughter of the originator. Alter as needed.

Corned beef and cabbage: Perhaps one of her English genes prompted Darlene to cook corned beef and cabbage more often than my mother did and more often than I have on my own. Her recipe was simple: it came from the plastic wrap on the package of corned beef. She cooked it in a crock pot overnight and added cabbage and potatoes when the recipe called for them. I don't remember that this dish was a great family favorite, but it was far more popular than the dreaded liver and onions that I sometimes cooked.

Pancakes and bacon: Saturdays were "pancake and bacon days" in every one of our houses. On camping trips, we counted on having pancakes and bacon at least once on every trip. Bacon and pancakes with coffee made at a campsite can't really be replicated in a kitchen, but they are a great meal to start a day, especially a Saturday when there is time for such a luxury.

On camping trips, I was as likely as Darlene to be the breakfast cook. At home, especially in Wisconsin, she cooked the pancakes and bacon while I played with the kids in the yard. As I mentioned elsewhere, we especially liked to burn a pile of brush in our Wisconsin yard early in the morning while waiting to be called in for breakfast. For me at least, that the sort of thing is what made America great.

Darlene sometimes had a reprieve on Saturday mornings in Wisconsin. If the kids and I were up early, we would slip away to McDonald's nearby and let her sleep. After breakfast at McDonald's, we would go across the street to Farm and Fleet, a large farm and truck supply store where the aroma of fresh tires told customers that adventure and good times were ahead. We bought candy and fishing worms at Farm and Fleet, but we took them home in separate containers. By the time we got home, Darlene was on her second cup of coffee and ready for the uproar of the day.

Ethiopian food: Darlene was a natural-born Hoosier girl of solid Kentucky stock, so it may be surprising to know that she cooked excellent Ethiopian food. There are two essential ingredients for Ethiopia/Eritrean food: a spice mixture called *ber-beri* and *injera*, a sourdough flatbread made from a fermented batter of *Teff* flour. Neither of these special ingredients is readily available in the United States.

My friend Isaac Joseph sent us our first *ber-beri* in about 1978. It came wrapped in plastic in a paper box so fragile that it could have broken in transit. The powerful smell might have aroused suspicions of customs agents, but the package made it to our house in Wisconsin. I had learned recipes for Ethiopian beef or chicken stew from an Ethiopian friend in Indiana, and I taught Darlene. She learned quickly and soon made better chicken stew—called *derho waT*—than I could. We both did well with *zigga waT*—the beef version. (I have capitalized the "T" in these food names to alert you to the fact that the "T" is produced with a popping sound in those words. I don't want you to sound like a *ferenji*—a foreigner.)

Darlene cooked both Ethiopian stews fairly often, usually with boiled eggs added to the chicken version. Her stew was always good, but the *injera* could be chancy. The most difficult part of Ethiopian or Eritrean cooking is the *injera*. It seems that authentic *injera* can be cooked only by Ethiopian or Eritrean women, and it seems that older women can do this best.

Truth to be told, when our family wanted Ethiopian or Eritrean food, we usually bought *injera* from an Ethiopian restaurant if there was one in town. If no restaurant was available, we concocted our own versions, some of which were actually edible.

Full disclosure: I have made some passable ersatz *injera* but never the real thing. Here is how I think it is done. First, mix *Teff* flour with water and let it stand for three days. It will ferment and form a gray or beige batter, depending on the *Teff* flour you have found. You then pour a portion of the batter on a very large, hot griddle covered with only the thinnest layer of oil. When it stops bubbling, take it off the griddle and begin again with another portion.

Tongue, heart, and liver: Some, including even our adult kids, may be surprised or even shocked to know that Darlene sometimes cooked beef tongue, heart, and liver. If it's any comfort, I don't think we ever had those body parts from pigs. In our defense, we never cooked brains, eyeballs, reproductive organs, or intestines. We didn't often have the three other delicacies I have named, but the fact that we had them at all is evidence that Darlene could be an adventuresome cook.

A nightmare dinner: Darlene liked to eat a wide variety of foods. I can't remember a food she strongly disliked. We once grossed out Matt by inviting him to share our dinner of liver and onions, Harvard beets, and fried cabbage. When I told him the menu on the phone, he declined my invitation and tenderly informed me, "Dad, that is the worst nightmare of a dinner that I can imagine."

In Her Own Words

*D*arlene did not keep a diary. I wish she had. I might know her even better now and know more about her professional life if she had kept a diary. Her thoughts, feelings, and insights are recorded mainly in her Bible, where she underlined and dated many passages, especially during her two cancer episodes. She sometimes wrote a short note to indicate what a passage meant to her. Once or twice she wrote "cancer" beside a sentence describing a threatening enemy. She underlined "He numbers our days."

On one of her chemo days in late 2009, Darlene said, "I have heard about a book for journaling about your life. Could you go across to Barnes and Noble to see if they have it?"

"Sure. What's it called?"

"I think the title is *Conversations with My Mother* or something like that," she said.

"I'll go look."

When she had settled in for the chemo treatment, I left the Cancer Center and crossed Michigan Street to the Barnes and Noble store. It wasn't obvious where such a book would be shelved, so I took the extreme step of asking a saleslady. The book was in stock. I discovered a companion book called *Conversations with My Father*. I bought both books and hurried back to Darlene.

We leafed through our books and thought about answers to the questions that were designed to guide us through the stories of our lives. The books are designed to be used by adult children to conduct interviews with their aging parents, thus the titles. We decided to fill in the blanks as though we were interviewing ourselves. We soon began spending afternoons or evenings filling in the blanks in those books, usually in separate rooms. Sometimes we would call to each other to clear up a question about a date or a place. It was work, but it was enjoyable work. We knew her time was short, and we knew we were doing something valuable. We wrote from time to time in 2009 and 2010, placing dates on the pages as we wrote. She made her first entry in July 2009 and her last entry less than a month before she died.

She wrote left-handed and I wrote with my right hand. She sometimes joked that lefties are smarter than other people; she may have been right. Her left-handedness was so natural that after her death it was hard to remember the fact that she held her pen like a right-handed person, not upside-down like some lefties.

Her book is mainly a factual record of events in her life: dates of births and weddings, names of family members and friends, major milestones, stories of pets and travels, and other important experiences. The book elicits only a few feelings and judgments, but the factual record provides insights into who she was. Darlene's entries now confirm many things I still remember about her, even stories from her childhood.

When I went through her book in 2018, I was reminded of things I remembered incorrectly and details I didn't know. It was as though she was sitting beside me, answering questions and reminding me of things I had forgotten, just like so many older married couples.

Neither of us completed our book, and we sometimes wrote in haste. Still, I am thankful that I have Darlene's own stories from life as she saw it. Her entries in *Conversations with My Mother* are a special treasure. They are in her own beautiful handwriting, and they are the most detailed writing she did about her life.

In March 2011, five months after Darlene's death, I had a feeling of panic about her book. I had only one copy. What if something should happen to that book? I took her book to a print shop and found a way to remove the text from its wire clamp binding. The printer then ran off copies for each of our adult children and for Darlene's two sisters. Even after distributing those copies, I have usually kept both books in a safe.

I know of no easier way to tell your children and grandchildren the story of your life than through one of those two books. At this writing, they are available directly from the publisher, Sterling Publishing. They are available online from Barnes and Noble, the AARP online bookstore, and from third-party sellers on Amazon.

This book, *The Summertime of Our Lives*, has been strengthened by facts that I found in Darlene's *Conversations with My Mother*. I haven't provided footnotes where her corrections or corroborations helped me, but I think you may enjoy this sample of Darlene's entries in *Conversations with My Mother*:

- Concerning her name, she wrote "My parents were expecting a boy who would have been named David Andrew. (My dad's middle name was Andrew.) When I turned out to be a girl, they decided on Darlene but couldn't decide on a middle name for me. My dad used to call me 'Darlin.' My uncle Frank called me 'Skip.'"

- When she cried as a colicky baby, Grada sang "In the Shade of the Old Apple Tree" when he held her.

- Her first memory was of a toy: "I remember playing with a metal chicken who 'laid' marble eggs if you pushed down on it. I was playing with it on our front sidewalk and fell on it, cutting my knee. I still have a scar from this. I remember playing under the branches of a willow tree in our yard and having pretend tea parties there. I remember our neighbors' persimmon tree. Sometimes we would get one which wasn't quite ripe and our mouths would pucker!"

- When her beloved Papa Huffman read the newspaper, he read it softly out loud.

- Grada's life in Kentucky had been difficult: "Daddy grew up in a large family near Railton, Kentucky. They all lived in a small house and were farmers. Daddy's father had a bad respiratory illness and became unable to work. Daddy, who was second youngest, and Ted, the youngest, quit school to help run the farm. Daddy would have been in about sixth grade then. They were very poor and the work was hard. Daddy was plowing a bottom field behind a mule on a hot day. He would stop in the shade to rest the mule. That day he decided there must be a better way to make a living than what he was doing. He and his brothers eventually moved the family to Indianapolis. The boys got factory jobs and supported the parents until they died."

- As a little girl, she and her friends played "elevator" with the sliding door of a closet.

- She used to ride her bike around Southport looking for her friends. If one was busy, she went to another.

- She didn't like roses because of the overpowering smell of roses at the first funeral she attended.

- Favorite activities with her friends were movies on TV, popcorn, pizza, boy talk, croquet, badminton, and swimming. Some of her friends were Connie Pavey, Bonnie Buffie, Phyllis Green, Bonnie Burris, Paula Morrison, Betty Gardner, Nancy McLaughlin, and Diane and Jim Norwood.

- She had a dog named Skipper who liked to sleep under Grada's truck and had an oil spot on his back to show for it. Skipper was hit by a car on Route 31. That was sad.

- She and some girls formed a club and called themselves "The Flames." They wore blue skirts and white blouses. Bonnie Buffie got them "blue flame" logo pins from the Gas Company. An initiation included walking blindfolded on cooked noodles, pretending they were worms.

- "I was also in Blue Birds, which is a pre-Campfire Girls club. After one year, we 'flew up' to be Campfire Girls. We had campouts and service projects. One time we collected packages of seeds to send to Ceylon (Sri Lanka). I still have my red scarf we wore."

- Some of the other kids had chocolate-striped cookies in their lunches at school. Darlene wished she could have cookies like that. She thought of them as "rich kid cookies."

- She never considered not going to college, and she loved the flexibility and freedom she had there. "I was majoring in biology and minoring in chemistry, planning to teach at some level. I went to medical school intending to teach and do research. As I got into the clinical rotations, I got more interested in practicing medicine. I really enjoyed my pediatric rotation—the kids as well as the staff doctors and residents. They seemed like my kind of people, so I went into pediatrics."

- On her first date with Nyle, she thought he was a good conversationalist, funny, kind, and good looking. She noticed that he liked the way she listened.

- "Meeting Nyle, courting, and getting married were all wonderful, and I felt God leading us in that."

- She wanted as many as six kids, but she was happy with three.

- Working so many hours in Indianapolis was something she regretted.

- Jenny and Anna baked a birthday cake for her when they were young girls. She loved it.

- Jake called her "Bada."

- Sam called her "The Airplane Grandma" because she had flown to Houston to visit.

- She had been brought up to be honest and hard-working. "I had the expectation that I could succeed at what I tried. However, I also think I had an inferiority complex which I still struggle with to some degree. Nyle says I had to become a doctor to counteract my inferiority complex!"

- "Many more women are working outside the home now. That is rewarding for the women as they use their talents. I think it has not always been good for the home and the children. Women have more legal rights, which is good. When I entered medical school, my class had 10% women. That had been the case for years before. Within a few years, the number of women in medicine and other careers had greatly increased."

- "I am thankful that I had the opportunity to have a career in medicine as well as home and family. When I was considering medical school, Daddy expressed some concern that a medical career would prevent or impede having a home and children. He didn't want me to miss out on this. I told him I thought that I could have a good quality family life as well as do medicine. Daddy said that he and Mother would support me in whatever decision I made—and they did! Daddy and mother were so proud of us girls and all the grandchildren!"

- Looking into the future, she wrote, "We are planning to stay in our house as long as we can. We like having room for everyone to come home for visits. It is great to have the kids come home. Nyle's parents followed this pattern of maintaining the family home for themselves and us to enjoy."

About the Author

*N*yle Kardatzke lives and writes in Indianapolis, Indiana. He retired after a varied career of teaching and school administration. He grew up near Elmore, Ohio, and graduated from high school there. He graduated from Anderson (College) University (Anderson, Indiana) and earned a master's degree and a PhD in economics from the University of California, Los Angeles. He has three children and ten grandchildren, and he is active in the Church at the Crossing, Indianapolis.

The author's other books are *Widow-man: A Widower's Story and Journaling Book* (2014), *The Brown House Stories: A Child's Garden of Eden* (2015), and *The Clock of the Covenant* (2016). All are available in print and Kindle editions on Amazon and from Barnes and Noble online.

Darlene and Nyle at Campsite 13 in 2005.

Request for Reviews

I have self-published this book. Few people know of it unless they have seen it online or have heard of it directly from me. Reviews on Amazon help readers choose which books to read. Your opinion is invaluable. Would you take a few moments now to evaluate my book on Amazon or any other book review website? Your opinion will help readers understand the nature of this book and decide whether it will be of value to them.

Thank you!